— *The* —
CHELSEA GREEN
READER

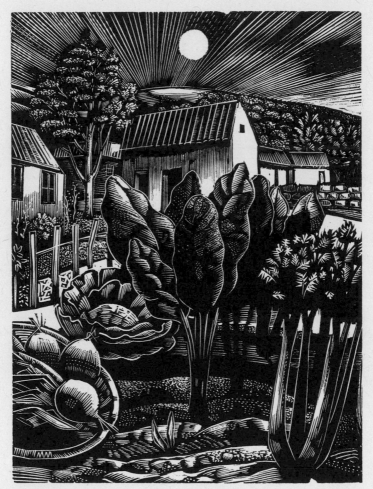

— *The* —
CHELSEA GREEN READER

SELECTIONS FROM 30 YEARS OF
INDEPENDENT PUBLISHING, 1984–2014

EDITED BY
BENJAMIN WATSON

FOREWORD BY
IAN BALDWIN

Chelsea Green Publishing
White River Junction, Vermont

Project Manager: Bill Bokermann
Project Editor: Benjamin Watson
Editorial Assistant: Lizzy Hardison
Copy Editor: Laura Jorstad
Proofreader: Helen Walden
Designer: Melissa Jacobson

Printed in the United States of America.
First printing November, 2014.
10 9 8 7 6 5 4 3 2 1   14 15 16 17

Our Commitment to Green Publishing

Chelsea Green sees publishing as a tool for cultural change and ecological stewardship. We strive to align our book manufacturing practices with our editorial mission and to reduce the impact of our business enterprise in the environment. We print our
books and catalogs on chlorine-free recycled paper, using vegetable-based inks whenever possible. This book may cost slightly
more because it was printed on paper that contains recycled fiber, and we hope you'll agree that it's worth it. Chelsea Green
is a member of the Green Press Initiative (www.greenpressinitiative.org), a nonprofit coalition of publishers, manufacturers,
and authors working to protect the world's endangered forests and conserve natural resources. *The Chelsea Green Reader* was
printed on paper supplied by Thomson-Shore that contains 100% postconsumer recycled fiber.

Library of Congress Cataloging-in-Publication Data

The Chelsea Green reader : selections from 30 years of independent publishing, 1984–2014 / edited by
Benjamin Watson ; foreword by Ian Baldwin.
    pages cm
  Includes bibliographical references and index.
  ISBN 978-1-60358-601-6 (pbk.) — ISBN 978-1-60358-610-8 (ebook)
  1. Sustainable living. I. Watson, Ben, 1961– editor. II. Chelsea Green Publishing.

  GE196.C48 2014
  304.2—dc23

                    2014038356

Chelsea Green Publishing
85 North Main Street, Suite 120
White River Junction, VT 05001
(802) 295-6300
www.chelseagreen.com

CONTENTS

EPILOGUE

FOREWORD

Thirty years ago Chelsea Green began its life in the refurbished ell of a white clapboard house in Chelsea, Vermont, on the town's south green, adjacent to the Orange County Courthouse. We began by publishing three books a year, doubling our output to six over the next three years. Not a lot of books, but each was scrupulously attended to.

From the outset we worked with the instincts of craftspeople: Each book was unique and each made very individual demands on us as the author's collaborators. Publishing, in our eyes, was a co-creative process. We were editorially and design-driven. We still are.

From the start our books were nationally noticed, garnering positive reviews and accolades and awards for our authors.

The company not only endured, but held on and eventually prospered through one of the most tumultuous periods of the publishing industry's five-hundred-year-old history, as the technological revolution known as the Internet shook (and still shakes) the entire industry to its foundations.

We were also a bit wild: In our first six years we published an illustrated fable, three novels, a photographic travel book, a biographical guide to Parisian cemeteries, several nature books, an art book, two or three memoirs, and a poetry book.

Jean Giono's *The Man Who Planted Trees*, illustrated with wood engravings by Michael McCurdy, published in our first year and still in print, went on to sell hundreds of thousands of copies over the years and set the tone for what we hoped to achieve. The story's hero, Elzéard Bouffier, served as a kind of lodestar, an example, for us as we struggled to find our own way in a highly changeable world.

To this day Giono's story is powerful and inspiring to readers who wish to shape a better world. It has inspired at least two of our subsequent books: Alan Weisman's *Gaviotas: A Village to Reinvent the World* (1998), about the legendary architect and activist Paolo Lugari's creation of a village of disaffected engineers and tinkerers who make revolutionary low-cost and low-impact technologies in the empty llanos of eastern Colombia. And Julia Alvarez's *A Cafecito Story* (2001), with woodcuts by Belkis Ramírez, which tells the story of a man who learns how coffee is grown and is empowered in the process.

Despite our varied interests we saw ourselves as an environmentally conscious publisher—and suggested that by the use of the word *Green* in our name. We valued things that were rural and decentralized, nature for its own sake, alternative ways of getting energy, growing food, and building shelter—in short, a culture that involved more beauty and less violence.

In 1989 we published the first of Eliot Coleman's books, *The New Organic Grower*, which went on to become one of the company's biggest revenue generators and helped establish the nation's organic, local agriculture and food movement. As Janisse Ray wrote many years later in her book *The Seed Underground* (2012): ". . . the farmer in all of us has roused."

That same year we published our first political book, *The Vermont Papers* by political scientist Frank Bryan and policy analyst John McClaughry, a book the *Los Angeles Times* proclaimed was "the Small Is Beautiful of American Politics." It was the first and only political book until much later in our story. But it, too, sparked an interest and a commitment in an important subject area that the company would eventually nurture and develop more fully.

By 1995, with the publication of Paul Gipe's *Wind Power*, Donella Meadows's, Jorgen Randers's, and Dennis Meadows's *Beyond the Limits*, Eliot Coleman's *Four-Season Harvest*, Michael Potts's *The Independent Home*, Gene Logsdon's *The Contrary Farmer*, and Athena and Bill Steen's and David Bainbridge's *The Straw Bale House* (one of our all-time best-sellers), Chelsea Green had created its niche as a publisher of books about sustainable living. The company had become not only more focused but also profitable. These were, each in its own way, pioneering titles; many of them were revised in the ensuing years and still sell as bedrock backlist titles. The backlist, books that sell over years and decades, are the sine qua non of any publisher, its spine if you will. The backlist helps pay the bills each month, making it possible to take a leap of faith with new, unproven, but promising authors and important ideas that we hope will someday make good backlist titles in their own right.

Chelsea Green has always had a nose for authors and subjects that are way ahead of the cultural curve. In 1991 we published Wolfgang Zuckermann's *End of the Road*, about reducing car dependency and "calming" urban traffic (a bit too far ahead of the curve, as it turned out). During the mid-1990s we began exploring the growing topic of permaculture, and co-published or distributed books from overseas before publishing some of the first American books on the subject like *Gaia's Garden* by Toby Hemenway and *Edible Forest Gardens*, the definitive two-volume reference on theory and design by Dave Jacke and Eric Toensmeier. Today permaculture is much more widely recognized, and it remains one of Chelsea Green's core subject areas. In 1997 we published a book about the now au courant subject of hemp farming, and in 1999, the first book about community-supported agriculture, Elizabeth Henderson's *Sharing the Harvest*, now in a revised edition.

This short list would not be complete without mentioning Sandor Katz's *Wild Fermentation*, which has become one of our all-time bestselling titles, despite being way ahead of the curve when we published it in 2003. By 2012, almost a full decade later, fermented food had entered the mainstream consciousness, and Sandor Katz's third Chelsea Green book, *The Art of Fermentation*, made it onto *The New York Times* bestseller list.

In 2004, under my wife Margo's leadership, Chelsea Green expanded its mission to include the politics—as well as the practice—of sustainable living. We published cognitive linguist George Lakoff's *Don't Think of an Elephant!*, about how significant the framing of ideas and values is to the successful conduct of politics, releasing the book just in time to make the pre-presidential-election conversation. It instantly took off, becoming the first of our four *New York Times* bestsellers, staying on the list for over a year and selling hundreds of thousands of copies. Three years later we published our second *New York Times* bestseller, Naomi Wolf's *The End of America*, warning Americans about the danger posed by the encroachment of corporate state power in their everyday lives and the consequent erosion of their civil rights.

In three decades we've been privileged to work with a great many talented and diverse authors. Some attracted us by their passionate commitment and personal heroism, in the fearless, persevering spirit of Elzéard Bouffier himself. One such author is shrimper-activist-writer Diane Wilson. *An Unreasonable Woman* (2005) is Diane's story of her against-all-odds battle with a giant chemical plant that she single-handedly forced to stop polluting the Gulf waters of her beloved Seadrift, Texas. Another is biologist-fisherwoman-activist Riki Ott, whose excruciating story—*Not One Drop* (2008)—is about the near-complete destruction of the fishing community of Cordova, Alaska, by the *Exxon Valdez* supertanker's massive oil spill, and about the protracted struggle of the citizens of Cordova to claim restitution from one of the world's largest and most powerful corporations.

We were privileged to also work with such outstanding human beings and scientists as Donella Meadows (1941–2001) and Lynn Margulis (1938–2011). Donella was the lead author of the original *Limits to Growth* that shook the world over forty years ago and continues to influence people worldwide through the two editions we subsequently published in 1992 and 2004. Her posthumously published book *Thinking in Systems* (2006) is one of our top-selling titles and leads our growing ebook sales list. Lynn Margulis was the co-creator, with James Lovelock, of Gaia theory, and one of the world's foremost exponents of an emergent theory of evolution that emphasizes the role of symbiosis in the unfolding mystery of life. We are proud to have published several of the books Lynn wrote during the last years of her extraordinary life as a scientist.

Over three decades Chelsea Green has published more than four hundred titles and worked with writers of varying kinds, *all of whom* have had original and worthy things to share, either as writers or as practitioners of special trades and disciplines—and sometimes both. Less than a quarter of these writers and their books are represented in this reader, an unavoidable limitation! Some of the writers selected here have written bestselling books; more of them, mid-list books; and some, books that didn't sell well at all. Yet each has commanded our interest and commitment as a publisher to help her or him realize what they want to say to the world.

As you read the short introductions to each author in this *Reader* you will see many of the books have won various national awards in their fields. The first book we published to win a national award—the John Burroughs Medal for "a distinguished book of natural history"—was Lawrence Kilham's *On Watching Birds*, which won in 1989. (In 2012 another Chelsea Green author, Edward Hoagland, won the medal for his *Sex and the River Styx*.) Lawrence Kilham died in 2000, but his son Ben is the author of *In the Company of Bears*, released in paperback this fall of 2014. Two generations, father and son, now live under one publisher's roof.

What then of the future? Does an independent publisher still have a role to play in a future dominated by the phenomenon of Internet-based self-publishing? In 2009 three of every four new books released were self-published. With an expected three billion online users by 2015, why wouldn't all authors simply create or beef up their own websites and join the herd? As the august publisher and editor Jason Epstein has reminded us, "Digitization makes possible a world in which anyone can claim to be a publisher," and asks who will "winnow what is worth keeping in a virtual marketplace where Keats' nightingale shares electronic space with Aunt Mary's haikus"?

The life of an independent publisher, believe it or not, has been made easier by the presence of the Internet and such entrepreneurial wizards as Jeff Bezos. No backlist title need now fear going out of print—ever. Everyone in the world has access to whatever book we publish, not only in an ebook format but, with print-on-demand technology, as a printed copy.

The question of our future relevance, however, will not be answered by us. Only our authors, past, present, and future, can tell us. And they will.

Chelsea Green was born from a single seed: the beauty of craft. Craft in writing and editing, in a story well told or a thesis superbly expressed. Craft in design, illustration, and production. Craft in generating sales "copy" and the word-of-mouth "publicity" that makes the story, the exposition inside a book's covers, leap forward, sometimes like wildfire, sometimes as slowly and steadily as an unnoticed turtle, using all the tools now at our disposal, most certainly including the Internet's proliferating social media, as well as through such old-fashioned activities as book tours and signings.

The notion of craft, of making books painstakingly, with an eye on their aesthetic identity and purpose, as well as their secular or practical one, still informs who we, some twenty employees at Chelsea Green, are and how we—all of us, in editorial and production, sales and marketing, distribution and business operations—like to publish. It's in our DNA as professionals.

Up until now most of our hundreds of authors have appreciated this care.

People are moved by what they read. That pertains whether they read an ebook or a printed one, and they want to connect with the writers who make their lives richer. Part of the publisher's role is to help make this vitalizing connection.

This nexus among author, publisher, and reader is, I believe, unlikely to wither anytime soon.

—*IAN BALDWIN*, cofounder and publisher emeritus
September 2014 • South Strafford, Vermont

PREFACE

When people ask me what I do for work I tell them I'm a book editor. More often than not they then ask, "Oh, does that mean you correct spelling and grammar?"

Well, yes, in a way . . . but then I go on to tell them about everything it takes to get a book into print. Searching for and signing up the best authors on topics that we want to publish. Nurturing and helping them develop their ideas. Giving structure and organization to the text and artwork. Making hundreds of design and production decisions along the way. Describing and positioning the book six months or more ahead of publication, so that salespeople and marketers can promote and sell it in advance.

To me, publishing is a lot like time travel. We work on books that in some cases may be years away from sitting on anyone's shelf or night table. We work on immediate deadlines, on books that are in editing or production for the coming season. And these books don't disappear after publication: We continue to sell them, often working with the author to promote them, update them, and keep them current and in print. The most successful ones have an impressively long life, one that spans decades.

It all makes for awkward conversation, though. When I'm asked, "What are you reading?" I often reply, "Something you'll be reading two years from now." It's exciting to be ahead of the curve, a little out of sync with the world.

This book represents a moment frozen in time—a snapshot of where Chelsea Green Publishing has traveled, throughout the intellectual universe, over the thirty years since its founding in 1984. Thirty years as a small independent publisher may or may not seem like a long time, depending on one's perspective. The fact that we have survived through all of the seismic shifts in publishing and bookselling that have occurred over the past three decades is, to me at least, nothing sort of astonishing. And we are gratified and incredibly proud that we are thriving today as an employee-owned company, continuing our mission to publish groundbreaking books on important subjects. The ideas and authors we publish are helping to build the foundation for our collective future—one that I firmly believe will be better, wiser, and more just and sustainable than our present age of transition and strife.

Each of the 106 books included in this anthology was originally published by Chelsea Green. The excerpts were chosen to reflect the broad areas where we have published over the past thirty years—from forays into literature and memoir to progressive political thinking, to highly practical books on building, agriculture, and other topics that embrace an underlying philosophy of sustainable living. Collectively, they define who we are as a publisher, showing where we have been and suggesting where we are going.

In fact, I like to think of these brief excerpts as individual stones in a cairn. A cairn is a landmark, a pile of rocks built by hikers high above tree line in the mountains. It grows larger and larger over the years as new hikers passing by contribute a new stone, or replace one that might have fallen. A cairn is there to confirm, even on a foggy day, that we are on the right path, and it indicates the way forward, to the summit.

Every book is a stone, or a brick in the wall, of an edifice that is always being constructed, constantly evolving, and never quite finished. Perhaps it's no coincidence that a publishing company is colloquially referred to as a "house." At Chelsea Green we continue to build, with our authors and their ideas, a great house, one that represents our deeply held values and beliefs, our hopes and our dreams.

—*BEN WATSON,* Senior Editor

ART, POETRY, FABLE & FICTION

HOPE

RONALD T. SIMON

—— *from* ——

The Man Who Planted Trees

Jean Giono
Wood engravings by Michael McCurdy

1985

Jean Giono, one of France's most celebrated twentieth-century novelists, wrote this ecological fable in the early 1950s. It was far ahead of its time. Chelsea Green persuaded the wood engraver and fine press publisher Michael McCurdy to make twenty engravings that dramatically enhance the book's simple but powerful narrative. For the first time—almost three decades after its publication in Paris in Vogue *magazine—the story appeared in book form in 1985. In time it became an international bestseller, and in 1992 Chelsea Green created an audio edition, with Boston's WGBH classical music host Robert J. Lurtsema reading and original music by the Paul Winter Consort. In many ways this book embodies the spirit of our company.*

THERE WAS PEACE IN BEING WITH THIS MAN. The next day I asked if I might rest here for a day. He found it quite natural—or, to be more exact, he gave me the impression that nothing could startle him. The rest was not absolutely necessary, but I was interested and wished to know more about him. He opened the pen and led his flock to pasture. Before leaving, he plunged his sack of carefully selected and counted acorns into a pail of water.

I noticed that he carried for a stick an iron rod as thick as my thumb and about a yard and a half long. Resting myself by walking, I followed a path parallel to his. His pasture was in a valley. He left the dog in charge of the little flock and climbed toward where I stood. I was afraid that he was about to rebuke me for my indiscretion, but it was not that at all: this was the way he was going, and he invited me to go along if I had nothing better to do. He climbed to the top of the ridge, about a hundred yards away.

There he began thrusting his iron rod into the earth, making a hole in which he planted an acorn; then he refilled the hole. He was planting oak trees. I asked him if the land belonged to him. He answered no. Did he know whose it was? He did not. He supposed it was community property, or perhaps belonged to people who cared nothing about it. He was not interested in finding out whose it was. He planted his hundred acorns with the greatest care.

After the midday meal he resumed his planting. I suppose I must have been fairly insistent in my questioning, for he answered me. For three years he had been planting trees in this wilderness. He had planted one hundred thousand. Of the hundred thousand, twenty thousand had sprouted. Of the twenty thousand he still expected to lose about half, to rodents or to the unpredictable designs of Providence. There remained ten thousand oak trees to grow where nothing had grown before.

That was when I began to wonder about the age of this man. He was obviously over fifty. Fifty-five, he told me. His name was Elzéard Bouffier. He had once had a farm in the lowlands. There he had had his life. He had lost his only son, then his wife. He had withdrawn into this solitude where his pleasure was to live leisurely with his lambs and his dog. It was his opinion that this land was dying for want of trees. He added that, having no very pressing business of his own, he had resolved to remedy this state of affairs.

The oaks of 1910 were then ten years old and taller than either of us. It was an impressive spectacle. I was literally speechless and, as he did not talk, we spent the whole day walking in silence through his forest. In three sections, it measured eleven kilometers in length and three kilometers at its greatest width. When you remembered that all this had sprung from the hands and the soul of this one man, without technical resources, you understood that men could be as effectual as God in other realms than that of destruction.

He had pursued his plan, and beech trees as high as my shoulder, spreading out as far as the eye could reach, confirmed it. He showed me handsome clumps of birch planted five years before—that is, in 1915, when I had been fighting at Verdun. He had set them out in all the valleys where he had guessed—and rightly—that there was moisture almost at the surface of the ground. They were as delicate as young girls, and very well established.

Creation seemed to come about in a sort of chain reaction. He did not worry about it; he was determinedly pursuing his task in all its simplicity; but as we went back toward the village I saw water flowing in brooks that had been dry since the memory of man. This was the most impressive result of chain reaction that I had seen. These dry streams had once, long ago, run with water. Some of the dreary villages I mentioned before had been built on the sites of ancient Roman settlements, traces of which still remained; and archaeologists, exploring there, had found fishhooks where, in the twentieth century, cisterns were needed to assure a small supply of water.

The wind, too, scattered seeds. As the water reappeared, so there reappeared willows, rushes, meadows, gardens, flowers, and a certain purpose in being alive. But the transformation took place so gradually that it became part of the pattern without causing any astonishment. Hunters, climbing into the wilderness in pursuit of hares or wild boar, had of course noticed the sudden growth of little trees, but had attributed it to some natural caprice of the earth. That is why no one meddled with Elzéard Bouffier's work. If he had been detected he would have had opposition. He was indetectable. Who in the villages or in the administration could have dreamed of such perseverance in a magnificent generosity?

To have anything like a precise idea of this exceptional character one must not forget that he worked in total solitude: so total that, toward the end of his life, he lost the habit of speech. Or perhaps it was that he saw no need for it.

—— *from* ——

In a Pig's Eye

Karl Schwenke

1985

Published in the spring of 1985, this book launched Chelsea Green in its native state and throughout New England. Karl Schwenke was a successful travel guide writer from Utah who befriended Helen and Scott Nearing when he and his wife, Sue, moved to Vermont in the 1950s to start life anew. Inspired by the Nearings' example, the Schwenkes built their own stone house and wrote an acclaimed book, Build Your Own Stone House, *still in print. Later the couple moved north to Newbury, Vermont, and raised pigs. This carefully crafted, often hilarious, sometimes sad tale of life lived with pigs and other beings in a small Vermont town was Karl's first work of fiction. Thirty years later it is still in print, a classic.*

WHAT BLACK AND HIS HELPER MAY HAVE LACKED in personal hygiene, they made up for in personal competence. In minutes, Black found a suitable beam in the barn from which to suspend his spreading yarn, and the boy unloaded the scalding tub. Without asking, he filled it with water from the barn faucet. Together they unloaded a rickety wooden table which they nestled up to the tub. Next came a large, hand-forged hook, a meat saw, and a communal wood scabbard holding efficient-looking knives and a sharpening steel. Finally, they wrestled a large pressurized gas container from the pickup and hooked it up so that a foot-long flame played on the bottom of the tub. Not a word passed between them as they went about their work. They seemed oblivious to my brooding presence.

"Where're the pigs?" Black's back was to me as he fumbled with something in the cab of his truck. The question startled me. A scant fifteen minutes had passed since they had pulled into the dooryard. Black turned, and he held a revolver in one hand and a knife in the other.

"Th . . . they're over here," I stammered, pointing in the direction of the two stalls around the corner. There was an irremediable lag between my brain and my tongue. Images were bouncing around in my skull; little pigs emerging from a bran sack; adolescent pigs gamboling across an open field under a midsummer sun; grown hogs, become piglets again as they cavorted under the rain of sweet-smelling cedar sawdust.

"Umpf," grunted Black. He spat a stream of yellow juice. I followed in his ripe wake as he turned the corner.

It is a non sequitur to talk of death or love rationally; once experienced, both defy description, and without experience, both are nonsense. Though it would be stoutly denied by most rural people, husbandry is a form of love (it is no accident that spouse is synonymous with husband) and the ultimate goal of all husbandry, be it of plant or animal, is to mourn the death of that which we nourished and loved. We call the wake a harvest celebration.

"Them two're good looking pigs," said Black when he came to a rest in front of the sows. "That'n," he pointed to the boar, "looks a mite peaked." In the sleety rain his flat black eyes seem to have taken on a sheen that matched the cold metal of the revolver. "Nawthin' pers'nal, but you don't look so hot yourself."

"Yeah," I replied lethargically.

He looked at me sharply. "You wanna go outside the barn while I . . ."

"No!" The vehemence of my response surprised me. Then more softly, "No, I reckon I'll stay."

He shrugged, and opened the door to the sow's stall. I forced myself to watch as he carefully lined the muzzle up between the sow's eyes. "Bang!" The sow's legs flew out from under her, and there wasn't a tremor as she died. Deftly Black drew the sharp blade across her throat, and the blood pulsed across the clean, fresh sawdust. "Bang!" went the revolver again. Black didn't waste any motions.

The smell of the fresh blood was everywhere, and despite my resolve, I pulled back. A grunt from the next stall made me turn, and I found the boar's bloodshot eyes fixed on mine.

Black emerged from the sow's stall and started to open the door to the boar's.

I put my hand on the latch. "Do you mind," I asked in as even a voice as I could manage, "if I . . . kill . . . this one?"

He shifted the quid on his cheek as he stared at me flatly. "No, I reckon not."

"Hold on a minute," I said over my shoulder, "I'll be right back." I started toward the house.

I was back a minute later, and Black and the boy stared bemused at the two bottles of homemade beer I carried.

"Drinking buddy," I explained shortly. I took Slack's revolver in one hand and the beer in the other as I entered the pen and kicked the door shut behind me.

When I came out again five minutes later I carried two empty bottles and the smoking gun. I did not try to hide the tears in my eyes.

Aloud I said, "The damned fool thought he was immortal!" Inwardly I was thinking, "but illusion is just about all we've got left."

——— *from* ———

Words and Images of Edvard Munch

Bente Torjusen

1986

Bente Torjusen, formerly director of Oslo's Munch Museum program for public education, teamed up with her painter-filmmaker husband, Clifford West, to create this pioneering art book exhibiting one of the twentieth century's great masters. The couple, both experts on Munch's life and work, realized one of the artist's unfulfilled dreams, which was to create a portfolio or book that exhibited both his words and his images in juxtaposition. The book exhibits a little-appreciated series of twelve Munch prints called "The Mirror" in their entirety for the first time, showing Munch's engrossment in the romantic and erotic encounter between a man and a woman, whose love is destined to be shattered. The image and words chosen here—Geschrei or The Scream—is, in the words of art critic Arthur Lubow, "an icon of modern art, a Mona Lisa for our time."

Geschrei

Ich fühlte das grosse Geschrei
durch die Natur

EDVARD MUNCH

I walked along
the road with two
friends—then the
sun went down
Suddenly the sky
became bloody red
(—and I felt
a breath of sadness
—a sucking pain
beneath the heart)
I stopped, leaned
against the railing tired
to death—over the
blue-black fjord and city
lay blood and tongues of fire
My friends walked
on and I was left
trembling
with fear—
and I felt a
big unending
scream go through
nature

—— *from* ——

Judevine

David Budbill

1991; second edition, 1999

Poet and playwright David Budbill, who lives in Vermont's Northeast King-dom, has what Wendell Berry has called a "loving interest in other people," especially poor, unnoticed rural people beset by poverty and adversity of a universal sort. "Without [Budbill] these people would not be heard from," claimed fellow poet Thomas McGrath. Budbill's widely produced play Judevine—*sixty-five productions in twenty-two states—is a dramatic stage version of the* Judevine *cycle of poems that Chelsea Green published as a complete collection for the first time in 1991. His dark, lyrical, and funny narrative poems bring to vivid life ordinary people of the rural North.*

SALLY TATRO'S PLACE
Even now, years after its desertion, and though it is
gray and sinking and its parts come apart, the house
still clings to a former grace—narrow clapboards,
fluted corners, a center door with frosted glass—
and, in addition to dishevelment, dilapidation,
the place suffers weeds high as the windows,
a porch roof fallen in, though it now
fades and withers, slips irretrievably away,

when I drive past I watch and think how it is like
old poetry where reference and allusion are obscure
but where, even after centuries, insight and need
still swell within the form, and I see in the

collapsing house the builder's passion rising
from design: this indestructible, eternal dream.

ENVOY TO SALLY'S PLACE
There was a fellow passing through who lived and worked
in New York City, an official of some sort down there at the
Metropolitan Museum of Art is what I heard.
He was summering up here, I think, and going down the road
when he spied Sally's place and was so stunned
by its beauty and calm, so taken aback by finding
such a work of art so far from anywhere,
he drove his car right off the road.

Roy comes up to him out of breath and says:
You okay?

And the gent turns around surprised and says:
Huh? Oh. Yes. Fine. Thank You.
and then says:

Does anyone here know how beautiful this place is?
Oh!

Roy didn't say much but did pull the fellow out
and he was on his way.

When Edith heard the story her mouth tightened as it does
when she gets mad and she said:
Yes, we know, or used to know.
It *was* a lovely place, but not now, not anymore.
What's beautiful about an empty house?
It's falling down, deserted, cold inside,
what's beautiful about that?

You should have seen that place when the Tatros
still were there, where there was flowers in the dooryard
and the barn wasn't falling down, paint on the clapboards
and wash on the line and the pastures clear of cows—
then it was beautiful. Now it's just an old wreck,
a picture for that fellow's old museum.

JERRY WILLEY'S LUNCH
Before Jerry got The Garage he worked for the Mountain
     Company down in Stowe
helping New York ladies get off the lifts,
all day on top of the mountain freezing his ass off
for two and a quarter an hour.
Jerry never brought a lunch, not once in all those years,
just six pieces of bread, a jar of mayonnaise and a soda which
each morning when he reached the mountain top he placed
inside the warming hut beside the skiers' lunches
left there so they wouldn't freeze

As Jerry said: I ain't eatin' salt pork and macaroni
when I got these. Then he'd unwrap half a dozen
skiers' sandwiches, extract a slice or two from each—
roast beef, corned beef, ham, pastrami—
rewrap them carefully and fix his lunch.

THE GASTRONOMIC TRYPTICH
WHICH IS SAM HINES' LIFE
Sam Hines divides his life like most of us
by years
but unlike most of us
he breaks each year apart
into three parts
not four or twelve.
Seasons and months mean nothing to him.
He never knows what time it is,
what day or week,
he only knows what time he eats.

When I feel the sun get higher in the sky
I begin to dream 'bout sugarin'
an' when we boil that first time
I go onto maple syrup right away
an' hit it hard
an' stay with it until it's time for trout.
Then I stay with them until the frost comes
an' leaves come down and I get the itch
to kill a deer. When I've got me one,
I stay with him right through the snow n' dark;
only I can't hit him hard the way I do the trout 'cause
he's got to last me 'til the sun gets back up here
an' I can go again onto the syrup.

Works good. Except those years I don't kill a deer.
Those are hard winters an' I'm use'ly always sick,
an' sometimes I'm so sick
I think I'll die an' never make it to the syrup.
But I always have, by Jesus—
only sometimes, Mister Man,
it's been awful close.

——— *from* ———

A Cafecito Story/El Cuento del Cafecito

Julia Alvarez
Woodcuts by Grabados de Belkis Ramírez

Originally published as *A Cafecito Story* in 2001;
English/Spanish bilingual edition, 2002

Julia Alvarez is an acclaimed poet, novelist, and essayist, so much so that in 2014 she was awarded the National Medal of Arts by President Obama. In 2002 Chelsea Green published her charming eco-fable, A Cafecito Story, *based on her experience with her husband founding Alta Gracia, a sustainable coffee farm and literacy center in the Dominican Republic. Alvarez writes about the rejuvenating power and cultural significance of reclaiming this coffee farm and returning it to traditional growing methods. This book isn't only a beautifully crafted story: It's also a reminder that fair trade and sustainable agriculture have the potential to positively impact hundreds of thousands of real lives.*

EVERY DAY AS THEY WORK TOGETHER, Miguel tells Joe the story of coffee.

How before the coffee can be planted, the land must be prepared in terraces with trees of differing heights to create layers of shade: first, cedros; then, guamas and banana trees.

Meanwhile, Miguel starts the coffee seeds in a germination bed. It takes about fifty days for the shoots to come up.

From the germination bed, the little transplants go into a vivero for eight months. Finally, when they are bold and strong, Miguel plants them on the terraces.

Then comes the weeding and the feeding of the plants with abonos made from whatever there is around. We say organico, Miguel explains, because we use only what nature provides for free.

After three years, si Dios quiere, we have a first harvest. We pick four times during the season which goes from December to March. Only the red cherries, of course.

Then the rush is on: we must depulp the cherry that same night or early the next morning. The pulp goes to our worm bed where we are producing our natural fertilizers.

The wet granos, we take to the river for washing. They must be bathed with running water for eight or so hours—a watchful process, as we have to get the bean to just that moment when the grains are washed but no fermentation has begun. It is not unlike the moment with a woman—Miguel smiles, looking off toward the mountains—when love sets in.

And then, the long drying process in the sun. Some of us, who cannot afford a concrete patio, use the paved road. The grains have to be turned every four hours. At night, we pile them up and bring them under cover. Woe to us if there is rain and we do not get our granos covered quickly enough! Wet coffee molds and ends up in the abono pile.

After about two weeks, if the weather is good, we bag the coffee—

Joe sighs with relief. I didn't realize so much work went into one cup! he confesses.

I am not finished, Miguel continues, holding up a hand. Once the coffee is bagged, we let it rest. A few days, a few weeks. We have only taken off the pulp but the bean is still inside the pergamino. So, after the rest, we haul the bags down to the beneficio to have this pergamino removed. Then we sort the beans very carefully by hand, since one sour bean in a bag can spoil the taste for the buyer. The seconds we keep for ourselves.

You mean to tell me that great coffee I've been drinking is seconds? Joe asks, shaking his head.

Miguel nods. The export grade is, of course, for export.

But your coffee is so much better than anything I've tasted in fancy coffee shops in Omaha, Joe notes.

That is because—as you told me yourself—you are a farmer's son, Miguel explains. You taste with your whole body and soul.

Until this moment of Miguel saying so, Joe did not know this was true. He remembers his father planting corn in rows so straight, God Himself might have drawn the lines with a ruler. While he worked, Joe's father would whistle a little tune as if he were in conversation with a flock of invisible birds.

Sometimes, as Joe works alongside Miguel, he finds himself whistling that same tune.

——— *from* ———

Rehearsing with Gods

*Photographs and Essays
on The Bread and Puppet Theater*

Ronald T. Simon and Marc Estrin

2004

Peter Schumann's Bread and Puppet Theater is likely one of the most important contributors to modern American theater, and surely the longest lasting. Since the early 1960s Schumann and his puppeteers have been pouring out work after work on every scale. In this collaboration Ronald T. Simon, a remarkable photographer, and Marc Estrin, a longtime puppeteer and novelist, identify eight archetypes engaged repeatedly by Peter Schumann and his crew. This book consists of parallel meditations on the themes of Death, Fiend, Beast, Human, World, Gift, Bread, and Hope. This selection is from Hope.

Does Bread & Puppet Give Me Hope?
Yes.
hope to be able to name names when names need naming
hope to see the slapstick in the tragic, the tragic in the slapstick
hope for tongues that can speak the unspeakable
hope that the glib may come unglued
hope that persistence will continue to persist
hope that the uninvented may already be born
hope that probity and integrity will triumph over want
hope in idealism at the helm
hope for the categorical imperative
hope in the rightness of Yes! for an answer
hope that I might someday play the accordion
hope that the great unicycle will roll on, upright
hope that the dead can actually rise BOOM CLASH
hope that the virtues—classical and theological—will triumph
    by Glover example
hope to be at demonstrations I don't attend
hope that you don't get only what you pay for and
hope that the best things in life will not be things

hope that unAmerican activity may triumph in the world

hope that the ever-renewable will continue to renew

hope that human reach will continue to exceed its grasp

hope that there is still an alternative to There Is No Alternative

hope that the New World Order may become new

hope that Hope will not be deferred, nor the heart be sick

hope that in this hell, hope need not be abandoned

hope that swords may also be beaten into puppets

hope that giants may still walk the earth

hope that *Lieb* will cushion *Leid*, and that *Welt* may be
    infused with *Traum*

hope that the earth will still green in the spring

hope that humans may be reachable and teachable

hope that our masks may show us who we are

hope that words can still have mottled meaning

hope that there is music still to be invented

hope that political power can grow out of barrels of guns that
    say BANG!

hope that we don't have to study war no more

hope that there is a shore for Michael's boat to row to

hope that the flowers have not gone anywhere

hope that Captain Kidd will never be caught and hung

hope that the children will not die, but will climb on their stilts
    and dance

hope that Death's dominion will feel like the necropolis—fraternal

hope that in the tightness of the times, we may get back to the
    truly basic

hope that Cheap Art can claim its place at the art table

hope that the wine and wafer will sustain and not be genetically
    modified

hope that we can learn to bear the terror of angels

hope for Simple Gifts and Sacred Harps

hope for the human need of garlic for good bread

hope that tickets to *Theatrum Mundi* will always be free

hope that humanity will not be all-too-human

hope that all ex votos be effective

hope that fire will always bake as well as burn

hope that neither bread nor puppets can ever be defeated

hope that morning meetings may always end in tired evening bliss

hope that simple light may rise out of complicated darkness
hope in HALLELUJAH!
hope that the last word may be *vollbracht*

—— *from* ——

Not in His Image

Gnostic Vision, Sacred Ecology, and the Future of Belief

John Lamb Lash

2006

Not in His Image *delves deeply into the shadows of ancient Gnostic writings to reconstruct the story early Christians tried to scrub from the pages of history. Author John Lash, a comparative mythologist, explores the richness of the ancient European Pagan spirituality—the Pagan Mysteries, the Great Goddess, Gnosis, the myths of Sophia and Gaia—and chronicles the annihilation of this Pagan European culture at the hands of Christianity.*

As Pagans, the GNOSTIKOI REJECTED the belief that suffering has a redemptive value. As theologians, they refuted the claim that divine intervention could alter the human condition. By rejecting the superhuman savior and refuting salvationist beliefs, Gnostics drew a frontal assault from those who were formulating and enforcing the doctrines of the Judeo-Christian redeemer complex. The brutal suppression of the Mysteries, the destruction of Gnostic writings, and the wholesale genocide of Pagan culture in Europe belong to the untold story of "Western civilization" and "the triumph of Christianity." This is the story as it was lived by the "losers." To reclaim Gnostic wisdom for today *and* merge Mystery teachings with deep ecology—the dual intention of this book—cannot be done without looking closely at what destroyed the Sophianic vision of the living earth, and why it was able to do so. The genocide of native culture in the classical world went on for centuries, but a cover-up has largely concealed this fact, and continues to this day. To expose the cover-up and reveal both the cause and scope of the destruction so wrought is the secondary, but no less important, objective of this book.

The redeemer complex has four components: creation of the world by a father god independent of a female counterpart; the trial and testing (conceived as a historical drama) of the righteous few or "Chosen People"; the mission of the creator god's son (the messiah) to save the world; and the final, apocalyptic judgment delivered by father and son upon humanity. Orthodox Jews accept all four points of the complex, but do not recognize Jesus of the New Testament as their Messiah, who to this day has yet to appear. Christians follow the dictum of the apostle Peter who addressed converting Jews as "a chosen race, a royal priesthood, a holy nation, God's own people" (1 Peter 2:9), thus, in one deft phrase, transferring the status of "Chosen People" from Jews to Christian converts. In short, Roman Christianity adopted the larval or tribal form of the redeemer complex from Judaism, and transformed it into a universal ("catholic") program of salvation. Differing views of these four components determine various factions of Judaism and Christianity as well as Islam, which also belongs to the trinity of Abrahamic religions, although it arose after the Gnostics were silenced, and hence did not figure in their critique.

Some Gnostics, such as Valentinus and Marcion, appeared to propose compromise positions on these issues, but the radical Pagan argument ruthlessly refuted all four points. Almost without exception, scholars and historians of religion today hold the view that the Gnostic movement arose within early Christianity: If this were so, Gnostic ideas would have merely been aspects of a vague kind of "Gnostic Christianity" that was gradually eliminated with the doctrinal definition of beliefs. But the evidence of the surviving materials clearly contradicts this interpretation. Gnostic Christianity is a retrofit contrived by scholars whose religious convictions prevent them from seeing, and admitting, that the greater part of Gnostic material was diametrically opposed to the Judeo-Christian ideology of salvation.

For Pagans and Christians alike, the four components of the redeemer complex were not merely dry theological issues. The Gnostic protest against the redeemer complex aroused an enormous wave of violence in converts to the salvationist creed, as seen in the murder of Hypatia. She was a *gnostikos*, a Pagan intellectual from the Mysteries, targeted by the righteous rage of people who pinned their faith on the Divine Redeemer. The mob that attacked her believed that their God had a unique way to overcome suffering, and this belief sanctioned them to inflict suffering to further His cause.

Belief in the redemptive value of suffering is the core dynamic of the violence, will to conquer, and genocide that drove the rise of Roman Christianity and released an ever-expanding wave of destruction across the planet.

Humans may commit violence for many reasons, they may seek to oppress and dominate others for a variety of causes, but when domination by violent force, both physical and psychological, is infused with righteousness and underwritten by divine authority, violence takes on another dimension. It becomes inhuman and deviant. Like countless others of her time, and in the centuries to follow, Hypatia was the victim of religiously inspired sectarian violence driven and fed by faith in the redeemer complex. What kind of world results if the power to dominate and control others, inflicting enormous suffering in the process, is sanctioned by a divine being who can at the same time redeem that suffering and release the perpetrators and their victims from that world's evils? Such was the diabolic system Gnostics found themselves facing after 150 c.e.

Salvation is not the crucial issue for humanity. Adaptation is. We *do* fit into the natural world, but not in any way that Gaia predetermines for us, as she does for other creatures. We are the novelty in *Her* nature. We are the singularity in Sophia's Dreaming, the exception upon which she relies in some way, if the seers in the Mysteries were right . . .

From time before reckoning indigenous people all around the world have observed the ways of nature and other species, and by doing so learned how to fit into their environment. By coercing us to "believe in an abstract reality which pits us against the earth that houses all organic worlds," patriarchy and perpetrator religion have almost totally destroyed the precious legacy of native wisdom, and the natives along with it. There are still some threads of indigenous sanity to weave into a future worth living, but in the end it may not be native savvy alone that ensures the survival of the unfinished animal. Loving observation, empathy, and respect for nature and other species can teach us a lot about how to live, but to resolve the question of our niche something more is needed: imagination, the luminous *epinoia*.

Imagination is the genius of humanity, and in each people of each region of the world it manifests a particular creative and innovative spirit—the *genius loci*, the local genius, or spirit of place. The Sophia mythos tells us that the Goddess charged Zoe, the immortal life force, with the task of implanting *epinoia* in humanity. To put it another way, we carry divine imaginative force as a somatic capacity, evident in the phenomenon of bioluminescence, as already noted. Imagination and vitality are crucially wedded in the human psyche and mutually anchored in the body. No ideology can ever defeat or deracinate this union.

NATURE &
ADVENTURE TRAVEL

JOHN WALTERMIRE

—— *from* ——

First Light

*Sojourns with People of the Outer Hebrides,
the Sierra Madre, the Himalayas, and Other Remote Places*

Ethan Hubbard

1986

*Ethan Hubbard left his job as a teacher in Vermont and in the early 1980s
began traveling with a 35mm camera and a backpack to out-of-the-way
places all over the world. His richly toned black-and-white photographs, alive
with narrative meaning, capture landscapes and people virtually untouched
by industrial culture. Hubbard's love affair with rural people, young and
elderly as well as adults who are solitary but not lonely, is made palpable by
his straightforward prose, and above all by his luminous photographs.*

FLYING LOW OVER THE CONTINENT from Sydney to Alice Springs, I saw
mountain ranges, red-orange and black, stretching as far as the eye could
see. The desert floor sprawled out to the west—dotted with intermittent
mining roads, cattle, and sheep stations. Three hours later we landed in Alice
Springs. Coming off the plane I was immediately aware of being in the middle of a vast desert. In the shade the temperature read 110 degrees. Beyond
the fences of the airport lay jagged mountains that seemed to bleed in the
afternoon heat, and yellow earth lay all around me, barren and cracked. We
boarded an air-conditioned shuttle bus that sealed us off from the desert we
had come to see.

On the way into town I saw the Aborigines. They sat in small circles, as
still as statues in the tall grass under shade trees. Even from the window of
the speeding bus they looked shockingly poor. They were shoeless and wore
ragged clothes. There was a ghost-like quality about them; it was as if their
bodies were still there, but their souls had long since vanished. I had the feeling that something monumental—disastrous—had happened to them. I sat at
the edge of my seat and stared. No one else on the bus seemed to notice them.

Alice Springs was a modern city of twenty thousand people in the heart of
the desert outback. Once an important cattle and mining center for the country's interior, it was now a major tourist center that catered to the wealthy
traveler. People came from all over the world to see the desert outback: the

quintessence of nothingness. The hardpan soil, blistering sands, blazing heat, and huge ominous sky seemed to fill tourists with wonder and make them thankful for their own cozy little niches back home in Germany or Yugoslavia.

Long before cattle and mining—all the way back to the last ice age—Alice Springs had belonged to the Aborigines of the western desert. It had been the holiest of their holy shrines, the very source of their game and water, the inspiration for their myths and ceremonies. But their land had been torn from them. Signs in store fronts in Alice Springs read: Proper Dress Code Enforced For Admittance: Pressed Pants And Collared Shirts. This local ordinance single-handedly disqualified most of Alice Springs' fifteen hundred Aborigines from even the most basic of civil rights. They were outcasts in their own land.

I began to go see the Aborigines on my bicycle every day. I took long rides around the edge of the city that took me to Hoppy's Camp, Three Mile Junction, and a sacred stone outcropping called the Howling Dingo Monument (once a major shrine to these desert people). At first the Aborigines did not know what to make of a white man coming to see them. But they did allow me to sit with them around their campfires at night, and on their stone piles in the shade during the day. I watched silently as old men carved boomerangs and worked stone into spearpoints that would never be used. Sometimes the old men and women taught the children how to paint the enigmatic designs of their ancestors. These fiery whorls and scrolls alluded perhaps to dream states that revealed the location of water or knowledge of the soul of an animal they intended to kill. The Aborigines spoke no English, so we communicated with each other with a handshake or a smile or laughter. Day after day I arrived and took interest in their lives, and slowly, ever so slowly, a feeling of trust and friendship developed between us.

When I saw how malnourished and hungry they were, I began carrying a knapsack full of food: cheese and sandwich meats, fruit and yogurt, cold milk for the dehydrated babies, tea and biscuits for the old men. Sometimes when I brought a carton of eggs for the group, the men and I made a fire of sticks and hard-boiled them in billy cans. Bringing food, of course, was only a gesture, not a solution. But I knew that a gesture often spelled the difference between giving up on life or going on.

For several weeks I continued to make daily visits to the encampments. New friends began to wave at me as I pedaled by: Willie, Eunice, Peter, Old Nosepeg, Kaapa, Winnie, Left Hand Jim, and Louie Paga. I joined them whenever I could, mostly at their stone piles, where they stared off into space or looked down at the ground for hours at a time. During these long silent vigils they waited for something that never seemed to come and seemed to hope for something to take away their struggle and pain. Old men held my hands and cooed, their long slender fingers folding over mine in unspoken trust.

The Aborigines were dying a slow, horrifying death. Their nomadic ways, their art, dance, music, and oral history, which stretched back to the last ice age—all they possessed—had slipped through their hands like sand. They endured this collective death with quiet resignation. Perhaps this acquiescence stemmed from their belief that this life was a mere shadow of the real world, that beyond it lay a greater reality.

——— *from* ———

Backtracking
The Way of a Naturalist
Ted Levin
Illustrations by Joan Waltermire

1987

In Backtracking, *naturalist, educator, photographer, and writer Levin travels from eastern maritime Canada to the Everglades to revel in the surprising behaviors of different wild animals, and along the way he explores his boyhood as a budding, irrepressible young naturalist on suburban Long Island. Author of two Chelsea Green natural histories (*Blood Brook *was published in 1991), Levin won the John Burroughs medal in 2004 for his third,* Liquid Land. *He is one of America's most outstanding writers on the natural world—whether it be wilderness, rural, suburban, or urban.*

THAT DARK FEBRUARY NIGHT, one of those rare midwinter nights when the sky is clear and the temperature is above freezing, I heard a fox call—a short run of sharp yips and barks, then a long, emaciated howl, smaller and daintier than the wild, drawn-out voice of a coyote. From the darkness beyond our peeper marsh, near the meadow's head where the land rises gently toward the ridge, another volley of barks and yips rose above the tree-tops and carried onto our porch.

All winter this fox had marked the snow, but tonight, as Orion climbed in the southern sky, he uncurled and stretched and sent an urgent message into the night. He never used a winter den. He slept in the middle of the meadow instead, head to the wind so the long outer fur of the guard hairs—rust-colored and silky, stayed still. Beneath those long protective hairs a wrap of dense under-wool held a warm envelope of air. Once his blood began to flow and his leg muscles loosened, the fox wandered into the night. After several steps he squirted urine on a withered milkweed stem then headed for a small pond tucked into a fold in the meadow. With his urine the fox had run a classified advertisement, announcing both his presence and his desire. More drops down the side of a cattail stalk.

Fox piss is strong stuff that has a faintly skunky smell, and he used it like semiprecious fluid—a few drops here, a few drops there—the pungent odor clinging to snow, stems, and cold air until it is washed away. If it is fresh, I can smell fox piss without bending down. But if it's old, then my dog— who can read withered urine—knows that a cunning (and horny) predator slightly bigger than a tabby has passed through the meadow. Five weeks before the equinox, as an annual jolt of testosterone coursed through the fox's body, he sought company, attempting to reestablish a pair bond with last year's vixen or to attract a new mate by pissing everywhere. His trail stained the snow and the air.

After marking the cattail the fox strode off along the edge of the pond, twice backtracking, when he heard tiny footfalls beneath the snow. At the head of the track pattern that resembled a buckled figure eight the fox crouched. He pinpointed a mouse by leaning into the sound, an ear cocked toward the ground, then drove up off his long thin hind legs straight into the air. At the height of the jump he jackknifed and his front paws struck the ground first, pinning a mouse securely beneath them.

According to J. David Henry, a wildlife biologist from northern Saskatchewan who has unraveled a great many vulpine mysteries, red foxes are built for those quiet airborne attacks. Using simple physics to prove his point, Henry compared the skeletons of a male fox and a male coyote. According to the principle of surface area to volume ratio, if a wooden block doubles its linear dimensions the column and weight increase by eight. Applied to mammals, a proportional increase in surface area per gram of limb bone should exist between fox and coyote, which also pounce. Henry found, however, that red foxes had 30% more surface area than the rule of squares and cubes predicts. Which is to say that red foxes have longer, lighter legs than one would expect for an animal of their size. They are, so to speak, the gymnasts of the canines, airborne little dogs that can float past the antipredator defenses of small mammals. They are lighter and comparatively leaner than coyotes.

The fox's four thin, dagger-like canine teeth punctured the mouse. In a gulp it was gone. From spring to pounce to bite, the fox had dispatched his prey with catlike precision. Red foxes, although members of the dog family, have several anatomical traits that converge with those of cats: their claws are semi-retractable, their pupils are vertically slit and the *tapetum lucidum*, that iridescent eye membrane that recycles light before it leaves the eyes and is the source of the animal's eye shine, is well-developed; their canine teeth, long and thin, are proportionally not as thick as those of coyotes. With all of these catlike qualities and with its comparative lightness, it is no wonder the fox launched into the air when it went after the mouse. Only when hunting snowshoe hare, woodchucks, or other moderately sized prey did he chase them dog-like.

Hare were scarce this winter, so Reynard padded through the snow, listening. His single line of tracks etched across the pond and meadow and up the apron of the ridge. A wider-chested animal, a raccoon for instance, would have marked the snow with all four feet while a long, thin, short-legged animal, a fisher or a weasel, would leave a series of parallel prints. But when the long-legged, thin-chested fox walked, his hind feet swung directly into the tracks of his forefeet. When he ran, all four feet marked the snow. I once shadowed a fox along the curve of a frozen brook. When it realized I was coming, it broke into a dead run. Its tracks, at first a leisurely line of prints spaced eight to twelve inches apart, exploded into clusters of four, deeper and more pronounced, with seven- to eight-foot gaps between them. But I was hours behind this fox, so he moved with assurance, varying his speed to suit his mood.

Wind had cleared with the crest of snow, exposing frozen ground unattractive to voles and unpromising for the fox. He crossed the ridge and headed down the south slope through the beech-maple woods, pausing only to piss. In the woods the snow was deeper and travel slower, so the fox plowed instead of padded, his long fluffy tail dusting the surface. Halfway through the ridge he caught scent of a vixen that had crossed the head of an adjoining meadow. His pace hastened. With ears bent forward, he yapped—short, sharp yaps—then pranced like a frisky colt. Alongside a prostrate sugar maple, amid a highway of deer moose prints, the vixen had left her mark, a few drops of bright red estrus blood amid a splash of golden-yellow urine. Color coordination had no effect upon the fox. Like a sensitive black-and-white film, his eyes registered only shades of grey. He knew from the blood's rich odor that the vixen, too, was ready to breed. Casting prudence aside, he howled and screeched then followed her footsteps.

By early morning he had crossed a brook along the back corner of an idle dairy farm, nearly a mile and a half from the ridge. A single set of tracks marked the snow. Her scent grew fresher, almost overpowering. Again the fox barked and yipped, waggling his tail in anticipation. A long line of prints snaked through the pasture. At the end sat the vixen. A dome of arctic air settled over east-central Vermont, warding off snow. The wind picked up, temperatures plunged. Dry snow swirled off the meadows into tiny frozen twisters that skirted the surface then vanished. And beneath that vaulted February sky, now flush with the rising sun, two red foxes came together.

——— *from* ———

On Watching Birds

Lawrence Kilham
Illustrations by Joan Waltermire

1988

Naturalist and scientist Lawrence Kilham spent a lifetime observing birds closely both in his own backyard and around the world. He was convinced that anyone who is interested can make unique discoveries about birds simply by watching them consistently and persistently. The robin or house sparrow can be as interesting as an exotic warbler or thrush. To be involved in the process of close observation takes you into the heart of a bird's life and the meaning of its behavior. Kilham is a deceptively humble master of the craft of bird-watching. On a family note, Lawrence is also the father of Ben Kilham, who published his own book In the Company of Bears *with Chelsea Green in 2013.*

WHEN I SPOKE TO A SCIENTIFIC COLLEAGUE about a sense of beauty, he said there is no such thing. Some people think a factory chimney is beautiful, and others think it is the opposite. For my part I think a sense of the beauty of nature is innate. It was probably implanted in our ancestors early on. The sense of beauty had homeostatic value for man living in a state of nature; it made him feel at home in the world and in balance with other living things. "I thought the sparrow's note from heaven, singing at dawn on the elder bough," wrote Emerson. Who knows but that our remote hunter ancestors had the same awareness? And who can say, scientifically, that we might be healthier and happier if this awareness was not dimmed by civilization? Dr.

M. D. Coulter, who thinks that the esthetic sense could involve medicine, wrote in the *British Medical Journal:*

> Who would not even now stop in their tracks at the sound of the nightingale, or feast replete on the sparkle of the sun on the fresh moving sea? To cast these aside is to ignore the legacy of a thousand ages . . . why do so many people seem untouched by great music or the beauty of the natural world? Partly because it is for some not freely available and also because so often it is denied them at their most impressionable age.

The mass of people, living lives of work, hurry, preoccupation, and anxiety, do not see nature's beauty. When they are unhurried and at peace with themselves, the world can seem incredibly beautiful to ordinary people: the stars at night, the morning after a snow storm, the flowers of spring. "I never see the dawn break or the sun set," wrote Emerson in his essay "Nature," "without reflecting 'what can be conceived so beautiful as actual nature?'"

A sense of beauty may be especially intense at moments of physical exhaustion or even of death. Lord Tweedsmuir (John Buchan) wrote of his experience in the Boer War that after a long trek following a late camp the night before, ". . . though savagely hungry, I forgot about breakfast. Scents, sights, and sounds blended into a harmony so perfect that it transcended human expression, even human thought . . . The world was a place of inexhaustible beauty . . ." And speaking of a small company marching into a heavenly valley in Vietnam, the military historian S. L. A. Marshall wrote:

> What they saw made the way seem remote and their misery incongruous. Given only a few minutes to enjoy the setting as they marched, they made the most of their opportunity. The picture thereafter would remain with them imperishably, for such is the nature of man under pressure. While excitement holds, the individual may rise above his prior limits. Woodrow Wilson Sayre, writing of his fight against death on Mt. Everest, put it in this way: "Surprisingly the sense of beauty is still sharp. How deep that sense must be within us. Even a man waiting to die will notice the loveliness of trees and sunlight around him." I have found this to be true of much humbler men, combat hands who, unlike Sayre, did not possess an acute awareness of an unusual instance of order in art or nature.

I have read, in an account of one of Hitler's death camps, of the intense feeling of beauty that came to a girl dying of tuberculosis when she saw a spray of apple blossoms outside her barrack window. Why should extreme fatigue or approaching death make some otherwise indifferent people perceive the beauty of the world? Could it not be that the pressures and anxieties of civilization are lifted at these times? Recall the way highwaymen and pickpockets were said to look so peaceful when riding through the gallows, as though they had nothing more to worry about. "You cannot perceive beauty," wrote Thoreau, "but with a serene mind."

Among naturalists, none appear to have felt the sheer beauty of the world more than British author Richard Jeffries at the time his health was breaking up and he was about to die. At this time, as he wrote in *Story of My Heart*,

> The familiar everyday scene was soon out of sight. I came to other trees, meadows, and fields. I began to breathe a new air and to have fresher aspiration . . . By the blue heaven, by the rolling sun bursting through untrodden space, a new ocean of every other day unveiled. By the fresh and wandering air encompassing the world, by the sea sounding on the shore—the green sea white-flecked at the margin and the deep ocean; by the strong earth under me.

I think it is because civilization imposes such heavy burdens that the best in us is often crushed. We do not think and feel as the great individuals we might be but only as members of the herd. How about scientists? Have they, by habits of precision and exactitude, risen above such things as beauty of the world? Certainly not some of the abler ones. John Tyndall wrote of Faraday, one of the most honored scientists of all time:

> What to him was the splendor of a palace compared to a thunderstorm upon the Brighton downs? What among all the appliances of royalty to compare with the setting sun? I refer to a thunderstorm and a sunset, because these things excited a kind of ecstasy in his mind, and to a mind open to such ecstasy the pomps and pleasures of the world are usually of small account. Nature, not education, rendered Faraday strong and refined.

Often when in the woods cutting trees and piling branches I look up at the white clouds and blue sky, at the sun on the snow and white birches, and, exhilarated by the mountain air, I exclaim to myself, "Oh, beautiful world. Oh, wonderful day." Nature is not something to do with other men. It's something to get us away, at least for a minute, from the turmoil of the natural world. The habit of watching birds and animals in beautiful places can, for a time, bring us closer to what we really are.

There are so many obstacles to our developing the sense of beauty. I wonder if too much preoccupation with intellectual matters does not kill the esthetic sense. Charles Darwin was exhilarated by the beautiful scenery when younger but spoke of losing the pleasure he formally took in it. Darwin, speculating on this phenomenon, wrote:

> My mind seems to have become a kind of machine for grinding general laws out of large collections of facts, but why this should have caused the atrophy of that part of the brain alone, on which the higher tastes depend, I cannot conceive. The loss of these tastes is a loss of happiness, and may possibly be injurious to the intellect, and more probably to the moral character, by enfeebling the emotional part of our nature.

Alexander Skutch, by far the greatest of living ornithologists, has retained his esthetic sense into old age. He writes of birds: "They charm us with lovely plumage and melodious song; our quest of them takes us to the fairest places, to find them and uncover their secrets, we exert ourselves greatly and live intensely." Frank Graham Jr., who went to Costa Rica to interview Skutch, reports that "his attachment both to natural beauty and the extraordinary moments when the mind and senses savor it, is intense."

I feel sympathetic to Darwin's perception that loss of the esthetic sense is regrettable, but I think losing it is not inevitable with age but results from simple neglect. If a behavior watcher thinks about the beauty of the places where he goes to watch birds as well as the birds themselves, and if he keeps an eye out for both, he may retain the enthusiasm he had for both into old age. Enthusiasm for the beauty of life helps to keep the brain alive. And there is a practical aspect to it. Things do not always happen when one goes out to watch birds. There can be long stretches when nothing much seems to be going on, as when watching by the nest of a pileated woodpecker. At these times I switch to thinking about how beautiful the world is, and instead of being impatient that the bird does not return, I find myself at peace with the world.

————— *from* —————

A Canoeist's Sketchbook

Robert Kimber

1991

Robert Kimber is a prolific author of nationally published magazine articles about canoeing, snowshoeing, and hiking in the wilderness of northern Quebec, Labrador, and Maine, where he and his wife, Ruth, live on an old farm. A widely published translator (with his wife), essayist, philosopher, and humorist, Kimber revels in the subtle joys and unexpected miscues of the wilderness experience. A Canoeist's Sketchbook *rewards even the most experienced paddler with tips on making your way in remote country, keeping your balance, and becoming attuned to realms of great, unaccustomed beauty.*

ABOUT THE BEST REASON I CAN THINK OF for owning and paddling a canoe is that it can take me into wilderness. And what, you may ask, is so great about wilderness? The silence, for one thing. In real wilderness, silence is not just quiet, which is the absence of noise. It is the voice of the living earth, unmuddied by aural clutter.

I live in the country, which is much quieter than the city, but even in the country there is a lot of noise: the cars of people commuting to work, the machines that build the houses, cut down trees, haul the gravel, paint the stripes down the middle of roads, fly around in the sky, split quiet lakes in half, whine across the top of the snow.

In the country, you experience blessed periods of quiet, and quiet surely is a great treasure. But in the wilderness you are surrounded by the voices of silence, they are a greater treasure still.

What else is wilderness? The water you can drink; the air you can see through; Mars climbing up over the horizon, splitting into a mirage of double Mars, and dancing a little jig with itself. Wilderness is a ghostly rainbow arching white across the night sky under a full moon.

There are lots of highfalutin texts about wilderness experience—visions, epiphanies, all manner of mystical stuff. Davidson and Rugge, who have spent enough time in the bush to know what they're talking about, have this to say about wilderness being "a quality of the heart, something *inside* [us].

Nonsense. The wilderness is plain open space, the sheer physical presence of the earth unwinding without us people."

That sheer physical presence can affect our inner state, but I think what is going on is pretty simple and straightforward. The "wilderness high" is no more nor less than the delight we take in all that plain open space, in a world absolutely free of our own clutter, a world that has not suffered the slightest infringement of man the tool-making, dam-building, road-building, mine-digging, tree-cutting, water-polluting animal. Just to see it all as it was in the beginning, that in itself is such a delight and a privilege that we get "high," which is simply to say that we are happier than we can ever be in the normal course of our lives.

The enjoyment of wilderness, it seems to be, is a privilege we should have to earn, not a right we can claim. And if we are going to have any wilderness left in this world, we'll have to establish a principle of earned access to it. That means we'll have to set aside large territories where aircraft are illegal. It means that if you want to get into real backcountry, you'll have to work to get there. You can't buy your way in. You can't substitute the power of petroleum and money for the truly earned power of knowing how to handle your boat on the river, to keep yourself warm and dry, to feed yourself, and take care of your companions as they take care of you. We'll have to make it illegal for mere wealth to buy its way into our remaining wilderness.

If you object that these are elitist ideas, let me try to convince you otherwise. Since when has travel by foot or by paddle been elitist? These are the most primitive methods of transportation known to humankind. Anyone who walks or paddles is reverting to the primitive. The elitists are the people in the airplanes, in the four-wheel-drive trucks, on the snowmobiles and ATVs.

And what about the old and the infirm? I think I'm old enough to address that question with some kind of realism. What will I do for wilderness if or when I'm too decrepit to walk or paddle into it? I'll do without. I'll regret it, but I hope I'll do my regretting with good grace, not bitterness. Because that is simply the natural course of things. When I am past the time when I have the physical strength to get where I'd like to go, then I'll yield that privilege to those who do. I won't ask that a road be built for me or a plane be hired for me, so that I can violate wild places out of my personal yen for them. They will get on without me. I am as grass. Grass withers, the flower fades; but the world that is wilderness stands forever.

—— *from* ——

Set Free in China

Sojourns on the Edge

Peter Heller

1992

*Bestselling novelist Peter Heller—*The Dog Stars *(2012) and* The Painter *(2014)—came to Chelsea Green with what would be his first book of adventure travel,* Set Free in China. *(It was followed by three other nonfiction works before Heller started to write novels.) The passage selected here from the book's title story reveals Heller's taut, edgy style that captures the intensity of living—and dying—on the eastern edge of the Tibetan Plateau, where the raging Dadu River has a rendezvous with a party of daredevil white-water kayakers from the American West.*

JUST AHEAD ON THE LEFT, I could see the line of the ledge we had noticed earlier. I paddled hard to the right, dropped around the ledge, and saw our fourteen-foot raft stuck beneath, riding the huge hole, empty, doing cartwheels.

A visceral knowledge, too complete and sudden for conscious articulation, can seize you. It's the heart-thump when the car hits an ice patch and slides toward a tree; you see the crash and can do nothing but cry out. I saw the tumbling raft, felt the shudder of tragedy, and thought, "Jesus, no—swimmers!"

Sprinting downstream, I saw a yellow helmet bobbing off the left bank. I flew toward it, pivoted and put my stern in the swimmer's face. "Grab the boat!" I yelled. "Grab the loop!" It was Liu, one of the Chinese mountaineers. I don't know if he was too panicked or didn't understand, but the current pulled him away before he could take hold of the kayak. In the same instant I saw a pile of logs just downstream, five feet from them a nearly submerged boulder, and stuck in the funnel between, a white helmet. Swiftly we were being sucked toward the jam. I stroked hard and hit the shore. "Swim!" I screamed to Liu. For God's sake swim. He didn't make it. His helmet joined the other.

Jumping out of the boat, I grabbed the throw rope and ran. I fell twice on the slick rocks, thinking nothing, thinking this is the way people die. Running beside me was Zhang, the Yangtze guide; I don't even know where he came from. We jumped onto the wet logs and clambered over them. All I could hear was tearing water and two men moaning. On the last log, each of us reached down, grasped the shoulders of Liu's life vest, and pulled. Zhang was yelling, adding his cries to the terrible chorus: Liu was his old friend. "One, two, three, *heave*!" we screamed, and by some miracle, we yanked him free. Zhang's desperate yells were the only thing gluing my hands to the vest and we fell back, sliding Liu up onto the pile.

We dragged him over to a big log, where we laid him groaning, face down, then scrambled back to the other man. Kim and Scott were right behind us, followed by Mark, who had been guiding the flipped raft and, like Zhang, had somehow been flushed out of the hole and made it to shore.

We seized the man, two on the life vest, two on the arms. Water was surging around his neck and into his face. *Heave*. He didn't move an inch. Fingers gathered to grip again, and somebody, maybe me, yelled, "*Now*!" Nothing. He was wedged like a stopper in a seam of granite. It was then that I knew, somewhere beneath the rush and screams and gripping hands, that this man would die. Sucking air, catching breath, I caught Scott's eye: He knew it too.

"My right foot." Those words, barely audible, came from the man. Kim and I lay across the log, holding his life vest and helmet. By now, he was too weak to keep his head above the pummeling current. Scott and Mark rushed back to shore to make a snag line, a weighted bag tied in the center of a rope that they would toss over him, let sink, and pull back, in the hope of freeing a leg. Reaching down shoulder to shoulder, Kim and I glanced at each other.

"Who is it?" I yelled. I could barely glimpse his face.

"It's Dave."

"Dave?" There were three Daves.

"Of Dave and Fiona."

I guess I can say that my heart broke then. Stretched across the log, holding Dave's head, images flashed: Dave in Chengdu giving each of the women a speckled orchid; sharing a bag of peanuts with the table; reaching out at dinner to place a hand on Fiona's leg. Generous and warm, thirty-eight years old, on his honeymoon.

The snag weight skipped uselessly over the heavy current. It was just no good.

We couldn't take the logs apart because they were all that allowed us to scramble out far enough to hold Dave up. Mark bravely stepped onto a jutting limb just below the funnel and got a line around Dave's waist. Dave Lamb quickly rigged a Z-drag—a rope with two opposed pulleys. The device could provide enough force to haul a fully submerged raft, but Dave didn't budge. They tried from upstream, downstream, the side.

Holding his head, trying vainly to keep water off it, I watched Dave go.

Death is simple. It surprised me, coming in clean and hushing everything. I wonder if there are hurricanes that really end abruptly in a whisperless silence. That's what Dave's death was like for me—at the end, it was a quiet relief.

———— *from* ————

A Shadow and a Song

The Struggle to Save an Endangered Species

Mark Jerome Walters

1992

Mark Jerome Walters is a wildlife veterinarian and naturalist, and the author of four books of natural history. A Shadow and a Song, *his second book (voted one of the ten most notable books of the year by Booklist), was aptly called by E. O. Wilson "an elegy for a vanished race, a labor of love" and "a beautifully written work." It is the story of how the Endangered Species Act failed a small songbird whose only remaining habitat lay in the path of the Kennedy Space Center, not far from Disney World. Walters chronicles in crisp, unsparing prose the struggle between the dusky seaside sparrow's advocates and adversaries. This excerpt is the book's last chapter, a moving summary of the bird's denouement and its impact on those few who fought for it.*

ORANGE GAINED NEAR CELEBRITY STATUS during his tenure at Disney World. Newspapers and magazines around the country published stories about him. Like an elderly statesman in his final days, Orange came to be described less as a living figure and more in eulogistic tones. His actual presence would pale compared to the anticipated historical legacy he would leave behind. A recap of Orange's life might have read like this: Orange began his public career on July 25, 1978 when he was netted and banded in the wild, north of State Road 50, in Brevard County, Florida. In 1980, he was again netted seven or eight miles south, unexpectedly, in the fork of the Beeline Expressway and sent in a sack to captivity at the Florida Game and Fresh Water Fish Commission in Gainesville. On April 20, 1981, on orders of Fish and

Wildlife, Orange was transferred to aviaries at the Santa Fe Community College Teaching Zoo, where he resided for the next two years. In September of 1983 he was authorized to be part of a crossbreeding program at Disney World and sent to Orlando. There he fathered a generation of part-duskies, producing an 87 percenter in 1984, and several more in 1985. Once he came down with a severe eye infection but, after treatment with an antibiotic, recovered, though was left partially blind. Orange produced three infertile clutches of eggs in 1986. Cook described the aging Orange as "middle-aged-looking, chubby, a little slower and less sure in his landings."

Throughout his ordeal as a captive bird, where others had grown more or less accustomed to people, Orange remained shy and solitary, if curious. Unlike the more outgoing Abraham, for example, Orange usually remained hidden in the broomgrass of his cage. He never sang naturally, as there were no other duskies to cause him to defend a territory. This is what Cook and his keeper noticed most. Only when they brought the same minute-long tape that he had heard hundreds of times before, was Orange coaxed into song.

At twelve years old, Orange was perhaps the longest-lived dusky ever, but as winter of 1986 bloomed into spring of 1987, it dawned on Cook that even this sparrow would not live forever. And when he died, so would the entire dusky race. Cook collected some final video pictures of Orange for posterity. Kale told Cook to keep some dry ice handy.

At about 4:30 pm on June 12, 1987, senior keeper Danforth went to check on Orange and the remaining hybrids. Orange seemed perky—so it was noted in the logbook she kept. She ran fresh water through the "ponds" and fed him wax worms and crickets. Orange sand loudly in response to recordings played to him that day. Over the next two days, all seemed well with the sparrow.

Sometime on the night of June 15 or early June 16, 1987, surrounded by the phantasmagoria of Disney World, Orange huddled on the sandy ground beneath the broomgrass and died. When Danforth arrived on Discovery Island early on the morning of June 16 and went to the aviaries, she noticed the cage to be unusually quiet. When she looked closer, she found Orange, lying on his right side by the pond, his wings slightly spread as if in a final attempt to keep from falling over. She fought off her emotions and tried to put into place the protocol. But first she picked him up and held him quietly in both her hands. An assistant keeper was feeding fruit to the toucans nearby. With the body of Orange in her hands, Lisa walked over to her and said, "This is the last bird; he's dead." Still cradling Orange in her shaking palms, Danforth walked silently to the backstage area of Discovery Island. She pulled a Ziploc baggy from a cabinet and slipped Orange's body into it, then placed him in an empty refrigerator. She didn't know exactly what to tell Cook, so she stood for awhile thinking about it. Then she called him at home—he was just getting ready for work—greeted him cheerfully as if nothing had happened, then blurted out: "Charlie, Orange is in a Ziploc bag in the refrigerator."

Cook paused, then said, "I'll be right there."

When Cook arrived he took Orange from the refrigerator, removed him from the bag, and put the chilled body on the counter. As the protocol dictated, Cool carefully cut him open and removed some tissues. He packed the specimens in the dry ice and sent them Federal Express to a geneticist at the University of Georgia for a genetic analysis. Others would go to a pathologist to determine the cause of death. Cook called Kale: "He's gone, Herb. Orange is dead."

The formalities completed, Cook stopped to think about what had happened. From that moment on, his life would be different. He later explained, "It was like watching a comet fade. I just cried when they were gone because no matter what I did, there could never be more duskies. I had rushes of memory—driving the birds from Gainesville, their singing in the aviaries in the spring and summer, their small nests tucked in the broomgrass. The aviaries went silent. Orange took the last dusky seaside sparrow song on earth with him."

—— *from* ——

The Safari Companion
A Guide to Watching African Mammals
Richard D. Estes

1993; second edition, 1999

It's one thing to be able to identify animals, quite another to truly observe them, understanding how they behave and why. Since its original publication in 1993, The Safari Companion *has been recognized around the world as the best field guide for wildlife enthusiasts traveling to Africa, enabling them to recognize and interpret courtship rituals, territorial marking, aggression, care of young, and other behaviors. Author Richard D. Estes, a renowned expert on the social ecology of African mammals, gives a detailed account of hundreds of species, complete with illustrations, in this wildlife classic. In addition to leading safaris, Estes is a research associate at the Smithsonian Institution Conservation and Research Center, an associate at the Harvard Museums of Natural History, and a trustee of the Rare Species Conservatory Foundation.*

To GAIN INSIGHT INTO WHAT AN ANIMAL IS DOING, it is necessary, first of all, to recognize the type of activity (or inactivity) in which it is engaged. It doesn't take any training to see that an animal is feeding, lying down, sleeping, or grooming itself. It doesn't require any special knowledge to figure out whether an animal's interaction with others of its own or another species is hostile, friendly, or sexual in character. In the case of an aggressive interaction, most people can guess, on the basis of the animals' bearing and movements, whether one antagonist is dominant or whether they are evenly matched. Play is another type of behavior that is usually easy to distinguish though hard to define.

Displays are behaviors that have been modified or ritualized by evolution to transmit information. Although displays, being designed for communication, generally attract attention to the performer, human observers may overlook or misinterpret some behaviors that convey information to members of the observed species. This is particularly true of maintenance activities, such as eating, sleeping, grooming, and excretion. Maintenance behaviors performed under stressful circumstances, such as when two males engaged in an aggressive encounter perform grooming or feeding behavior, are called displacement activities.

To the discerning observer, displacement activities convey information about the performer's emotions and intentions. By taking into account the context in which maintenance activities occur, how often or vigorously an action is performed, and the sex and age of the performers, you too can tell when maintenance activities double as displays and interpret their meaning.

For example, a lone wildebeest bull standing on his stamping ground or a topi bull standing on a mound are engaged in at least two and probably three behaviors other than simply standing. A topi or wildebeest advertises his presence and territorial status by making himself conspicuous. Territorial males typically stand with heads raised, whereas all non-territorial individuals keep their heads below shoulder level except when on the alert for possible danger. This bull is also monitoring his surroundings, ready to repel rivals and detain approaching females, or flee from predators. Meanwhile, he is chewing his cud and digesting the grass he has been eating.

Many mammals use urine and feces for social communication, especially for scent-marking their territories. Most antelopes and carnivores, as well as rhinos, hippos, and hytaxes, regularly deposit their dung on established middens or latrines, or on prominent landmarks.

A pile of dung at the spot where the animal eliminates is a sure sign that it is using a regular latrine and not simply excreting at random. Scent-making is usually performed in a more purposeful, brisk manner, more often and more sparingly than random excretion. In many species, the act of elimination has evolved into a visual display, a stereotyped performance that advertises the actions and status of the performer.

Elimination postures are often distinctive and different not only between but also within species, depending on age, sex, and social status. The use of elimination postures as visual displays is most developed in species that live in open habitats and scent-mark in plain sight of their neighbors. Dogs and their wild relatives are a familiar example: urinating with cocked hind leg identifies an adult, high-ranking male. Jackal pairs both urine-mark their territory, but the female uses a different posture. Cats have their own particular way of spray-marking with urine.

Dunging is the prevailing mode of territorial marking among antelopes, though there is considerable variation in the associated postures. Urinating and defecating in sequence on dung middens is a territorial display in gazelles and their relatives, the dwarf antelopes. Wildebeests, by contrast, barely even lift their tails when defecating, but territorial bulls call attention to the act by first pawing vigorously with their forefeet.

Although everything an animal does is important to a researcher engaged in studying a particular species, displays, especially visual displays and other signals that convey information within and between species, are most interesting to visitors and the main focus of this book. Thanks to the years of study of African mammals carried out by researchers over the past generation, even first-time visitors can aspire to recognize and understand these signals.

—— *from* ——

The Northern Forest

David Dobbs and Richard Ober

1995

In the 1990s a battle raged over the uncertain future of the Northern Forest—the Great North Woods that stretch from Maine to northern New York State. Paper companies were going out of business, and large landowners, including multinational corporations, were putting large tracts of land up for sale. In a region where the local people depend on the forest for their livelihood and cultural traditions like hunting and fishing, it wasn't entirely clear what conservation meant, or whether it would be a good or a bad thing. In this book Vermont journalist David Dobbs and New Hampshire conservationist Richard Ober tell the intimate stories of Northern Forest residents, who together share a complex, fragile, but ultimately hopeful vision—one that balances ecology and economy.

THE PINE DIDN'T SHUDDER UNTIL THE BLADE of the ax had sunk more than a thousand times.

When the man had started chopping the tree an hour earlier, only three seconds would pass between each swing, before another chip would fly off the hardened steel and another seam of pitch would bubble out. Slowly he had deepened the cut into a wedge four feet across the trunk.

Now the swings were coming further apart as the man labored in the thin winter air. Under his canvas trousers and wool shirt, clammy sweat glued his skin to his long underwear. Fifty feet away, an ox stood staring into the snow. Occasionally the huge animal trembled, jingling the iron and leather rigging draped over its shoulders.

When the pine shuddered, the man stopped and wiped his face on his frozen sleeve. Stepping back through the snow, he looked up the trunk. Deep furrows of bark ran straight up unbroken to the first branches sixty feet above the ground; the crown, swaying slightly, was another hundred feet higher. The man walked around the trunk to check the pile of trees he had felled to cushion the big pine's fall. Dropping the smaller birch and spruce and fir trees into a lattice had taken two days of tedious work, and he wanted to make sure the pine landed squarely in the middle. Once the tree was on the bed he would butt the trunk into 16-foot logs, wrap a chain around each log, and pull them off with the ox. From there it was a short drag to the bank of Baskahegan Stream, where the logs would sit until ice-out in April. He would leave the cushion trees to rot, even though several were more than two feet across. They were worthless and the winter was getting old. Before the river started to run, he had more pines to drop.

He turned back to the pine and hefted his ax.

The tree had sprouted a hundred fifty years earlier when a small, lightning strike fire had rushed along the Baskahegan. The blaze took out the thick canopy of hemlock, spruce, and beech trees that had shaded the river bank for centuries. With the sun flooding forest floor, birch, white pine, pin cherry, and poplar seedlings pushed up through the blackened ground. Struggling against the hardwoods and underbrush, the pines fought to dominate their columns of light. They grew a foot straight up every year, wasting little energy on horizontal branches. Within fifty years, a few of the pines had outraced the hardwoods and were spreading their branches in the sun. The shade in the forest deepened. The pines dutifully dropped cones, but their progeny couldn't compete against more shade-tolerant trees whose seeds were still present, deep in the soil. As the ground cooled beneath the pines, tiny fir seedlings spread throughout the forest. Underneath the firs, and eventually overtaking them, were the slower growing and stronger spruce, interspersed with beech and maple. Eighty years after the fire, the fir was dying back and the spruce trees were 60 feet tall, fighting the hardwoods for space. As the decades passed, the spruce trees fattened under the canopy of the pines.

The woodcutter had found the stand of pines the previous fall, in September 1818, during a scouting trip from his hometown of Bangor. He had made his way on foot up the shore of the Penobscot River, turning east along the Mattawamkeag Stream toward the uninhabited wilds above Baskahegan Lake. During the first part of his journey, he had come across clusters of freshly cut stumps where woodcutters had worked the winter before. By the time he reached the point where the north-flowing Baskahegan Stream runs into the Mattawamkeag, he was in a virgin forest. Climbing a ridge and shimmying up a tree to get his bearings, the woodcutter immediately spotted the tall pines, their soft green crowns standing out in sharp relief against the reds and yellows of turning hardwood trees and the blue-green spires of spruce and fir. The pines were hugging the western bank of Baskahegan Stream five miles to the south; beyond that he could see the dark waters of low-lying Baskahegan Lake.

The woodcutter returned to Bangor. He sketched a rough map and went to see the government land agent to pay for the rights to cut pine on twenty acres of uncharted land. He gathered his team and stocked up on supplies. In mid-December, after a foot of snow had fallen and the ground was frozen, he left town with three other men and two oxen. The men walked, and the oxen dragged a long sled on two wooden runners. Under the sled's canvas tarp the men had stowed sacks of beans and flour, salt pork, a small barrel of molasses, axes, whetstones, wool blankets, and a few personal belongings. When they reached the Baskahegan, they built a twelve-foot-square cabin of balsam fir logs and filled the chinks with moss. Off to one side they erected hovels for the oxen. They made beds out of logs and lined them with fir boughs and blankets. In the middle of the cabin was an open fireplace for cooking and heat. A hole in the roof above vented the smoke.

Every day from dawn to dusk the woodcutters cut pine. They hunkered down in their cabin only during the fiercest storms. By the end of March, they had stockpiled sixty logs, 16 feet long and ranging from 30 to 60 inches across. When the first spring freshet of April started to move the ice floes downstream, the men broke camp and packed up the sled. At the river's edge, they carved an identifying symbol into the ends and side of each log. Then, using iron-tipped wooden pry bars known today as peaveys, they rolled the logs into the rising river. Over the next six days they walked along the shore of the Baskahegan and the Mattawamkeag, poling the logs through tight spots with long pick poles. At the Mattawamkeag's confluence with the Penobscot, southeast of Mount Katahdin, the men turned their logs over to a river-driving crew working from double-tapered boats called bateaus. Two weeks later the drive landed at a water-powered sawmill on the bank of the Penobscot in Bangor. Millyard workers hauled the logs out with horses and separated them by the loggers' identifying marks. By then the woodcutters were back in town, planning how they were going to use the fee from the mill to finance the next winter's cut. They'd have to look even harder, they knew, to find a good vein of pine.

——— *from* ———

The Lost Language of Plants

The Ecological Importance of Plant Medicines to Life on Earth

Stephen Harrod Buhner

2002

Stephen Harrod Buhner is a master herbalist, psychotherapist, and expert on indigenous spiritual traditions. This 2003 Foreword Book of the Year Silver Award Winner exposes the dangers to the environment posed by pharmaceuticals and other synthetic substances that people use for health and personal body care. In addition he shows how plants, the original chemists of Gaia, contain phytochemicals that provide the fundamental communications network for the Earth's ecosystems, including how plants communicate their healing qualities to humans and other animals.

FROM THE BEGINNING WE HAVE BEEN SURROUNDED by the presence of plants; it is not only upon the soil, other plants, or the insects that the aromatics of the plant world fall. They fell upon our species as well; all during our long growth we breathed them in. The Artemisias nursed more than plants; they were outriders for more than trees.

In Africa, southwestern Asia, Greece, Iran, Syria, Spain, and Italy humans lived amid steppes of Artemisia. As Delores LaChappelle remarks: "The persistent odor of [sagebrush] accompanied humans as slowly, over generations, they moved further north and into the Paleolithic cave areas of Spain and France. Then, as the climate changed, the persistent odor of the [Artemisia] steppe moved further north into the areas where humans later learned to grow cereal grains. Throughout all this period of human development" our species was immersed in the volatile aromatics of the Artemisias. They preceded us wherever we went; they have called us to them wherever they grew.

Plant chemistries, unlike pharmaceuticals, are released into the world for a reason. Each chemistry a word imbued with import, all together a language that possesses its own grammar and syntax. Its own underlying epistemology. Scientists study the vowels and consonants and how they are put together to form plant words, but they do not study their meaning, nor the intelligence or intent that gives rise to that meaning. Too often they insist there is no meaning, for, as anyone can see, plants have no brain. Still, each complex assemblage of expressed plant chemistries is a sentence of communication, carrying specific messages, imbued with meaning. And the world receives those meanings and responds.

Plant communications are like stones in water. The ripples they create move throughout ecosystems; they wash up against us. That we take plant words in through our nose or our skin or our eyes or our tongue instead of our ears does not make their language less subtle, or sophisticated, or less filled with meaning. As the soul of a human being can never be understood from its chemistry or grammar, so cannot plant purpose, intelligence, or soul. Plants are much more than the sum of their parts. And they have been talking to us a long time.

───── *from* ─────

Sippewissett

or, Life on a Salt Marsh

Tim Traver

2006

Tim Traver's Sippewissett, *a biography of a salt marsh that doubles as a meditation on the science of place, is heir to a rich tradition of nature writing. Akin to classics like Aldo Leopold's* A Sand County Almanac *and Annie Dillard's* Pilgrim at Tinker Creek, *the book forms an eloquent bridge between ecology and memory, science and art. A Nautilus Book Award Silver Winner in Ecology/Environment/Sustainability.*

WHEREAS IN JUNE AND JULY EVERY MEMBER of the marsh community clamors to be productive, and every day something new lifts up its head, in August I walked into the marsh to find life silenced but for a consortium of song sparrows. They seem to have taken over, perched on top of midget junipers on the dunes or on the gray nubbins of bayberry. As stark as the August sand itself with their gray eye stripes and dark breast spot, song sparrows sang from clumps of grass, chunks of driftwood half buried in sand. They wanted to be barely above the lowly sand, enough to be seen and heard, but not enough to be captured and eaten. In August, the white sand of the dunes was crisscrossed by the tracks of sparrows and mice and traced by the tall wands of bright green dune grass *Amophila breviligulata*. Now there's a pair of words, a Linnaean creation: *Amophila breviligulata*. They sound together like the title of an Italian opera. And in form they make such an arousing song, stretched like a green skin drum over the dunes.

How will we lose this place? How will we keep hold of it? What threatens? Is it sea level rise and hurricane floods? Too much privacy or not enough? Is it the loss of the reflective self? Or is it sand? John Teal has written about sand and the sand dunes of this marsh. He bemoaned their loss and asked questions a scientist should ask about the impact of the loss of sand dunes to the life and health of the salt marsh lying in their lee. When dunes disappear, salt marshes become more vulnerable to storms. And as the channels in a marsh fill with sand sweeping in with strong incoming tides, the pattern and depth of the twice-daily tidal influx changes. Teal wondered about the fate of Sippewissett and all marshes in an age of global warming and rising sea levels. What happens when the dunes disappear and winter storms and hurricanes intensify?

Thinking back to the tall dunes of my unfettered youth, I wondered if we had brought them down. Here the once tall dunes created an enticing world: mansions full of hidden rooms. As kids we couldn't seem to stay out of them. But marine dunes are delicate, vulnerable to human disturbances as innocent as footprints that displace and crush *Amophyla* roots and provide the merest opening to wind and storm waves. We used these dunes for play, jumping, rolling. At night, more than once, we made driftwood fires here, drank too much beer, and with sand-plugged ears slept under the stars.

Far worse, perhaps, than all our play, was the house once built here. Dunes are designed to move and shift, to drop back and move forward—Taoist warriors—and thus bear up against the full frontal assault of winter storms. Their strength is in their movement and continual rebuilding. Their strength is in time. Houses need stability and are not compatible, generally, with migrating dunes. The man who built a house on the dunes drove pilings down deep into the stony substrate beneath. He dug his well, found water, and lined it with tiles. At first the house lay somewhat hidden, tucked inside the hills of sand and the roves of grass, but then the dunes moved again and opened tunnels to storm winds. Now, thirty years after the house was built, the concrete footings and a twisted rusted pipe that was its water well are all that's left, visible at low tide fifty yards off shore. Fiddler crabs have found a home in the shallow tide pool the old well tile makes, and the pipe's rusted red mouth gapes up out of sand like an eel. It's almost as if the house had never been. The three chunks of concrete tile, half submerged in sand, face east like monuments to the sun. They contain the mysterious runic etchings of the enduring barnacle.

——— *from* ———

Javatrekker

Dispatches from the World of Fair Trade Coffee

Dean Cycon

2007

Dean Cycon is the founder of Dean's Beans, an organic coffee roaster in western Massachusetts that was one of the first "direct trade" companies in the coffee business, working with farmer co-ops throughout the world's coffee-

lands. For Dean, who is equal parts entrepreneur, activist, impresario, actor, and showman, this book was the perfect vehicle to highlight the people he met in his travels around the world—the peasant farmers who grow one of our favorite staple crops. Funny, informative, and engaging, this book won a Gold Medal for Travel Essays in the 2008 Independent Publisher Book Awards.

ETHIOPIANS ARE PROUD TO SAY that their country is the only one in Africa that has never been colonized. While this is technically true, the Italians did try in a colonialist version of keeping up with the Joneses. After all, the British, French, Germans, Dutch, and even Portuguese had African colonies; why shouldn't they? The Italians used the new tactic of aerial bombardment with the banned mustard gas to burn villages to the ground and strafed fleeing civilians, but the best they could do in the heat and dust of the African Horn was to grab Eritrea to the north and hold Ethiopia through the early years of World War II. But the Italians left an indelible legacy in Ethiopia. All over Jimma, the manhole covers read "Pisa Foundry," spaghetti is on every menu, Ethiopians say *ciao*, and—most significant of all—the Italians introduced the espresso machine. America should hang its lattéed head in shame at the number of espresso machines that are found throughout the Ethiopian countryside. Every hamlet, with or without electricity, has at least one. Famous Italian names like Cimbali and Faema adorn these ancient marvels. Hand pumps pressurize many rural units, manned by kids in tattered T-shirts who can pull a shot like Dr. Illy himself. The milk comes in fresh every day, carried by nomadic cowgirls in hollow gourds decorated with leather straps and beads. The milk tastes curiously smoky; the girls invert the gourds over a charcoal fire each night to kill any germs from the day's carriage.

Jimma is also a region where the old religion and social system still survive, albeit *sub silentio*. Here, among the mosques and churches that pepper the landscape, people still practice Quallu, the animist worldview of an older Oromo society. One night in Jimma we pass an Irreessa, an outdoor prayer ceremony held before the harvest. During this ritual, a farmer will become *ayyaana*, inhabited by the Quallu spirit. The spirit will take the prayers and work on them in otherworldly realms, speaking through the mouth of the possessed farmer.

Probably more than anywhere else in Ethiopia, the people of this region have coffee in their cultural blood. Every day in most households begins with a coffee ceremony. Tadesse takes me to the small house of sixty-year-old Hadjj Hussein, a co-op member, to experience the ritual.

Hadjj Hussein lives far out of town. As is the case for many Ethiopian farmers, his coffee is "sun dried," meaning the coffee is processed by laying the coffee fruit out in the sun to dry like raisins. These are then picked up by the co-op and taken to Addis for further processing. Farmers sun-dry coffee when they are far from a coffee washing station that would allow the beans to be soaked and fermented in water immediately after harvest, and where they live in dry regions like Jimma or Harar. Sun-dried coffee sells for less than half the price of wet-processed coffee, so the farmers are that much poorer. Hadjj Hussein has fifteen children and twice as many grandchildren. I can't tell which are which. Supersized families are not uncommon among rural Ethiopians. Back in Yirgacheffe, Tasew Gebru at seventy is about to have his tenth child, who will be named Toduru, meaning "What Will the Neighbors Say?" When he is born he will be Uncle Toduru to seven nieces and nephews in their early teens.

One of Hadjj Hussein's younger daughters, twelve-year-old Rehima Hussein, comes out of the house swathed in brown-colored fabric, her head wrapped in a proper Muslim white head scarf. She is the same age as my oldest daughter and carries that same shy smile. Her sisters spread sweetgrass on the ground and burn frankincense to purify the air around us. Fourteen-year-old Minah stokes a small charcoal brazier. Three-year-old Nejat sits dangerously close to the glowing coals. Rehima puts an old blackened skillet on the brazier and places several handfuls of green coffee beans on the skillet. She stirs the beans with a wooden spoon until they are smoking and cracking like popcorn—the first sign the coffee is nearly ready. Rehima skillfully stirs the beans until they are almost black.

"The coffee is ready when it is the color of a chicken's eye," says Hadjj Hussein approvingly. Yes, I did spend several minutes trying to look into the eyes of the few scrawny chickens in his yard, but to no avail. They were too fast for me.

Rehima pours the beans into a wooden mortar and crushes them with the rhythmic movement of a pestle, humming the whole time. She empties the ground coffee into a clay coffee pot, a *jabana*, the symbol of Ethiopian coffee. There are giant mock *jabanas* at the entrance to many coffee towns in Ethiopia. Rehima pours boiling water into the *jabana* and swishes it around for a minute. Her sister brings out a tray of porcelain teacups, like the ones at a Chinese restaurant.

"We bought them in Jimma market," says Hadjj Hussein proudly. "They are made far away in China."

Rehima pours each cup. She begins about six inches from the cup and pulls the *jabana* up to three feet away as she fills it. Each filling is a little ballet of black liquid. We each receive a cup. This is *abol*, the first round. We drink it quickly and say, "*Buna gari*" (Good coffee). There is a second round, the *tonah*, and then the third, the *beraka* or "blessing" round. *Beraka* is an Amharic word. It shares ancient roots with Hebrew and is thought to have been introduced to Ethiopia by the Queen of Sheba and the early Semitic migrations. The Oromo, though, are not a Semitic people. They are Black African pastoralists who migrated throughout this region over the centuries and have been "internally colonized" by the Amharic peoples for a long time. But at least here, during the coffee ceremony, such things are not discussed. *Buna gari*. The ceremony has ended and the day's work can begin.

—— *from* ——

Sex and the River Styx

Edward Hoagland

2011

Edward Hoagland has been called the best essayist of his time by such literary giants as Philip Roth, John Updike, and Edward Abbey. Chelsea Green was honored to publish his twentieth book, a collection of essays that span his childhood exploring the woods in rural Connecticut, his days as a circus worker in the 1950s, and his travels around the world in his later years. Whether reflecting on aging, love, and sex in a deeply personal, often surprising way, or expressing his wonder at wild places, Hoagland brings the genre of nature writing to new heights. As novelist Howard Frank Mosher writes in his foreword, Hoagland "could fairly be considered our last, great transcendentalist." This excerpt comes from his essay titled "Small Silences."

Now, ANIMALS LIVE EVEN MORE in the present than we do. They are geographic or hierarchical in organization, operating by rote or scented memories of previous hazards and good fortune, seeking food with smaller brains but not wistful about it, as you'll notice watching a fox glance up at suet in a birdfeeder without wasting energy in pining after a bite. Short and brutish has been a description of their lives ("brutish" being somewhat tautological), but certainly the lives of what are called the megafauna are getting shorter while ours grow longer. Some people scarcely know what to do with their bonus time—doubled life spans, plus the round-the-clock availability of artificial light—because nature doesn't deal in bonuses. The sun rises and sets when it did a million years ago, with daylight altering by immemorial increments as the planet rolls. It doesn't award you an extra hour if you have a deadline. *Can you make it?* nature asks instead, if it says anything at all. But secondly and curiously, I think, it speaks in terms of glee. Glee is like the froth on beer or cocoa. Not especially necessary or Darwinian, it's not the carrot that balances the stick, because quieter forms of contentment exist to reward efficiency. Glee is effervescence. It's bubbles in the water—beyond efficiency—which your thirst doesn't actually need.

Bubbles are physics, not biology, and glee, if the analogy is to carry far, may be an artesian force more primordial than evolutionary. To me, it's not a marker for genetic advantages such as earning more, but an indicator that life—the thread of Creation, the relic current that has lasted all this way—is ebullient. Still, you might argue that the choosiest females select not just for strength and money or its zoological equivalents, but for the superfluous energy that humor and panache imply. The woodpecker drumming an irregular tattoo on my tin roof in the spring is not mechanistic in his ritual, as if merely to prove that he could dig big bugs out of a tree and bring them to his mate. His zest and syncopation is like when you watch two fawns gamboling with a doe, or a swaggering vixen mouth three meadow mice that she has killed to fit them all between her teeth for the trip to her den. Such surplus moments relax us and serve a tonic function—triumphal for the vixen, toning the fawn's reflexes, letting the woodpecker pause unexpectedly to listen for an answer.

The gamboling, like a kitten's stalk, prepares an animal for the hunt or being hunted, and the youngster that enjoys it most may wind up savviest. But the glee I mean is less utilitarian, more spontaneous, and a kind of elixir that needs a bit of peace to germinate. How does one account for the passive, concentrated happiness of listening by a lake to the lap and hiss of rustling water, watching the leaves jiggle, the poplars seethe and simmer? The lake is ribbed with ropes of wind and strands of sun between cloud shadows. The contours of three hills delineate the comely way that brooks feed into its blue bulk, and otters, loons, mergansers, animate it (the far mile curving out of sight), so that you'd hardly need to invent a loch "monster" for drama. And yet you can wake up nearly anywhere and experience a comparably high-pitched serenity. Glee is not complacency—in the middle of a roaring city it may seize you—and I think of it as possibly generated at life's origins, like a filament from, or footprint of, that original *kick*. Nature seems more than Evolution, punctuated or otherwise, and the Creationists may be onto something when they insist that it is an effusion of God's glory. Their god isn't mine, but glee may be a shard of divinity.

——— *from* ———

In the Company of Bears

What Black Bears Have Taught Me About Intelligence and Intuition

Ben Kilham

Originally published as *Out on a Limb* in 2013

Bestselling author Elizabeth Marshall Thomas called it "the most insightful book about animals written in the last 100 years." But to Ben Kilham, In the Company of Bears *was a labor of love—a way to share his discoveries from years of raising orphaned cubs and observing bears in the wild. He has found that black bears, once considered solitary, form friendships and alliances; abide by a code of conduct that keeps their world orderly; and even help out other bears in need. Kilham was, as a youth, barred from getting a traditional science degree by his struggles with dyslexia. Today his unique findings continue to interest bear researchers worldwide, and his observational skills have been compared to Jane Goodall's.*

EVER SINCE RAISING LITTLE BOY AND LITTLE GIRL, I was increasingly drawn into the bears' world. From the beginning, questions emerged about how bears behaved and why—questions whose answers came slowly, as the information and evidence began to pile up and patterns emerged. Though I certainly didn't know it at the start, the cubs' behavior would become powerful backup evidence for much of what I observed later among adult bears. Yet I had to spend two decades learning how bears communicate in order to finally make sense of the whole system.

I also had to grow comfortable with conducting my own personal experiment—doing things my way with no expectations of success, only to learn the way I was born to. In preparation for raising my first set of cubs, I searched the scientific literature to see what had been written on the subject. There were only two studies related to rehabilitation or behavioral research with black bear cubs. One was by a scientist who released six-month-old cubs to the wild and found that they were still alive three months later. He concluded that orphan bear cubs older than five months could survive by themselves in the wild. The study had a major impact in the wildlife community and was used to justify leaving orphan cubs in the wild or returning rehabilitated cubs to the wild at that very young age. I was stunned. Even as an amateur, it was clear to me that the study was simply drawing a convenient conclusion.

Wild bears spend eighteen months with their mothers. Surely there must be a reason for this. How could anyone come along and just say, "Hey, let's take away two-thirds of that time and I bet things will work out fine"? It's counterintuitive. The bears' lengthy cub-rearing strategy is the result of more than five hundred million years of evolution—and yet scientists believed that it could be reduced to five months? The biggest stress for any bear is surviving the winter, but the study did nothing to explain how the cubs were going to build up the required fat reserves without their mothers to show them how to find food or fend off competing bears. This was perhaps my first real exposure to the fact that, in many ways, we have become so detached from the natural world that we can't even trust our own instincts. We look for meaning in other people's theories, even when those theories directly contradict what we can see with our own eyes.

The nice thing about studying natural systems, though, is that when in doubt, you can always go back to nature: I was determined to find out what cubs learn during those eighteen months. I discovered distinct developmental stages that clearly affect bears' ability to explore—and survive—on their own. I also formed a relationship with one of these cubs, Squirty, that would last well into her adulthood—offering me a rare window into her world and the world of other wild bears around her.

One spring day back when Squirty was a cub, I climbed a steep trail with her and her two siblings, Curls and The Boy. The bears were seventeen months old, almost ready to leave home, and I knew from experience with the first set of cubs—Little Boy and Little Girl—that it was time for them to interact with wild bears, even if it meant they'd spend the night out in the woods instead of safe in their fenced enclosure on my property. I led the way up the trail, confident that the cubs would later retrace the route without me. The next morning, off they went by themselves. When I went to look for them, using the signal from The Boy's radio collar to track them down, they raced off down the other side of the mountain as soon as I got within earshot. That night, the cubs did not come home.

The following day was foggy and rainy, and the wind kept my scent away from the cubs. I snuck back up the mountain, and there they were, feeding in a beech stand. When they finally heard me—I stepped on a twig, which broke with a loud snap—they ran up the nearest tree, terrified. That's when I saw their newfound friend, an adult female wild bear who was not about to let me harm the cubs. She came at me in a false charge, a common behavior that says, unequivocally, "Back off." This wild bear was protecting my own cubs from me!

Just then the wind shifted, and the cubs caught my scent. Down they scampered, making the noise I've come to know as the "moan of recognition." The wild bear simply sat down and watched. The cubs rubbed all over me, masking my scent to prevent me from scaring off their wild friends. (Amazingly, afterward I was able to walk around that beech stand with wild bears paying me no attention.) And then each one in turn bit me on the arm, hard enough to leave a bruise but not to break the skin. They were punishing me for interfering with their friends—in much the same way your daughter or son would be furious if you decided to hang around during their teenage party.

MEMOIR & BIOGRAPHY

ERIN ACKERMAN-LEIST

—— *from* ——

Permanent Parisians

An Illustrated Guide to the Cemeteries of Paris

Judi Culbertson and Tom Randall

1986

Permanent Parisians *was the first of a series of offbeat travel guides to the most interesting cemeteries in Paris, London, New York, and California. Culbertson and Randall, experienced writers and travelers well versed in art, literature, and music, believe that the world's great cemeteries are its unacknowledged museums, where great three-dimensional art and stories mix, out of the limelight, and release the elixirs of the past. The series was extremely well received in the book trade. The selection here, describing the outsized life of the composer Hector Berlioz, is but one of many fascinating Parisian stories unearthed by the authors.*

HECTOR BERLIOZ *b. December 11, 1803, La Cote-Saint-Andre; d. March 8, 1869, Paris.* If Hector Berlioz were alive today, his behavior would be labeled obsessive-compulsive by clinicians; but that would take all the fun out of it. He was the quintessential romantic, a man given to extremes of emotion and for whom half-hearted opinions did not exist. With a great shock of reddish brown hair topping his intense hawklike features, his appearance matched his temperament. And like a hawk, little escaped his notice. His exquisite sensitivity invariably resulted in passionate outbursts. On more than one occasion his midperformance opinions thundered through the concert hall. "Not two flutes, you wretches—two piccolos! two piccolos!"

Berlioz was an example of the rare composer who cannot play the piano. Raised in the town of his birth, he was only mildly encouraged in his musical studies. Never was the parental eye cast toward music as a career. Medicine was to be Hector's profession, chosen by his physician father. In due course he attended medical school, but the charnel house stench of the dissecting room and the lure of music were too strong. Moving to the Paris Conservatoire, he quickly made up ground while retaining the unorthodoxy of the self-taught. He was revolutionary. His harmonies and modulations were new, and his ear for color and orchestration were unmatched. His use of themes foreshadowed Wagner's idea of leitmotivs. Berlioz reveled in the idea of a large orchestra and fully utilized all its color and power to express his heightened emotional messages.

Music was his medium, but love was at the core of his life. His first love, at age 12, was Estelle Duboeuf. She was 18 and barely knew he existed. His most famous love was Harriet Smithson, the Irish actress, with whom he fell in love at a distance. He terrified her with his ardent love letters and a visit to a rehearsal where, upon finding her in the arms of an actor, he let out a shriek and fled the hall. She became the beloved, the *idee fixe* in his famous *Symphonie Fantastique*, which depths the hallucinatory hell his love puts him through; it includes her participation in a mocking, orgiastic dance at a witches' Sabbath.

Several years were to pass before they met again. In the interim, Berlioz was spurned by another woman. Not without a sense of humor, at least in retrospect, Berlioz described in his wonderful *Memoirs* how, in close succession, he vengefully plotted her murder (he was to gain entrance to her house disguised as a chambermaid), attempted suicide (a passerby rescued him from drowning), then, drained of his passion, he spent the three happiest weeks of his life in Nice. He eventually married Harriet in 1833, but within five years, spurred by her drinking and his romantic yearnings, he found love in the arms of the lovely Marie Recio Martin, an aspiring opera singer with a voice like a cat's. They lived together for years, finally marrying seven months after Harriet died in 1854. Marie died eight years later.

The two women were united when Harriet's remains were moved from the smaller Montmartre cemetery before it was razed. Berlioz, there for the exhumation, described how the gravedigger "with his two hands picked up the head, already parted from the body. . .[and then] gathered in his arms the headless trunk and limbs, a blackish mass which the shroud still clung to. . . ." And so Berlioz had his last encounter of the fantastique with his Harriet.

At age 60, lonely and tired of life, Berlioz still pursued his romantic obsessions. He attempted to renew his very first love affair, making a pilgrimage to his old summer home to renew the sensations of his childhood love and then going on to see Estelle. Cordial, but not reciprocating his love, she did allow an occasional visit, and letters passed between them. For Berlioz it was a solace which saw him through to the end.

—— *from* ——

Goodbye Highland Yankee

Growing up in the 1930s—a Memoir

Scott E. Hastings, Jr.
Illustrated by Michael McCurdy

1988

Folklorist, teacher, and writer Scott Hastings wrote this entertaining memoir of growing up in Vermont and New Hampshire's Upper Valley. His stories vividly evoke a unique time and place, a culture that has since disappeared, but is not yet entirely forgotten in our present age of cell phones and online connectedness. Laurance Rockefeller hired Hastings to travel the length and breadth of Vermont for over a decade to assemble under one roof the finest collection of nineteenth-century farm technology and domestic artifacts in New England at the Billings Farm Museum in Woodstock, Vermont.

IN THE 1930S WE STILL CELEBRATED the Fourth of July with passion and élan. True, our activities could not compare to Dad's feat, around the year 1918, of setting off a substantial charge of dynamite on the ledges above McIndoe Falls and smashing almost every window in the village. (He and the other boys had no idea the ledges ran straight under McIndoes right down to the Connecticut River.) The resultant seismic tremors shot through the village like a dose of salts.

Our own efforts paled by comparison. Yet, viewed beside today's feeble observances, it was a wonderful day to be alive. The week or two before the Fourth saw days of frenetic activity as we kids gathered every penny we could scrape up. Piggy banks were smashed with abandon. Even our cherished Indian head pennies, still in circulation as coin of the realm, went into the pot to purchase fireworks. Two of the town's emporiums suddenly and miraculously sported shelves bending under the weight of numerous, gaudily packaged instruments of explosive potential which went to provide our armament for the Glorious Fourth.

The store of choice was a narrow, hole in the wall kind of place run by a tough old Sicilian named Joe. Joe stocked firecrackers of every size. These ran the gamut from deadly green five-inchers and yellow two-inchers in dull oily-looking coverings to brightly colored standard inch-and-a-halfs and braided strings of tiny red lady fingers. He sold the ubiquitous sparklers and Egyptian snakes, skyrockets, pinwheels, and Roman candles for the blackness of Fourth of July night. For the day, he offered a teeming multitude of devices with built-in bangs, booms, and gloriously noxious smells.

We used to carefully fold two standard firecrackers in the middle, cracking them and exposing the powder. Then we set them, broken ends facing each other, and touched off the rag powder with a glowing bit of punk. The resultant brief, hissing conflagration, we called a cat and dog fight. The lady fingers we painstakingly unbraided and set off one by one, for the great depression lay heavy on the land. We could not afford to waste them in one profligate, continuous explosion. We were up long before the stars left the sky on the great day. Out on the grass, the dew-silvered cobwebs foretold a fair and sultry day. A few scattered, high-intensity explosions, here and there around the neighborhood, soon told us who was up and ready for action.

Jim Slattery's dad loved the Fourth. He always kept on hand a big sack of carbide filched from the railroad. Jim and I'd fill a bag with the coarse tannish-white pebbles, grab the mop bucket, newspapers, a bottle of water and some matches, and head for the field up back of French's Gardens. Once there we'd put a small heap of carbide on the ground and sprinkle it with water. The bucket went on top, upside down with a stick under it to keep an edge up. When we smelled the acrid stench of acetylene we lit a long spill of rolled-up newspaper and touched off the highly explosive gas leaking out from under the bucket. The result was a thrilling, drawn out, muffled *whumph*, immediately following which the bucket flew up into the sky and kept going until it was a mere black speck—seemingly as high as the moon still palely gleaming a little above the horizon. We tried this once with a forty-quart milk can and a good big pile of carbide. The heavy can lifted off the ground somewhat ponderously and then kept going. When it reached its apogee it seemed to shift sideways in the sky and Jim and I were hard put, for a second or two, trying to figure which way to run to get out from under it.

After this, we sneaked the much battered mop bucket into Jim's house, ate some Wheaties, and resumed our pursuit of the festive Fourth. The rest of the morning we gathered with the other neighborhood kids for an orgy of detonating the sundry explosives we had managed to accumulate. Unwary passersby, especially girls, dodged and danced among the small brown, paper-wrapped torpedoes we bounced among them. Soup cans burst into shreds under the impact of shiny red cherry bombs' explosions. A granite fence post, with a transverse hole bored through its top, magnified to the roar of a cannon the sound of a five-incher touched off within. Aerial bombs, squat vertical tubes mounted on green-stained wooden bases, threw their charges high into the sky. The resultant clanging, ringing explosions roaring across the heavens brought frightened mothers rushing to the doors all along the length of the street.

By noontime we had exhausted our ammunition except for those few fortunate enough to possess the spectacular skyrockets, pinwheels, and Roman candles reserved for the evening's show. These were packed with chemicals, which upon detonation lit up the night sky with far-ranging showers and streaks of vari-colored lights and trailing streamers of smoke. Lampblack gave red and nitrate pink; lycopodium burnt with a brilliant sheen of rose-colored flame; camphor shone dead white and verdigris a handsome green.

Between the morning and the evening's conflagrant activities, however, there was a one-man fireworks show. The premier event of the day for us kids, it was staged by old man Touhey, who timed it to enliven the dull hours of the early afternoon. And until one fatal July Fourth in the late thirties, it had taken on the trappings of an annual event.

Promptly at one o'clock, Touhey, who lived with his wife in a small bungalow at the top of our street, appeared on the bank beside the road above his garden. His yearly burden on this short walk was a tattered bransack full of fireworks. One by one, he set these off. Bangs and booms and crumps and muffled thuds reverberated among the cabbages and broccoli. The serried ranks of vegetables took heavy casualties, but the redoubtable Touhey merely grinned and said he planted them only because his wife made him. This was a sentiment with which most of us heartily agreed and we urged him on with cheers.

Touhey was notorious for his method of ignition. He would bring the fuse of the explosive device to the glowing end of the inch-long cigarette permanently pasted to his lower lip. When the fuse lit he would hold the thing in his hand for a moment or two before throwing it, all the while grinning with an air of accomplished bravado. It was well known along the street that Touhey sometimes took a drop more than was good for him. This day, as things turned out, was to be no exception. Halfway through the bag, he extracted a particularly nasty-looking piece of work, a dark green firecracker of truly monumental proportions. The thick black fuse looked none too long. To further complicate matters, the thing turned out to be what we in the trade called a "quick burner." Touhey turned to us, his captive audience, and held out the giant cracker.

"Just look at that, old boys. Old Joe got it special for me. Just wait'll you hear *it* go off!"

Slowly, lovingly, he raised it to the glowing tip of his cigarette. The fuse lit with a splutter of sparks and Touhey held it out casually at arm's length, watching it closely with narrowed eyes. Suddenly it turned on him! The fuse gave a quick *fffsssst* and the cracker exploded with a thunderous *crack!* right in his hand. Loud as it was, it could not drown out Touhey's howl of agony and indignation at the fingers of his hand split open. There followed a moment of shocked silence as he gazed, astounded, at the wreck of his hand. Then Mrs. Touhey (who had been expecting something like this for a long time) rushed out with a towel. She wrapped his poor hand in it and led him, staggering, back into the house. Pretty soon Doc Wilson drove up. When he left, half an hour later, Mrs. Touhey appeared at the door. We were still there, waiting to get news of how Mr. Touhey was faring.

"You boys can have the rest of them goddamn fireworks," she offered. "Touhey's going to be O.K., but he said he never wants to see a firecracker again as long as he lives."

We set 'em off during what was left of the afternoon, but the zing had gone out of the day. Things picked up that night, however, when long after dark, Johnny McAdoo had a blue light from a defective Roman candle roll down one shirtsleeve and out of the other. Right after that Charlie Samuels put a big skyrocket into Ora Newton's chickenhouse. Before the fire department could put it out, the smell of spent fireworks had become inextricably mixed with that of roast chicken.

—— *from* ——

John Burroughs
An American Naturalist
Edward J. Renehan, Jr.
1992

Ed Renehan, now the author of more than twenty books, published his first biography with Chelsea Green—of John Burroughs, the East's counterpart and contemporary of the West's great naturalist John Muir, who is more widely familiar. Burroughs (1837–1921) knew such luminaries as Ralph Waldo Emerson, Walt Whitman, Oscar Wilde, and Henry Ford, among many others, and Renehan restores the once famous essayist and naturalist to his rightful place in American letters.

JOHN BURROUGHS WAS THE IMMEDIATE CONTEMPORARY of the robber barons who fathered the brownstone and cast-iron urbanization of the post-Civil War expansion. He had been born in the same decade as virtually all the tycoons who rose to define the values, mores, and industrial pace of the era. Burroughs was born in 1837. One year before him, in the same Catskill village, Jay Gould first saw the light of the world. Andrew Carnegie was born in 1835, J.P. Morgan in 1837, and John D. Rockefeller in 1839. Two other contemporaries, Mark Twain and Charles Dudley Warner, supplied a name for the epoch these moguls came to define in the title of their 1873 book, *The Gilded Age.* Twain and Warner saw the decades that these men shaped as being characterized by money lust, hardness, and cynicism. It was a time, in Twain's words, "of incredible rottenness." Burroughs's close friend Walt Whitman expressed a similar emotion in *Democratic Vistas,* where he wrote, "The depravity of the business classes of our country is not less than has been supposed, but infinitely greater."

In his most perceptive moments, Burroughs cited a direct link between the frantic urge for money getting and the alienation of man from nature. The chief business of America in the latter half of the nineteenth century was the taming and plundering of the wild landscape. The great fortunes were all based on either harvesting the natural wealth of the country in oil, coal, and lumber, or on building the industrial infrastructure of the railroads and cities that was so quickly displacing forest and meadow. Burroughs wrote in a letter to his friend, the farmer and poet Myron Benton, that he believed the removal of populations from the country to the city was "nothing short of a spiritual catastrophe." The migration from rural districts to urban neighborhoods and pursuits signaled for Burroughs the loss of a sense of place—the all-important umbilical between man and land with which he believed the soul thrived and without which it withered.

Burroughs often used the metaphor of the steam locomotive to represent the monolithic machine that was all things industrial and urban. The steam train sliced through the virgin forests like a knife and put riders in a false relationship with the reality of the natural world. "We are removed from nature and life by the whole distance of our wealth and refinement," he wrote in his journal on January 17, 1866. "The earth is overlaid with inventions and improvements . . . A man may live now and travel without hardly coming in contact with the earth or air. He can go around the world in a parlor. Life is intensely artificial . . . The ambition now is to get wealth and die a Christian—become rats if necessary to achieve these ends."

Despite the fact that he was generally mute with regard to the industrial excesses of his era, there is one important thing that redeems Burroughs. In essay after essay, he tried to instill a new, modern element of faith into the faithless decades of the Gilded Age. In their novel, *The Gilded Age*, Twain and Warner proposed that the country as a whole had entered into a malaise defined entirely by the worship and pursuit of money. Twain suggested that like the heroes of another civilization, America's multi-millionaires were being made into pharaohs. Their pyramids were the iron rail lines they laid, the steel suspension bridges they built, and the factories where many labored for the aggrandizement of the few. The agnostic Twain went so far as to suggest that cold cash was the closest thing to a God that modern man possessed—the one great common denominator. "Who is God, the one only and true?" Twain asked readers of the *New York Tribune* in the fall of 1871. "Money is God. Gold and Greenbacks and Stock—father, son, and the ghost of same—three persons in one; these are the true and only God, mighty and supreme." The cynical Twain may have correctly isolated the poison that was invading America's soul, but he recommended no antidote. Burroughs did.

For Burroughs, the Christian tenet of sin followed by redemption found its analogy in the citizens of cities who returned to seek the pleasure and solitude of the wooded countryside. As in the stories of St. Paul and Thomas Aquinas, knowledge of God was all the sweeter and all the more profound following salvation after a fall from Grace. Burroughs suggested that the idea of the city was born of fear and sin. Rude and barbarous people needed cities. The necessity of defense had built the first cities—Ur, Babylon, and Carthage. The weaker the law, the stronger the city. "After Cain slew Abel he went out and built a city," wrote Burroughs. And he suggested that it was calculated greed and a crude lack of faith that had laid the foundation for every city since. Hence, Burroughs argued that the city was "older" than the country. "Truly, man made the city," Burroughs wrote, "and after he became sufficiently civilized, not afraid of solitude, and knew on what terms to live with nature, God promoted him to life in the country." It was only after his abdication of the forest to industrialization that man could realize the true sanctity of nature. It was only after seeing the hell of the urban that he could realize the heaven of the rural. Only after sin could he find redemption.

Burroughs's third book of nature essays, published in 1879, was titled *Locusts and Wild Honey*. In his preface, Burroughs hinted that the title of the book was an allegory. Burroughs's allusion was to another John, John the Baptist, "the voice crying in the wilderness" who "fed on locusts and wild honey." The modern prophet Burroughs proselytized for a new church of the woodlands. The new and most necessary baptism was a baptism in nature. Amid the trees, by forest streams, he believed one could find a cure for the vanity and vexation of spirit that the growing American industrial colossus doled out in such generous portions. In days of increasing urbanization and "scientific barbarism," wrote Burroughs, the woods could set one free.

—— *from* ——

Loving and Leaving the Good Life
Helen Nearing
1992

In this last of the many books written by Scott, by Helen, and by both together—the most famous of their joint authorship being Living the Good Life *(1954)—Helen chronicles her life and times with her famous renegade husband, the radical-economist-turned-homesteader Scott Nearing. Together they pioneered the back-to-the-land movement in the 1930s and later, drew admirers and wannabes from all over the world to visit them in their self-built home in southern Vermont (and subsequently on the coast of Maine). The Nearings had an intimate connection, albeit an indirect one, with the early years of Chelsea Green's life in publishing (see the foreword to this* Reader*), and so it seemed natural for us to be Helen's publisher. The excerpt chosen narrates Scott's death, or as Helen would say, his passing.*

A FRIEND AND NEIGHBOR ASKS HIM toward the end: "What are you thinking these days?"

After a pause he answered: "It is a rare opportunity to have lived so long and to have experienced so much—and particularly advantageously located to speak out. We, Helen and I, have been together for half a century. Have had a unique position together—to have worked as a team.

"I am particularly concerned with society. The particular social pattern we call Western civilization is progressively breaking up. Is there a future for it? After a hundred years in it I can speak with a certain amount of authority.

I am profoundly concerned that the human race does its job thoroughly and persistently till it is complete.

"What is its job? The earth is a speck of dust in an enormous expression of life; one grain of consciousness in the totality. The human role in this drama has been more or less thoroughly muffled. We are fumbling with the ball. We have frittered away our time. Can we hold together and remake and rebuild something more worthwhile? I would like to make my contribution toward producing and creating a better world. This is what we are here to do.

"It is that which occupied my mind these last days of my life."

I took down on tape recorder this conversation two months before he died. "My purpose? My purpose is to live the kind of life that will mean the most to you, to me, to the universe immediately around us, and to some part of the universe that lies a little beyond what we see around us.

"In other words, I may be at the portal of a doorway, of looking at least into another type of being, another type of existence, another type of experience."

"You welcome that?" I asked.

"I have no choice. It's like asking if I expect the sun to rise tomorrow. The life people have been living is so far away from the real purpose. We've got to stop fooling around and move toward a new way of life.

"Do the thing you believe in. Do the best you can in the place where you are and be kind.

"I'd like to get people into the habit of living physically and mentally in such a way that when they get all through, the earth can be a better place to live than it was.

"Sit back and be comfortable? That's no way to be. Sit up. Move forward. Keep going. I'd like to get out and plant potatoes; cut wood, anything constructive.

"I would like to live as long as I'm useful. If I can be of use, I would like to go on living. If I can't even carry in the wood for you, I might as well go."

He might as well have quoted the words of the ailing king of France in *All's Well That Ends Well:* "'Let me not live,' quoth he, / 'After my flame lack oil,' . . . Since I nor wax nor honey can bring home, / I quickly were dissolved from my hive / To give some laborers room."

A month and a half before Scott went, a month before his hundredth birthday, while sitting with a group at the table one day, he said: "I think I won't eat any more." He never took solid food again. He deliberately and purposefully chose the time and the way of his leaving. It was to be methodical and conscious. He would cast off his body by fasting.

Death by fasting is not a violent form of suicide; it is a slow and gentle diminution of energies, a peaceful way to leave, voluntarily. Externally and internally he was prepared. He had always liked Robert Louis Stevenson's "Glad did I live and gladly die, and I lay me down with a will." Now he could put this into practice. He himself inaugurated his own technique for dying: let the body itself give up its life.

I acquiesced, realizing how animals often leave life—creeping away out of sight and denying themselves food. For a month I fed Scott just on juices when he wanted any liquids: apple, orange, banana, grape, whatever he could swallow. Then he said: "I would like only water." Yet he did not sicken. He was still lucid and spoke with me, but his body was extremely emaciated. The life force in him was lessening.

A week more on water, and he was completely detached from life, ready to slip easily into that good night. His body had dried up; now it was withering away, and he could tranquilly and peacefully retire from it. I was with him on his couch and quietly urged him on, the morning of August 24, 1983.

Half aloud, I intoned an old Native American chant: "Walk tall as the trees; live strong as the mountains, be gentle as the spring winds; keep the warmth of summer in your heart, and the Great Spirit will always be with you."

"You don't have to hold on to anything, my love," I murmured to him. "Just let go of the body. Go with the tide. Flow with it. You have lived a fine life. You have done your bit. Enter into a new life. Go into the light. Love goes with you. Everything here is all right."

Slowly, gradually, he detached himself, breathing less and less, fainter and fainter; then he was off and free, like a dry leaf from the tree, floating down and away. "All . . . right," he breathed, seeming to testify to the all-rightness of everything, and was gone. I felt the visible pass into the invisible.

Our love affair had lasted half a century and still goes on now, eight years after he died at the honorable age of a hundred. The love continues on my part, and on his side, too, I believe. From where else could come the glad certainty every morning, evening, and hour of the day that I live in love and am charged with it—outgoing and incoming. Since the day Scott died, I have had a sense of his continued being. As Winnenap the Shoshone medicine man said: "If the dead are truly dead, why would they still be walking in my heart?" Scott remains a large part of my life—a permanent presence.

Krishnamurti, in one of his later books, wrote "There can be no lasting happiness in relationships." I found happiness in my relationship with Scott even after his death. I believe in love after death as well as in life after death.

———— *from* ————

This Organic Life
Confessions of a Suburban Homesteader
Joan Dye Gussow

2001

Joan Dye Gussow, who for many years taught nutrition education at Columbia University, wrote this very personal, feisty, entertaining memoir about living and growing her own food in the suburbs of the Hudson River Valley. Interwoven with her own story are issues of local food, food miles, and the environmental impact and quality of what we eat. All of this sounds like standard fare today to well-read people, but at the time Gussow was one of the first to write about and popularize these themes. Subsequent food writers like Michael Pollan have acknowledged their intellectual debt to Gussow's clear-eyed, clearly written works.

SINCE GARDENING HAS GIVEN ME such an intimate relationship to dirt and its ingredients, I'm continually surprised by the anxiety that contact with the possibly contaminated seems to cause people. Most people who visit my garden do not have my positive relationship to dirt. They're always a bit startled when I graze in the garden, picking and eating one leaf or another. And when I pull a carrot, wipe off the clinging soil on the clover path, and offer it to them to eat, they glance around for a sink.

I suppose it's inevitable that people raised with little contact with soil, or with the process whereby even garbage can be transformed, think of all dirt as simply the opposite of clean. That might not matter if the way people thought about soil didn't affect their attitude about what's clean—and what's important. But our fundamentally negative view of "dirt" means that we don't really understand the need to protect it. Dirt on the windowsill, dirt on the front steps, dirt on the patio, is to be wiped or swept or hosed. What you wash off your produce, invisible or not, is dirt. Mommy shouts at her little boy, "Don't put that in your mouth, it's dirty." And if a positive thought is given to dirt, it's simply what underlies our tennis courts, roads, foundations, golf courses, or, closest to home—lawns. The fact that soil is the basis for life on the planet is largely forgotten, with consequences that were vividly illustrated only recently in our own village.

Piermont is much like a coastal Italian hill town—except our ocean is the mighty Hudson. Most of the houses are not on the flatland next to the river where I live, but stacked along small winding roads up the flanks of the steep woodsy hillside behind me. When storms hit, the worst damage almost always occurs right along the river. A northeaster or a hurricane churning up from the south lowers the barometric pressure and pulls up the tide by a couple of feet, and then blows in along with torrential rains. So when a huge hurricane came plunging up the coast and all I got was twelve inches of water in my yard—no damage to the boardwalk, no floating boards or logs or plastic—I didn't think to wonder what had happened elsewhere in the village.

I should have been alerted, I guess, by the fact that the water filling my yard—clear in the early afternoon—turned muddy before dark. But the electricity went off about then, and my bedroom ceiling started to leak, so my thoughts were elsewhere. I live almost exclusively with my back to the river, so I didn't notice what was going on behind me until someone appeared at my door the next morning to ask how I had made out. It turned out that this time the hillside had taken the biggest hit.

When rain falls on a forest, or even a single tree, the trees' leaves take the impact, allowing the water to come down gently enough to soak into the soil, which is held in place by the trees' roots. In recent years, many giant "river-view" houses have been built on lots gouged into the steep Palisades, uphill from the major road that runs above the village. Their wealthy owners all cut trees, of course, so they can enjoy the view of the river they have paid so much for. But when trees are cut and a house planted on a steeply sloping lot, a driveway paved, and a deck laid out back, heavy rain that falls on all these impermeable surfaces runs off and pours down onto a few square yards of soil—most of it covered with a (largely impermeable) lawn. What began as a heavy rain then becomes a river that rips away everything in its path.

So when water coursed down the hillside past these treeless mansions and onto the road, it took soil as it went. Following the path of least resistance, it ran through the front doors and out the backs of four houses newly built just below the road, depositing mud wherever it met an obstruction. Then it raced downhill, carrying everything moveable with it: roads, backyards, retaining walls, garage roofs, and, by luck alone, no houses—this time. When the flood reached flat land, the road and the houses adjacent to the river, it spread out and settled, blocking the main street with mud and boulders, filling the front yards and basements of the riverfront homes directly in its path with brown sludge, and flowing slowly down the street in my direction.

As the mud flowed past my house, it filled the sidewalk and my narrow front border, doing no damage. The worst of it flowed by, poured into the parking area south of my house, and then down onto my dirt and wood-chip driveway, which it covered with two inches of mud. Word got around town that I was the only homeowner in Piermont happy to have received this soil bounty; the driveway needed raising anyway. My plan now is to sow clover there, since it's obvious that we need to build topsoil wherever and whenever we can.

——— *from* ———

A Handmade Life
In Search of Simplicity
Wm. S. Coperthwaite
Photographs by Peter Forbes

2003

William Coperthwaite was a teacher, builder, designer (especially of yurts), and writer who explored the possibilities of true simplicity on a homestead on the north coast of Maine. In the spirit of Henry David Thoreau and Helen and Scott Nearing, Coperthwaite fashioned a livelihood of integrity and completeness—buying almost nothing, providing for his own needs, and serving as a guide and companion to hundreds of apprentices drawn to his unique way of being. Richly illustrated with luminous color photographs by Peter Forbes, the book is a moving and inspirational testament to a new/old way of life. A Nautilus Gold Award Winner in Ecology/Environment.

ANOTHER FACET OF BEAUTIFUL LIVING WILL BE an "intimate, personal, kinship relationship" with nature—knowing and being known by nature. Life should be a search for harmony—not a battle, not a challenge—neither dominating nor contending with nature but seeking harmony.

Not only is a more personal relationship with nature desirable but so is a more personal relationship to the world of things, from food to clothes to rocks in the garden wall. We need to surround ourselves with things made with care and attention.

One of our pressing needs is to build a more personal sense of our world. The role that emotional security plays in developing a happy, productive, and concerned person cannot be overstated. If we desire to eliminate prejudice, there is no better place to start than to create personal, meaningful relationships with our surroundings.

For example, washing dishes is a chore for many. There are too many of them, and all too often they have no personal meaning. But when the dishes we use are few, made by ourselves or our friends, or personally sought for their beauty and chosen because they are strong and easily cleaned, each as perfect an example of its kind as we can find, then the experience of dishwashing has been known to change its nature.

Have you ever had the experience of apologizing to an inanimate object? When we drop a cup and break it, we violate its nature. All things, be they living or inanimate, have their own nature, spirit, or essence. Whenever we come into contact with anything, we either promote or hinder that essential nature. Unless we seek to understand the nature of the things that surround us, we will be a hindrance rather than a help to our world.

Developing sensitivity and awareness by searching for the basic nature of things is the road to understanding. When we drop and break a cup, we do violence to its spirit, its purpose, and to the work of the artisan who shaped it. We owe the cup an apology.

Whether running a canoe aground, dulling a chisel on a nail, or puncturing a tire—instead of cursing, we owe an apology. You may respond that the object has no feelings. I would tend to agree with you. But apologies are both given and received, and the effect on the giver may be more important than the effect on the recipient.

——— *from* ———

An Unreasonable Woman

A True Story of Shrimpers, Politicos, Polluters, and the Fight for Seadrift, Texas

Diane Wilson

2005

When Diane Wilson, fourth-generation shrimp-boat captain and mother of five, learned that she lived in the most polluted county in the United States, she decided to fight back. She launched a campaign against a multibil-lion-dollar corporation that had been covering up spills, silencing workers, flouting the EPA, and dumping lethal ethylene dichloride and vinyl chlo-

ride into the bays along her beloved Texas Gulf Coast. Along the way she fended off scorn, bribery, character assassination, and death threats. Finally she realized that she must break the law to win justice, and resorted to nonviolent disobedience, direct action, and hunger strikes. Wilson's vivid dialogue resides somewhere between Alice Walker and William Faulkner, and her dazzling prose brings to mind the magic realism of Gabriel García Márquez, replete with dreams and prophecies.

MOST SHRIMPERS WILL ADMIT THEY GO TO SEA as much for the silence as for the catching of shrimp. At least in the beginning they do. The shrimping was incidental and wasn't what they were really on the water for. If they were lucky they remembered, but if not then they never escaped what years of toiling with nets and poverty and bad weather could exact on a fisherman. So a fisherman's original reason could switch like babies switched in a hospital. Then ten years down the road, a fisherman could suddenly look up and say, "Who the hell is this baby and what is he doing with me?" And the sea that had been the liquid part of his life and had given him balance and purpose and had whispered in his ear who he really, really was, was suddenly nothing more than a backbreaking job.

So I kept my boat, the *SeaBee*, as quiet and as uncluttered as possible. Only nobody was happy about my shrimping alone, and particularly Momma, who said the water was a gravedigger and they were gonna find me drowned out there one fine day. Just see if they didn't.

She told my daddy, Billy Bones, a dozen times a day, "Go talk to that son of yours and make him give her a job on land. That job at the fish house!"

Billy Bones said it was a waste of time. He rarely saw Froggie anymore and the only times he did was to watch him through the kitchen window, carrying one of his shrimp nets out of the barn and into the back end of Froggie's truck.

"That boy would take my underwear if I didn't have 'em on," Daddy said.

Billy Bones had quit the bay. Officially, so his nets were fair game. He had walked off his shrimp boat on the very day he had forgotten to tighten a bolt and all the oil in his engine had drained out and ruined a brand new engine. He was seventy-three years old and said he would never set foot on a boat again. He was too old and too stupid. And Daddy never did. But still he pined like a man in the desert dying for want of something. Only he was too stubborn to admit it. Still, whenever I said where I had went shrimping, his eyes would flare like coal in the wind. "That's a good place," he'd say. "I've spent the night out there, nearly right on top of that spot."

Sometimes when I wanted to shrimp someplace new, I'd get Daddy to draw a map of the area. A cut into Spirit Center Bay. The lay of Panther Point Reef. I'd stick my finger on the paper and he'd slap it away, saying, "Leave it alone. I'm doin' it. I ain't that old yet."

So as resolutely as Daddy quit the bay, I worked alone. I left in the dark and came home to the kids by evening. It was the spring run on brownie shrimp, and for several months there was a time and a pound limit. As long as the net was picked up by two o'clock, the game wardens didn't care what time a boat got to the docks. It just mattered to the fish house. No fish house wanted to stay open for hours, waiting on a few straggling boats. Still, I was usually the last boat in. After their last drag, most captains hauled their nets on board, and while their deckhand culled the catch, they headed for the docks. I didn't. I sat in the middle of the bay (the only boat for miles) and culled the catch in silence. Then I iced down the shrimp and washed off the deck, and after hanging the net in the air with a block and whip line, I steered for the docks.

The truth was I was happiest on the bay and loved that it never changed, even when I left. The water had the same smell and the same sounds that I remembered, and it no more changed than the blood in my veins changed. I didn't need to be told that I had went off and danced wildly, then come back tired and weary and lay down hard at her feet. She was the one thing that didn't quit when everything else fled like a fire was driving them.

Every evening and most mornings I took the *SeaBee* through three rituals. I pulled off the engine hatch and squatted over the engine (one boot on the deck and the other on the head of the diesel) and checked the oil gauge and the day tank's water level. Then I squeezed down between the hatch and the engine and crawled to the stern of the boat and poked at the stuffing box. If there were only a couple of drips of water where the shaft made its way to the outside of the boat, then that was good. There was nothing a shrimper obsessed over more than a loose stuffing box where the sea rushed in and a boat sank beneath him.

The *SeaBee* was forty-two foot long, ten years old (not old in boat years), and had one of the tightest keels in the harbor. She never leaked and rarely needed the automatic pump that was as critical to a shrimper as the single white mast light that identified a shrimp boat as a shrimp boat when coming down a channel at night next to a mountain-sized barge.

The day I stepped on the railing the boat groaned. The wind was high in the rigging and flipped my hair and shirt collar, so I went inside the cabin and took an old yellow slicker off a nail. Then I put both the thermoses of coffee on the catchall. I never hooked up the radio. It was gone—swiped off the boat when some hoodlums made a run on all the boats at the docks.

Then I let down the net and threw the ropes off the bow and stern and headed out of the harbor. Even though I had been off the boat for a while, it took only seconds to remember how a boat felt and sounded when she hit deep water. I didn't need a depth meter to tell me where I was. It was pitch black and I knew already.

The sky was half cleared in front with fast-moving clouds, and the moon was sinking. Behind me the town was black, except for the yellow harbor lights. I hadn't pulled the cabin door shut, so the wind came from the back door and it came in through the front windows I had propped open with sticks, and there it met on my front slicker. I stood with both hands on the wheel, feet spread to take the roll of the sea. I never bothered to sit in the captain's chair. The chair had swiveled once, but didn't any more. I never used it unless I was in the middle of a drag, and then I would prop my boots on the cabin wall and stare out to sea.

Now and then I glanced down at the lighted compass that floated in its own little water world, bobbing due south with a little east in it. The compass was bolted too. Everything I didn't want on the cabin floor was bolted. The stainless steel thermoses just rolled. I had given up on glass ones long ago.

I didn't have a map, but I knew where I was going: due south, across the intercoastal canal, then into the middle of San Antonio Bay for an early morning drag. In the fall, when the shrimp season was legally longer and time didn't play such a huge role, I could go farther into the bay or into another bay entirely. The spring run narrowed the options. If money was to be made at all that day, the first drag was the most critical. Shrimping usually went downhill from there.

Generally shrimp settled at night, but by early morning they were either lying in bunches somewhere beneath the surface of the water or were scattered like buckshot across the bay. The scattered trend made shrimping a bore, but the captain would have a fairly good idea of what he would catch for the day, and a deckhand would have a field day. A shrimper scratching for scattered shrimp just needed to put in some dragging time, and he didn't need to check his try net every fifteen minutes to see what in the heck he was catching because he knew exactly what he was catching. So his deckhand lay around half a day, sleeping on a homemade icebox and eating up all the groceries.

When shrimp bunched and offered the captain the possibility of a large catch, the situation changed radically. The shrimper got excited. The deckhand got excited. Then they both jumped all over the back deck and the captain lied up a storm on the radio, saying things like he wasn't catchin' a cryin' thing or he was thinking about taking his boat and headin' for the house. That lie was so common that every shrimper who heard it knew it for the lie it was and picked up his net and headed straight for the one lying.

The games on the radio were partly the reason why Baby quit shrimping. Games and the competition. Baby didn't want to be in a race with nobody. Baby wanted shrimping the way it was when he was still in his momma's belly and maybe that little bit of time afterwards; that summer long long ago when he worked with his uncle and his daddy and there had been a possibility of finding a spot on the bay that hadn't been drug twice, and he didn't have to spend half his time checking the water to make sure it wasn't some other shrimper's mud trail he was dragging through.

I don't know when it started changing. I just know it changed. Shrimpers quit believing there was a bay that hadn't been drug or a reef or a mud flat that hadn't been searched. The day the shrimpers realized that, they started figuring a means to overcome that loss. A bigger engine. A bigger net. Double the propeller. Then an hour or two less sleep. And in their rush to overtake their loss, they tried hard to avoid the dead dolphins and the buzzards that flew at the water's edge. Then when the red tide and the brown tide and the green tide came and their nets came up empty, the shrimpers simply threw them over again. There was nothing else to do. They were fishermen. They couldn't quit. But if one did, he never fully recovered. He was a dead man walking.

I was no different. I couldn't imagine a time when southern Gulf water didn't fill it. At times it pained me, the water with its grand-daddy wave and its great-granddaddy wave. They weren't dead. None of them. They were just back there. Back there. I could almost sling my head in that direction.

If I didn't know who I was, I sure knew where I came from. A direction from rather than a description of, which, I suppose, was the reason why every time the water dipped me and the *SeaBee* and rolled us in the warm salty night I was closer to home than I had ever been, and it was the closest thing to dreaming while being awake that I had ever known.

So I listened to the water and watched the compass, and those two led me and the *SeaBee* crazy into the night. It was intoxicating. I was drunk on as addictive a thing as was ever poured from a bottle. I sang to myself, The sea, the sea, the crazy old black sea.

———— *from* ————

The Man Who Hated Work and Loved Labor

The Life and Times of Tony Mazzocchi

Les Leopold

2007

Labor expert Les Leopold's thriller-like biography of the late Oil, Chemical, and Atomic Workers Union leader Tony Mazzocchi recounts his struggle to address the toxic exposure of tens of thousands of workers that led to the passage of the Occupational Safety and Health Act, including his work alongside that of nuclear whistleblower Karen Silkwood. Mazzocchi, the Rachel Carson of the US workplace, forever changed working conditions in American industry—and it made him enemy number one to a powerful few.

I FIRST MET TONY MAZZOCCHI A FEW MONTHS before he met Karen Silkwood. I was a graduate student who had come to his cramped union office on 16th Street in Washington, DC, hoping to enlist in his radical occupational health and safety movement. Tony had other plans for me and for the movement. His idea was impossibly simple—and perhaps simply impossible. He wanted to build a new working-class economics crusade, and he wanted me to help.

"Look," he said, "I think the post–World War Two boom is over. Workers should be ready to learn about the problems of capitalism." All I had to do was follow the same steps Tony had taken to launch the health and safety movement. First we'd design a course. Then we'd write a popular book based on the course. "Just don't use a lot of Marxist jargon," Tony said. Presto, a new movement would be born! I tried to believe him.

That fall, David Gordon, the noted radical economist, piloted our new political economy course for members of the Oil, Chemical and Atomic Workers International Union (OCAW) at the Rutgers Labor Education Center in New Jersey. No surprise: We did not spark a mass movement. But it did lead in 1975 to the creation of the Labor Institute in New York.

I would work at the Institute for the next thirty-plus years, first as a staff member and later as its director, helping Tony with his countless schemes. During his period of exile from OCAW, Tony showed up on the Labor Institute's doorstep. And after his second marriage collapsed, he even moved in for a while with our family in New Jersey, pasta and canned tomatoes in hand.

I was drawn to Tony's intelligence and his unwavering commitment (as well as his anchovy sauces). Tony didn't just preach about the need for great social changes: He acted each day to create them. But as fiercely as Tony fought for his ideas, as tenaciously as he held on to his principles, he was a kindhearted soul with an earthy, self-deprecating sense of humor. Unlike so many people who rise to leadership, Tony did not have an ego you constantly had to tiptoe around. He almost never got angry, or blamed anyone, or felt slighted. He was brilliant but referred to himself as a "hoople-head" who got things done because he had just enough brains to surround himself with smart people.

Tony was a big-picture organizer who couldn't sit still. All the time I knew him, he traveled the country incessantly, crusading for universal health care or a labor party—leaving too little time to spend with his six children from two broken marriages. He would start ten projects at once, tossing the details around like confetti while others swept up behind.

Yet he could be meticulous when it came to cooking, woodworking, home repairs, or cement work. He once spent three days taking apart a broken dishwasher piece by piece rather than call in a pro. And kids from all over (including mine) still have three-foot-long wooden fish he carefully cut out for them to paint at birthday parties.

Tony's method for radical social change was joyous and communal, involving stimulating conversation and lots of raucous meals with friends. Hopelessness and resignation were not in his repertoire. For inspiration he loved to read history, and his most forward-looking notions often owed a debt to the past. As an autodidact, Tony never recognized (or even noticed) the boundaries between different occupations and different fields of study. He eagerly collected information from everywhere. Then it all bumbled around in his unconventional mind, often producing ideas that catapulted him decades ahead of the curve.

As early as the 1950s, when the term *environment* was nowhere on the political radar, Tony learned about nuclear fallout and began integrating environmental concerns into his critique of capitalism and his union work. His environmental radicalism grew in the 1960s and '70s when he realized that corporations were willingly exposing workers to toxic, even lethal, substances to increase productivity and profits. In the late 1980s, Tony was arguing that global warming might force us to fundamentally alter capitalism. He believed that the struggle of capital against nature was *the* irreconcilable contradiction that would force systemic change.

For me, Tony conjured up a labor movement that didn't really exist, but just might. This movement would be militant and green. It wouldn't just fight to protect the workforce from toxic substances—it would *eliminate* them. It would bring about radical changes that would stop global warming. It would give workers real control over the quality and pace of work and over corporate investment decisions. It would champion the fight against militarism and for justice and equality. It would win life-enhancing social programs such as free health care. It would dare to create a new political party to counter the corporate domination of the two major parties. In short, it would make good on its potential to transform American capitalism into something much more humane.

------ *from* ------

Up Tunket Road

The Education of a Modern Homesteader

Philip Ackerman-Leist

2010

In Up Tunket Road, *author Philip Ackerman-Leist explores through his own experiences what it means to be a modern homesteader. He and his wife, Erin, moved to rural western Vermont and had to piece together—often from other locals—just how to build a life on the land. The learning curve was steep and not always easy, but the lessons Ackerman-Leist gained by experience are now shared with his students at Green Mountain College. Whether writing about his time in the Southern Tirol, North Carolina, or Vermont, the author's personal story is both enjoyable to read and instructive for would-be Thoreaus who wish "to live simply" on the land.*

ELECTRICITY'S GREATEST POWER IS PERHAPS not its ability to make life more efficient—personally or ecologically—but rather its capacity to transform luxuries into needs. This transformation of desires into expectations is a product of our relatively uncritical mode of consumption. Our collective disregard for where we are headed is pushing us to the brink of national—if not planetary—crisis. A national or international debate on our collective need to reduce consumption has little meaning if we are neither accounting nor accountable for our own household consumption of resources.

Tracing the ever-shifting line between need and luxury should probably be one of the first points of household discussion. The Pew Research Center has examined data tracking American perceptions of household necessities and luxuries back to 1973. They recently discovered a significant increase in the number of items that Americans consider necessities in the decade between 1996 and 2006. Those items that were considered necessities by more than half of the survey respondents in 2006 included, in ranked order: a car, a clothes washer, a clothes dryer, home air-conditioning, a microwave, a TV set, car air-conditioning, and a home computer. A cell phone nearly reaches the top half but falls short at 49 percent.

Interestingly, a more detailed analysis of the Pew Research Center data reveals that the higher one's income, the more likely one will be to consider certain items as needs rather than luxuries. Furthermore, rural residents consider fewer items to be necessities than do inhabitants of cities and suburbs. But what surprises and disturbs me the most is that the trend of shifting more and more luxuries into the needs category has endured for more than three decades, to the point that the most basic modern necessities, such as lighting, refrigeration, and running water, are automatically assumed to be needs, and thus have completely disappeared from the list.

Every time an item on the list of necessities becomes a given and disappears from the list altogether, we up our culture's base level of consumption. Not only that, but technological privileges can quickly become expectations, and the potential for thoughtful dialogue and debate about technology and consumption is greatly diminished. We are faced with the peculiar task of simultaneously reinventing necessity and reclaiming contentment.

According to the World Values Survey data, American happiness is not increasing at a rate commensurate with our increase in technological "necessities." It is also not clear that we are healthier as a society, given the dramatic rise in national rates of obesity. One might even make the argument that all of our labor-saving devices are forcing us to work more, as more Americans are working more than forty-nine hours per week while fewer persons are working just forty hours per week. And, of course, it seems inevitable that we exercise less as a result.

In the end, we can (and should) debate what these data really tell us about what we're doing to ourselves. Up to this point, homesteading in the American tradition has primarily been an individual response to a perceived misguided cultural trajectory. In other words, homesteading has been, in some ways, an individual-centered SOS—Save One's Self.

What is clear and different now—in contrast with Thoreau, the Nearings, and others in the American homesteading tradition—is that the homesteading movement's greatest potential contribution to society is no longer the salvation of the individual by means of rural exile. Rather, homesteading ventures and values need to focus on cultural and civic engagement—with a keen eye on energy—and not just in rural areas but also in comfortable suburbs and even the most difficult urban environments. First person singular has been the pronoun guiding the American homesteading tradition up to this point. But first person plural is the pronoun a good ecologist simply must use.

So we find ourselves in a world with ever-clearer ecological limits, a dilemma framed by the constraints of the law of entropy. Our likely sense of aporia, of having "no way out," is the sum total of our collective wild abandon, perpetuated by generations but intensifying in the hastening currents of our contemporary technological cascade.

If the homestead still has a place in the changing American cultural landscape, then it must be a place where we can actively ask questions . . . and try to better understand the incompleteness of our carefully lived answers. What we will probably find is that we can indeed control our technological cascade—collectively—much better than we can control its ecological consequences.

It's daunting, to be sure. But I have faith. There is a door, if we choose to open it. I'm reminded of it whenever I hear our college motto *Lux fiat*: Let there be light. The motto was undoubtedly meant to be a testament to the power of education. I subscribe to that belief, but, for me, it is also a reminder of a much-neglected gift.

According to the US Department of Energy, enough light hits the surface of the earth in a single minute to meet the current energy consumption of our entire human population for a year. We can idly sit back and let government and industry capture that energy for us. Or we can stand up, spurred on by a basic understanding of entropy, and begin to lay claim to that light ourselves—with gardens, forests, livestock, and renewable energy technologies.

Despite the small scale of rural, urban, and suburban homesteads, we have entropy on our side. Entropy is, in large part, a function of distance and the energy transformations required to provide our necessities. So harvesting the light and transforming it into useful energy to power and warm our daily lives can best be done right at home . . . or, perhaps better yet, in the neighborhood.

It's all about wise choices and smart technologies—in that order.

—— *from* ——

Diary of an Eco-Outlaw

An Unreasonable Woman Breaks the Law for Mother Earth

Diane Wilson

2011

In Diary of an Eco-Outlaw, *activist, former shrimper, and all-around hell raiser Diane Wilson picks up where she left off in her first book,* An Unreasonable Woman, *which told of her battle to save her bay in Seadrift, Texas. As it turned out, that fight was just the beginning—a launching pad that led her to take on Union Carbide for its failure to compensate those injured in the Bhopal disaster, co-found the women's antiwar group Code Pink to protest the wars in Iraq and Afghanistan, attempt a citizen's arrest of Dick Cheney, famously cover herself with fake oil and demand the arrest of former BP CEO Tony Hayward as he testified before Congress, and otherwise become a world-class activist against corporate injustice, war, and environmental crimes. As George Bernard Shaw once said, "All progress depends on the unreasonable man." In this case, make that "woman." Wilson has been jailed more than fifty times for civil disobedience, and has forced progress where progress was hard to come by.*

AS FENCES GO, DOW'S WASN'T SPECIAL. It had a hard metallic sheen and a nice roll of razor wire winding down the entire length. It could have been a prison fence just as easily as an industrial fence and my mind went to that industrial fence as naturally as a kid with a stick goes to a low-hanging hornet's nest. It was just a matter of time before the thing got whacked. Only I wasn't gonna whack Dow's fence. I was gonna climb it. After that, I didn't know. Then I saw the biggest tower in the plant and it was clearly visible from the highway. The ethylene oxide tower. I was going to climb Dow's tower and chain myself to it, I decided in an on-the-spot kind of way. Maybe I'd drop a banner.

After the shift workers left, I sat for a long while in my truck, patting the steering wheel and jiggling the truck keys. Okay, what next? I decided to drive my blue truck into the Dow plant. Check out their security. Now, that drive into the plant should have set off a few alarms. After all, I had sat in my blue truck for thirty days in front of their plant and Dow's security should have noticed when my blue truck drove inside their gate. Then, too, it was post-9/11, and six months before Congress had questioned corporate bigwigs like Dow about the potential for terrorist takeover on their big fat tanks full of explosive chemicals. Corporate bigwigs like Dow had responded that they had no need to reduce their stockpile of chemicals because they had high high fences. Such security the world had never seen. Well, if my truck was any indication, that was not true. Dow's security was flat zero and the parking lot was blank as a movie screen. No guard shack. No video cameras. No motion detector. I decided in ten seconds flat that I could get over Dow's fence.

As monkey wrenchers go, I was pretty fast. I definitely did not spend an enormous amount of time beating my good ideas to death even though I knew I should. (Chalk that assumption up to our rational-leaning education in the Western world.) So I gave myself twenty-four hours to make good on my fence-scaling idea and so far my plan had only one item and that was: Get a disguise.

Seadrift was bordered by water. On one side was San Antonio Bay and on the other side was Espirito Santo Bay. Beyond the bays was the Gulf of Mexico where the gas and oil industries launched a fleet of double-decker derricks that were manned twenty-four hours, seven days a week, with hard-hat-and-goggle-wearing workers. And every time gale-force winds whipped up in the Gulf, there came a flotilla of hard hats, goggles, twigs, seaweed, and plastic Coke bottles floating into the bays and in due time they all arrived in our harbor and on our beaches.

So everybody in Seadrift owned a hard hat. Some owned a few more, but shrimpers owned the most because they caught at least one hard hat a day in their shrimp nets. Usually shrimpers decorated their fences with the hard hats, nailing a hard hat to every corner post in the yard. The shrimper wives were more creative and turned the hats upside down on their front porch and used them for bird feeders or flower pots or someplace for a cat to sleep. I had half a dozen hard hats myself in a corner of the closet and I had been waiting on the day when they would be useful.

That evening I eyeballed a blue hard hat that was weather-worn and marked-up. No self-respecting worker would doubt another worker in that hat. I figured it was the best Dow ID I could get in the amount of time I had left to get it. Now what? Chains! I needed chains. Every shrimper on the planet has a barn full of chains. A truckload. A shrimp boat load. Chains

chains. We were poor white trash but we had a fortune in chains. However, the chains from my shrimping days were rusting into a coppery-colored death and Dow's security could snap them like chicken bones with a cheap pair of pliers. I needed something big. Something as thick as my little pinkie finger. And a lock. Maybe two locks. Maybe three!

The next morning, during my noon break from the plant, I called my little auntie June Bug to come sit in my truck while I used hers to run to the Western Auto store in Seadrift. The Western Auto was into some hard economic times and had been through several owners. The last owners were the hardest hit because shrimping was dying and the town was dead even though the chemicals plants were hatching like rabbits and doing just fine. So the latest owners had the store in total air-conditioned shutdown. Only a single glass door was held open with a brick. I walked across the gritty cement floor and wandered among a few scattered shelves where once there had been dozens. A young girl walked up and asked me what I wanted. Chains and locks, I said.

How much? she asked and I said I didn't know. Let me try it out first. So I wrapped some heavy chains around my wrists and tried to imagine myself chained to something. Then I tried to imagine what I could use to cover the chains and locks so Dow couldn't cut them off so easily. The girl watched me with a puzzled look that grew more puzzled by the minute. She was young and inexperienced about shrimpers and their gear but she definitely knew that shrimpers didn't measure out chain by wrapping it around their wrists.

Even so she never said a word. She just sold me the chain and five locks and handed me the receipt. Oh, I don't need the receipt, I said, and walked out. It was later that I heard that for days after our sale, the young girl had agonized, envisioning the FBI coming to Seadrift and arresting her for being a co-conspirator in my plot to take over the plant.

—— *from* ——

Good Morning, Beautiful Business

The Unexpected Journey of an Activist Entrepreneur and Local Economy Pioneer

Judy Wicks

2013

In this heart-lifting business memoir, Judy Wicks recounts a girlhood coming of age in the 1960s, her experience co-founding the first Free People's store (now Urban Outfitters), her accidental entry into the world of restaurants, the emergence of the celebrated White Dog Café, and her eventual role as an international leader in the local-living-economies movement. Van Jones wrote that hers was "a living, breathing tale of the new American dream in action." This memoir of an entrepreneur who would change not only her neighborhood but also her world won a Gold Nautilus Award and prompted Paul Hawken to write, "Judy Wicks' brilliance redefines what a business can be. . . . There is nothing here you will learn in business school."

SINCE MY COMING OF AGE DURING THE 1960S, I had questioned the role of business in our society and then, at La Terrasse, had seen that business was not about money, but about relationships. With my own restaurant, I wanted a mission statement that recognized this.

What was the mission of the White Dog Café? The satisfaction and pleasure of our customers gave me part of the answer. Gradually, I came to believe that the purpose of business is to serve. Yes, serve—the very thing I had rejected in my adolescent days as unimportant . . . and not cool. And it was not just about serving our customers. The White Dog would be a "full service" restaurant in more ways than one: we would serve our customers, serve one another as fellow employees, serve our community, and serve our natural world.

Because I didn't view profit as part of our mission, but rather a tool to better serve our mission, I did not make decisions based only on short-term profit. After being inspired by walks in the woods to purchase renewable energy, I discovered that it would cost the business about seven thousand dollars more a year. If our mission had been to maximize profits, I would not have been able to justify the decision to make the change to renewable energy. But because our mission included serving nature, this was an opportunity too good to pass up. At the same time, we were serving another part of our mission—our community—by putting less coal-burning pollutants into the air and creating less hazardous nuclear waste.

By being an early adopter of renewable energy, we helped make the cost go down in the long run. As the first business in our state to buy 100 percent renewable, we received a lot of press and several awards. Our customers and community were appreciative of our choice, and I can't help but think that sales increased more than enough to cover the difference in cost.

There were often hard choices to make—trade-offs to consider—between our several business stakeholders. At the end of the year, once I saw how much we made in profits, I would decide what changes we could afford to make in the coming year to better serve our four-part mission. Should I increase benefits to better serve the employees? Install a solar hot water system to better serve nature? Make larger contributions to worthy causes in our community? Each year I tried to do something more in each area. Employee benefits far exceeded industry standards—including paid holidays and vacations, contributions to their retirement funds and health insurance coverage, as well as opportunities for travel, education, and loans. Even the tipped employees, traditionally excluded from any benefits at all, received all these benefits after a certain length of employment, which eventually was after one year. To maintain a fair distribution of resources, I kept the wage gap between our highest and lowest salaries capped at a ratio of 5:1—meaning the managers, including myself, did not draw a salary more than five times that of the lowest-paid dishwasher. So when we had the resources to raise salaries at the top, I made sure we raised the entry-level pay rate as well. A key factor in my own financial security was owning the real estate that housed my business. My rental income allowed me to be more generous with benefits for the staff, which I continually increased over the years.

Being a socially responsible business, I came to see, was a continual journey rather than a state of perfection. There were so many things I wanted to do that would advance our mission of service, but we couldn't afford them all. This was especially true in the early years when we were hanging on by a thread. Not only were we not able to pay a living wage back then, or pay me at all, but also I once had to ask all the employees to accept a pay decrease to the minimum wage of just over $5.00 an hour in order to get through the slow summer months. Luckily, they stuck with me. Maybe some felt that the mission of the White Dog was their mission, too.

———— from ————

Slowspoke

A Unicyclist's Guide to America

Mark Schimmoeller

2013

Mark Schimmoeller's account of his solo unicycle journey across the United States is much more than a memoir; it is by turns a love story, a travelogue, even a delicately wrought philosophical treatise on the virtues of slow, contemplative living. Disarmingly sweet and often funny, the book reflects on not only the people and places he encountered during his trip, but also the courtship of his wife, their homesteading life together in rural Kentucky, and their fight to save a parcel of old-growth forest abutting their property from development.

IF I HAD BEEN IN A CAR, I would not have noticed the possum's expression. Recently hit on a road just west of Wilkesboro, North Carolina, the possum offered up a look of resistance. There seemed to be two extremes: going so fast you couldn't see the dead animals on the road or going so slowly that you adopted their expression.

During breaks, I scribbled diligently in my notebook, wanting to communicate everything I saw. To what result, I wondered. That I didn't know this answer compelled me to record everything, in search. I no longer wrote while unicycling, preferring instead to keep my arms out like oars in the air.

Just past the Kerr Scott Dam and the first hemlock trees I'd noticed in North Carolina, I talked with an old beekeeper sitting on a truck tailgate. He told me about five big tulip poplar that had been recently cut down. He was sitting there, he said, trying to get used to not seeing them.

I could, if I went slowly enough, develop an eye for what was no longer there, such as those tulip poplar. Yet it occurred to me that there were limits, too, to slowness on a unicycle, that the pace should inch just ahead of sorrow. As I headed west, toward a blurred outline of the Appalachians, I wondered if, in fact, there was a correlation between slowing down and increasing awareness. An answer that surfaced—that awareness and velocity weren't directly correlated but that someone going quickly may notice different kinds of things than someone going slowly—startled me. What then would be an optimal pace? If my sole aim were slowness, I could go more slowly walking. As an added bonus, the world would be less wavy.

In a couple of days I found myself inside the Appalachian Mountains, on the way to the home of Mel Resfield, my North Carolina contact. The Roby Martin Road in the Pisgah National Forest had steep ups and downs, slowing considerably the already negligible progress I'd make in a day. Going uphill, I would walk. Downhill, I'd ride. A horseback rider passed me and informed me that I was doing it the hard way.

One night I camped on a flat-surfaced boulder jutting into a river. There, water crashed against rock. If I looked at the river in a particular way, I'd find myself traveling upstream. Kneeling, I leaned over the rock and dipped my plastic water carrier into the river—in an instant it was full. On the other side, multiple rhododendron blocked my vision, keeping it at the bank. A leaning hemlock almost touched the current.

Dusk came. I lit a fire and cooked rice and thought of another principle for A Unicyclist's Guide to America: Relax the emphasis on arrival.

Yet was that a valid way to travel, to live?

Questions came and left. I felt that my body was getting stronger.

I woke up to a cold morning. A heavy dew settled on everything except the rock, which curiously stayed dry. I walked away from that camp, the sound of water on rock disentangling itself from me until I was left by myself, loose on the road.

ORGANIC GARDENING & SMALL-SCALE FARMING

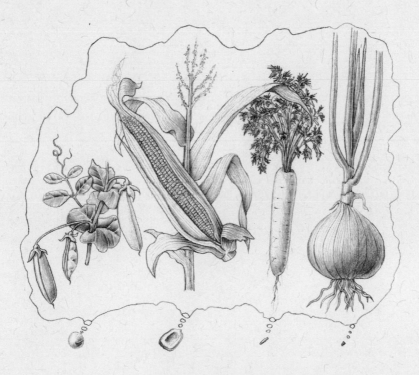

———— *from* ————

The New Organic Grower

A Master's Manual of Tools and Techniques for the Home and Market Gardener

Eliot Coleman

1989; second edition, 1995

In a very real sense, Eliot Coleman's The New Organic Grower *is the book that started it all for Chelsea Green—encouraging our ongoing commitment to books on organic gardening and sustainable farming. But it also became the standard reference for anyone interested in producing vegetable crops efficiently and profitably. Coleman's innovative thinking and careful testing of practices like soil blocks, ergonomically designed hand tools, and season extension have made this book a perennial bestseller. Today Coleman is one of the elder statesmen of the organic movement and spends much of his time passing on his vast knowledge and experience to a new generation of market growers—the New Agriculturists.*

WORKING WITH LIVING CREATURES, both plant and animal, is what makes agriculture different from any other production enterprise. Even though a product is produced, in farming the process is anything but industrial. It is biological. We are dealing with a vital, living system rather than an inert manufacturing process. The skills required to manage a biological system are similar to those of the conductor of an orchestra. The musicians are all very good at what they do individually. The role of the conductor is not to play each instrument but rather to nurture the union of the disparate parts. The conductor coordinates each musician's effort with those of all the others and combines them in a harmonious whole.

Agriculture cannot be an industrial process any more than music can be. It must be understood differently from stamping this metal into that shape or mixing these chemicals and reagents to create that compound. The major workers—the soil microorganisms, the fungi, the mineral particles, the sun, the air, the water—are all parts of a system, and it is not just the employment of any one of them but the coordination of the whole that achieves success.

I remember a conversation I had a few years ago with a Kansas farmer in his sixties who farmed some 700 acres. His methods were considered

unconventional because he had always farmed without purchasing herbicides or pesticides and bought only small quantities of lime and phosphorus.
I asked him on what theory he based his farming. He said there really wasn't
any theory that he knew of. It was simply the same now as it had ever been.
He mentioned a favorite book of his, a 1930s agricultural textbook that
stressed the value of biological techniques such as crop rotation, animal
manures, green manures, cover crops, mixed cropping, mixed stocking,
legumes, crop residues, and more. He said he used those practices on his
farm simply because they worked so well. The book never mentioned any
"theory" and probably never knew one. The book referred to these biological techniques as "good farming practices."

My Kansas friend assured me that by basing his crop production on those
good farming practices his yields were equal to and often far better than his
neighbors'. He saw no yield increase from soluble fertilizer when he had
tried it. His crop rotation and mixed-farming system made weeds, pests,
and diseases negligible problems. When fertilizer prices rose he felt secure as
ever because his production techniques were so fundamentally independent
of purchased materials. And as long as those good farming practices worked
and continued to make his farm profitable, he would continue to use them.
He concluded by saying that if there were any theory involved, he would call
it "successful farming."

I have long followed similar good farming practices—biological techniques—in my system. The secret to success in agriculture is to remove the
limiting factors to plant growth. These practices do that by efficiently and
economically generating a balanced soil fertility from *within* the farm rather
than importing it from without. They power the system through nurturing
the natural processes of soil fertility, plant growth, and pest management
and enable them to work even better. In the words of Cole Porter, they
"accentuate the positive." When chosen carefully and managed perceptively
so as to take full advantage of specific aspects of the natural world, these
good farming practices are all the farmer needs. As a further bonus they
eliminate such negatives as soil erosion, fertilizer run-off, and pesticide pollution at the same time.

—— *from* ——

The Contrary Farmer

Gene Logsdon

1994

The Contrary Farmer was Gene Logsdon's first book for Chelsea Green, but he was already a well-known writer, having published ten practical home-steading books for Rodale Press. The title came from Logsdon's long-running column in New Farm *magazine (and, more recently, his blog of the same name). But it also reflects his personal, intelligent, and often humorous or poignant essays on agriculture and rural living. Since this book's publication, Logsdon has continued to write and publish prolifically, with several more Chelsea Green titles to his credit, and even a few novels. Today he remains one of the strongest and most popular voices of rural America.*

IF HUMANS SUDDENLY VANISHED FROM THIS LAND, in just fifty years the forest would take back its domain. I think of that often as I look out over the countryside of field and village from the edge of my woodlot, my little citadel of native forest in the land of everlasting cornfields. Even after fifty years, the courthouse and grain elevators and St. Peter's church steeple that I can see from my mailbox would surely still stick out above the tree tops. But for the most part, a traveler in 2043, hacking his way through the under-brush, would stumble upon the crumbling, moss-covered houses and stores, and feel no differently than an archeologist discovering a time-lost temple in the green jungles of Ecuador. When I plant trees, I smile a little, thinking how absurd, in a way, is my work. Nature would gladly plant the whole humid world to trees if we would only get out of the way.

There are enormous risks involved in imposing the psychology of black-top on a forest ecology. When we separate our soil and climate from their natural role of growing trees, we also separate them from their ultimate source of fertility and ourselves from ultimate sustainability. We do know better, but knowledge is not enough to keep civilization after civilization from disappearing back into its degraded soil to be eventually covered again by trees—or if things have gone too bad, covered with desert or radioac-tive dust. In "Conquest of the Land through Seven Thousand Years," W.C. Lowdermilk's classic 1938 report on the effects of "civilization" on the earth, there is a photograph that shows one of the four groves of cedars still growing where the biblical "cedars of Lebanon" once flourished. Amidst a few ancient cedars on the grounds of a monastery, the photo reveals cedar seedlings growing in great abundance. Outside the stone wall that protects this green sanctuary from goats and humans, the land is a rocky moonscape of desolation. As Uncle Ade used to say, you couldn't raise an umbrella on land like that if you stood on a sack of fertilizer.

Lowdermilk found the same tragic condition on Chinese mountainsides, where the forest groves of Buddhist monasteries were the only living green in a jumble of rocks and ravines from which the soil had all eroded. An overpopulated society had cut every tree for fuel while its livestock grazed off every blade of grass for food. Below, on the flood plain of the Yellow River—China's Sorrow, as it used to be called—he observed how silt from the mountainsides continually filled the river bed, causing the water to rise and flood the rich farmland. With a stubbornness that defies belief, Chinese farmers built up dikes, century after century, to hold the river at bay, until the water level was higher than the farmlands around it. (The Mississippi River now flows past New Orleans between levees that also lift it higher than much of the city.) Periodically, floods broke through the levees and drowned the farmers. In 1856, 1877, and 1898, for example, the Yellow River flooded and killed *millions* of people on the densely populated plains on either side. This was, in fact, how northern China controlled its population for a while. Let the river do the killing. Let war and famine help. Let us forget the future and the past; on lust let no restraint be cast. Not until the last decades of the twentieth century did China recognize that stabilizing population with birth control just might be a better way. Will the rest of the world realize? Not yet. China farmed for forty centuries with amazing productivity before it admitted that increasing food production merely increases birth rates.

Tree groves and cultivated fields are both essential to the agricultural survival of human civilization. Trees grow where rainfall is ample, the same places where crops can be grown without irrigation. Trees are big signposts that say: "Farmer, sink your plow here." But trees are also signposts of caution: "But beware. Erase us from this landscape and you too will be erased."

—— *from* ——

The Apple Grower

A Guide for the Organic Orchardist

Michael Phillips

1998; second edition, 2005

Everybody used to say (at least everybody east of the Rockies) that you couldn't grow apples organically; the pests and diseases were just too hard to lick without regular chemical spraying. Nonsense, says Michael Phillips, an orchardist from northern New Hampshire. Our grandparents and great-grandparents were "organic" growers by default. What did they know that we don't? When this book first appeared, it was the only practical work on growing apples organically and profitably, on a small commercial scale. Since that time, with the development of kaolin clay, neem oil, and other organic treatments, almost no one claims that organic is impossible. This author, and this book, both were instrumental in creating that sea change in thinking.

AN ORCHARD IS MUCH MORE THAN THE SUM of the fruit trees growing therein. A rich soil underfoot teems with microbial life on which healthy trees depend for both nutrient breakdown and nutrient absorption. Herbs and wildflowers provide homes for hundreds of species of insects, some of which directly balance pest populations. Birds fill the air with song and also play a role in this predator-pest balance. Woodpeckers are the percussion section, drumming out borers and moth pupae beneath the bark. The soil, air, sun and rain perfect the background harmony in which a tiny cell grows to become a bud to become a blossom to become a pollinated ovary to become the beautiful apple in your hand.

An orchard floor favoring broadleaf weeds and flowering herbs is more suitable for fruit trees than a grassy turf. Fescues and other types of perennial grasses have dense root systems that apples avoid, but goldenrod, buckwheat, plantain, and clovers are more congenial about sharing the humus. Mixed cover like this also provides food sources for voles as an alternative to tender tree trunks. Raspberries in or near the orchard are another example of a tree friend. Unlike blackberry canes, which harbor summer disease inoculum, raspberries lack the waxy cuticle that sooty blotch calls home. Predatory mites, however, do favor this bramble fruit, and its blossoms furnish nectar for certain beneficial parasitoids. Raspberry canes compete very little with apple trees for nutrients and water but hinder the growth of grasses that do. And though you might get scratched trying to pick fruit from a standard-size tree surrounded by raspberry canes, what's tastier than a ripe berry on a summer orchard stroll?

Our great-grandparents often planted berries down the rows of a developing orchard. That way, they could enjoy several seasons of small-fruit production from the cultivated ground before the orchard trees filled in their allotted space. Beans provide both a marketable crop and nitrogen fixation on their leguminous roots. Such interplanting is an appropriate form of biodiversity, so long as the soil is built up and protected. Vegetables such as potatoes or winter squash can be followed with cover crop rich in organic matter. The planting aisleway decreases in width as the tree roots seek out the enriched earth. Shallow cultivation here does not overly compromise young roots because permanent roots that are encouraged downward access moisture and subsoil nutrients. The resulting good tilth from added organic matter more than compensates returning feeder roots with rich humus. Deliberately leaving crop ground for vegetable production between every few rows of orchard certainly abets airflow. Letting go the notion of a soil-block orchard—"monoculture or bust"—allows more management options on a diversified farm. Small orchards will reap diversity benefits from nearby borders of native plants in addition to the creative expression provided by crops interplanted between the trees.

Biodiversity applies to overall farm management as well. An underlying principle of biodynamics is that of the farm as its own organism. You might say the biodynamic farm has the ability to be sufficient unto itself without relying on outside inputs. Sir Albert Howard, in his book *Soil and Health*, shared this observation about fruit growing on the Indian subcontinent just prior to the First World War: "The tribesmen invariably combined their fruit growing with mixed farming and livestock. Nowhere, as in the West, did one find the whole farm devoted to fruit with no provision for an adequate supply of animal manure. This method of fruit growing was accompanied by an absence of insect and fungal diseases: spraying machines and poison sprays were unheard of: Artificial manures were never used . . . The quality of the produce was excellent: The varieties grown were those which had never been in cultivation in Afghanistan for centuries. Here were results in disease resistance in striking contrast to those in Western Europe."

The constant advancements in technology and science to overcome the natural world will not be the final answer in crafting a sustainable orchard.

Biodiversity brings into play nature's subtleties, many of which, quite frankly, we have yet to appreciate, let alone understand. The one human card we can throw into this grand mix of life shouldn't be overlooked either: more people involved in agriculture on small farms everywhere are ultimately part of the diversity needed to provide sustainable solutions.

—— *from* ——

Sharing the Harvest

A Citizen's Guide to Community Supported Agriculture

Elizabeth Henderson with Robyn Van En

1999; second edition, 2007

Robyn Van En was one of the first farmers to operate a CSA (Community Supported Agriculture) farm in the United States. Her influence and energy helped found today's vibrant and growing CSA and local food movement. Though her life was cut tragically short in 1997, her friend and colleague Elizabeth Henderson—herself a CSA farmer and a tireless advocate for organic standards and social justice—took up the banner and wrote Sharing the Harvest, *which remains the definitive work on organizing and operating a CSA, with examples drawn from farms all across the United States and around the world.*

WITHIN THE MEMORY OF PEOPLE STILL ALIVE, fruits and vegetables grew on the outskirts of most major cities. Market farms across the Hudson River in New Jersey supplied the vegetable needs of New York City dwellers. Apple orchards blossomed in the Bronx. Since that time, urban, and then suburban, sprawl has paved over cropland and planted houses and highways where cabbages used to grow. Food production has shifted to where it is most "efficient," where bigger machines can maneuver over larger, flatter fields, where chemicals and technology reduce the need for horse and human power, and where crews of poorly paid migrant workers do their jobs and then move on.

The global food system plays economic hardball. A vicious speed-up has been going on in the countryside. In 1950 a farmer could support a family with a herd of twenty cows; today two hundred are needed to eke out a living. Where once a 160-acre "section" produced enough grain for a family's livelihood, today 1,600 acres with a much greater yield per acre is just barely enough to keep a farm in business. Increasingly large and specialized farms produce basic commodities, yet rural areas no longer feed themselves. The Field to Family Community Food Project states, "Iowa is a 'textbook example' of the effects of an expansive industrial food system. The state's agricultural production, focused on grain and livestock, is highly specialized for export purposes, and because there are few food processing industries based in the state, almost all of the food consumed by the state's 2.8 million citizens (including that derived from the basic commodities produced in the state) is imported. The state depends on such imports for essentially all of its vegetables and fruits."

Until the twentieth century, the United States was largely an agrarian society. As recently as 1910, one-third of the population, some 32 million people, lived on farms. The Dust Bowl, the Depression, and World War II drove 9 million people off the land, but those major upheavals pale in significance compared with the decimation of the farming population that followed the restructuring of farm price supports in the 1950s. In 1937 there were 7 million farms; by 1993 less than 2 percent of the population was left on only 2.2 million farms—so few that the U.S. Census Bureau announced it would stop counting them.

—— *from* ——

Natural Beekeeping
Organic Approaches to Modern Apiculture
Ross Conrad

2007; second edition, 2013

In recent years the serious decline of honeybees has captured the attention and concern of beekeepers, farmers, environmentalists, and the general public around the world. Ross Conrad's book was the first comprehensive modern work on how to keep bees organically, using techniques like breeding and herbal treatments rather than increasingly toxic—and only temporarily effective—chemicals. Conrad's intelligence, experience, and gentle philosophy have made him famous among Vermont beekeepers, and Natural Beekeeping *demonstrates to both home and commercial apiculturists that there are viable and earth-friendly alternatives to the chemical merry-go-round.*

DESPITE WIDESPREAD BELIEF TO THE CONTRARY, the term *organic* does not mean that the final crop or product is free from toxic chemical contaminants.

This mistaken perception has taken hold primarily due to the efforts of manufacturers and marketers, who have successfully promoted the notion that organic products are pure and chemical-free. Meanwhile, because of the success of this viewpoint, resentment has built up among many bee-keepers, who feel that the organic label relegates their own commercially produced honey to second-class status. What was once considered a natural, healthy product is now deemed inferior, when, in fact, the final products of conventional and organic production may not be all that dissimilar in terms of their chemical composition.

At its inception, the organic approach traditionally referred to a management style and philosophy that is biological in nature. Rather than being a statement about product purity, *organic* was all about the big picture. It referred to approaches that care for the life in the soil and minimize the use of nonrenewable inputs and energy sources, such as those derived from petroleum. Organic principles embraced an attitude of fairness and care in regard to our common environment, as well as social concerns such as the welfare of farm workers. One of the original aims of organic agriculture was to establish a sense of stewardship for the Earth, embracing human-scale operations that fit harmoniously with the landscape and local community. Although it was certainly possible that organic management practices would result in a cleaner product, it was not the primary focus. Instead, organic management sought to mimic the natural world in its efforts to be sustainable, with the ability to be carried on indefinitely, as nature has proven herself to be. For example, organic farmers have long relied on beneficial insects that feed on pests in order to reduce crop damage, such as the large-scale release of ladybugs to limit the population of aphids on a crop. Some farmers and growers use traps on a regular basis. These traps mimic the effect of natural predators by removing unwanted insects, often by luring the unsuspecting victim using a synthetic version of a natural pheromone attractant. These are just a couple of the approaches to pest control that copy the ways in which the natural world will spare some plants over others from the damaging effects of insect predation. Although these types of approaches may have little impact on the quality of the final crop, they are integral to the organic philosophy that stands behind the finished product.

In contrast, one of the guiding principles of the industrial model that has been developed by Western culture is the desire to maximize production. When applied to agriculture, this typically results in the drive to push biological organisms to the limits of their capacity. Unfortunately, the focus on increasing our harvest seems to distract our attention from the quality of the crop that is being produced and the health of the plants or livestock that are doing the producing. In the dairy industry, for example, the cow that historically produced 15 to 20 pounds of milk a day and lived for fourteen years or more in a healthy, relatively disease-free state has today been bred to pump out an average of 90 to 120 pounds of milk a day and has to be sent to the slaughterhouse within three or four years, simply because she becomes exceptionally prone to sickness and disease from the stress of the forced increase in milk production. The poor cows are literally worn out. The humble honey bee is similarly affected by our efforts to artificially boost the size of its honey crop. Activities such as the use of chemical mite controls or the feeding of sugar syrups and pollen substitutes, although beneficial to honey production in the short term, ultimately may weaken the vitality of the hive and increase its vulnerability to diseases and pests such as varroa. As a result, such management tools should be used sparingly, if at all.

Our industrial model encourages large-scale production under the "economy of scale" argument that has been the drumbeat of US schools of agriculture since the end of World War II. That is to say, "If you want to be profitable, you must grow larger."

The same pressure for farmers to increase in size applies to the beekeeping industry. Aside from the inexperienced or inattentive hobbyist, it is the large commercial bee outfits that have had the hardest time preventing their hives from collapsing due to varroa, disease, or colony collapse disorder (CCD). Reports of winter losses exceeding 40 percent and attributed to either mites or CCD have been all too common among those with 600 hives or more. In truth, the number of colonies an experienced beekeeper can manage success-fully in this new era is likely to be lower than those of pre-varroa/pre-CCD years, at least until new strains of bees have been developed that are either extremely resistant or outright immune to these challenges.

Part of the allure of chemical pesticide use is the economic benefit that can be reaped by a reduction in labor—a cost that reflects the investment in time, and the attention to detail, required by nontoxic organic approaches to pests and disease. With the chemical approach proving itself to be less than satisfactory in many ways, those in the beekeeping industry may find themselves having to decrease their hive-to-beekeeper ratio to match their colonies with the amount of labor available to keep their hives healthy. The number of hives that a single beekeeper can inspect and treat in a timely manner is limited. This is especially true when one considers all the unexpected issues, from bad weather to flat tires, that typically arise and cause delays, forcing one to fall behind schedule. As conventional chemical treatments become less effective, the shift to nontoxic, labor-intensive management techniques will require new approaches and technologies to make up for these increased labor demands.

———— *from* ————

The Winter Harvest Handbook

Year-Round Vegetable Production Using Deep-Organic Techniques and Unheated Greenhouses

Eliot Coleman

2009

Best-selling author Eliot Coleman is something of a perfectionist. Before he releases any new information in print, he makes sure that his advice actually works in the field and on his farm—sometimes taking several years to test and refine a particular technique or system. Years after his first Chelsea Green book, The New Organic Grower, *was published, Coleman brought out this elaborated, improved system of growing and harvesting crops year-round, even in cold climates like coastal Maine. His longtime goal has been to prove there is no "off-season" for farming, no matter where you live.*

IT IS IMPORTANT TO STRESS THAT what has been accomplished to get organic farming from the early pioneers to where it is today is the story of a groundswell of natural truths flourishing in the face of a passel of corporate/industrial lies. I remember the situation very well as it was when I started back in 1965. The forces were definitely arrayed against us. The defenders of the chemical side, claiming that organic farming was foolish and impossible, were the U.S. Department of Agriculture with its scientists and its enormous budget, all of the land-grant universities and the smaller schools of agriculture, the extension service, every feed and seed store in the country, and of course the enormous money and power of the massive agrochemical industry. On our side, claiming not only that organic farming worked but that it worked much better than chemical farming, were a few old-time large-scale farmers who had never bought into chemicals in the first place and a bunch of idealistic young newcomers who wanted to farm and who found the concepts of organic farming totally in line with their thinking about humanity, sustainability, and the welfare of the planet. When a study came out in 1977 from Barry Commoner's group at Washington University in Saint Louis showing that, in a side-by-side paired comparison, a group of Midwestern organic farmers were just as successful as their chemical-using neighbors, it was the first major eye-opener of the world to come. The other side had had no idea we were that good. There were some newspaper and magazine articles, but far less press than this should have received if the public had been aware of the massively unequal array of forces on the opposing sides. In my mind what had just happened was the equivalent of a junior high football team splitting a couple of games with the Steelers. The type of press those football games would get is what this incident deserved.

The first of a number of studies positive to organic farming had begun appearing in the early 1970s. I had a friend at the USDA whom I used to call on the phone as each one of these studies appeared. He was consistently dismissive. The first one I told him about was a very positive study by a French farmer's organization. "Ha!" he scoffed, "The USDA isn't going to pay any attention to a bunch of French farmers." A couple of years later a significant study was done by the Dutch Department of Agriculture. "Ha!" he scoffed, "The USDA isn't going to listen to the Dutch Department of Agriculture." Then the Washington University study came out. "Ha! The USDA isn't going to listen to Washington University." I had lost touch with him by 1980 when the USDA's own very positive study, *Report and Recommendations on Organic Agriculture*, came out, but I would not have been surprised if he had said, "Ha! You don't expect the USDA to pay attention to the USDA, do you?"

In other words, the myth that organic farming could not work was so ingrained, so much like a religious belief, that it was accepted out of hand by agricultural-university faculty members who were not reading the published literature in their own fields (or if they were reading, they weren't paying attention). And, of course, none of them had ever investigated it in person. The difficulty of dealing with them reminded me of Max Planck's famous quote: "A new scientific truth does not triumph by convincing its opponents and making them see the light, but rather because its opponents eventually die, and a new generation grows up that is familiar with it."

—— *from* ——

The Resilient Gardener

Food Production and Self-Reliance in Uncertain Times

Carol Deppe

2010

Carol Deppe is a remarkable woman who holds a PhD in biology from Harvard but who for years has made the garden her laboratory, breeding and improving numerous seed varieties in the public domain. In this book she tells gardeners and small farmers how to grow, store, preserve, and cook with the most important staple crops—ones we can use to sustain ourselves and our neighbors through both good times and bad. With the growing concern over our changing climate, erratic weather events, shaky economic times, and dwindling resources, this book teaches valuable skills all gardeners need to know.

THE SEASONALITY OF "GREEN" VARIES with the region. The true New Englander expects his densely planted landscape to be green and lush all summer. In fall, when much dies, he celebrates the "fall colors." When the ground is covered with snow, he doesn't complain about the lack of green, but rather, comments upon the pristine cleanness of the white blanket that covers all summer sins. Nor does he bemoan the naked, leafless, dormant deciduous trees in winter. Instead he notices their essential shapes and comments on the myriad patterns and shades and kinds of bark.

I'm a westerner, a scion of the Willamette Valley of Oregon. I appreciate the lush greenery of spring as much as any New Englander. But by midsummer, I expect the natural rhythms to be changing and slowing down. By August, I expect the dominant shade in the landscape to be the yellowish-brown of grass doing what it makes sense for natural things to do at this time of year . . . to go dormant. Like most Oregonians, toward the end of August, however, I am getting restless and eager for the return of the winter rains. I watch and evaluate those first few sprinkles in September. In response to each, I am asking whether it is just a sprinkle or a real rain—a rain that begins to re-hydrate the soil and wake up all the sleepers. I sniff every breeze for rain. When the first real rain comes, like most Oregonians, I rejoice, as humans often do, by running around and exclaiming over the rain and commenting about it to everyone who will stand still long enough. Sometimes I even go for a walk in that first real rain. I welcome it back by getting thoroughly and happily drenched, an act that is impossible in summer.

The leaves begin to fall from the deciduous trees. Most don't turn any spectacular color first. Yellow is usually the best we get. But I don't mind. The few swaths of bright red on the hillsides don't arouse any particular emotions other than a reminder to avoid those places. That's the poison oak. Our fall color isn't red or even yellow so much as green, the green of everything waking up, coming to life, germinating. Our winter, too, is mostly green. The occasional few days here and there with snow on the ground are fun but get old fast. What I want is green. There are at least a hundred shades and kinds of green. I love them all. Spring is green and the rains cease. Early summer is still green, but the natural cycle (and the natural yard) is winding down. Then comes August in soft yellows and browns, a time of rest.

There seem to be more garden writers from New England than from elsewhere. Those of us who live elsewhere need to be careful not to be bamboozled into trying to impose a New England pattern on places where it doesn't belong. The Oregonian or Californian or Washingtonian who wants a green lawn in August is, in essence, saying to that lawn: "Be a New England lawn!" We lowland westerners should be landscaping with appropriate natives and adaptable imported plants that can thrive on our natural cycles, not trying to impose the patterns of alien regions.

National and state boundaries don't mean anything to plants. I will do better with lowland-adapted, dry-summer-adapted Mediterranean natives than native plants from eastern Oregon or even natives from a few miles away—but a mile higher. What plants care about are specific climates and temperatures and patterns of rainfall.

Those who live in truly desert areas have additional problems. They need desert-adapted plants. But in addition, they need a different concept about planting densities in their landscapes. A commonly stated rule is that most plants have roots that extend about as far down and around as the top growth of the plant extends up and around, or a bit beyond. That isn't true of desert plants. Desert plants often have root systems that are manyfold wider and/or deeper than the aboveground plant. Some have very deep roots specialized for reaching deep reservoirs of moisture. Some have huge expanses of shallow roots designed to grab every molecule of rainwater the instant it touches the ground. A yard landscaped with desert plants must mimic desert plant spacings. The desert-living human gardener adopts the patterns of the desert and learns to appreciate the spaces and rocks and sand as much as the plants in his sparser plantings.

One of the most joyous things we can do is to find our place, the land we fit into, the land where we belong. Having found our place, we snuggle into it, learn about it, adapt to it, and accept it fully. We love and honor it. We rejoice in it. We cherish it. We become native to the land of our living.

—— *from* ——

The Small-Scale Poultry Flock
An All-Natural Approach to Raising Chickens and Other Fowl for Home and Market Growers
Harvey Ussery
2011

Carrying on the tradition of edge-pushing agricultural books, this almost immediately became a bestselling title for Chelsea Green, even considering the myriad other chicken books on the market. The difference: None of the others offers a practical and integrative model for working with chickens and other domestic fowl based entirely on natural systems. As Joel Salatin rightly puts it: "Harvey Ussery has spent a lifetime developing and show-casing a truly viable poultry model that is ultimately carbon-sequestering, hygienic, neighbor-friendly, and food-secure. . . . this book is about a call to heritage, to the wisest of wise traditions in food security and relationships."

GALLUS GALLUS—THE RED JUNGLEFOWL, at least in good part the ancestor of domestic chickens—did not have housing; and I've heard from intrepid flocksters who follow suit, allowing their chickens to live outdoors, fending for themselves and roosting in trees at night. That is the cheapest housing option, but it certainly opens the field to the neighboring predators. Equally problematic, chickens have a tendency to revert to the feral state if not kept in close association with their keepers. A tree-roosting flock would be too wild for my taste. It is *housing* as much as any other factor that keeps our birds *Gallus gallus domesticus.*

Chickens' notions about housing conditions parallel our own. In summer we want shelter from the broiling sun. In winter we want to be out of the wind. We can bundle up against cold temperatures per se, but a sharp wind in the winter cuts to the bone. The chickens are bundled up in a layer of feathers, among the best of all natural insulation, so they're ready for the cold—but windchill is as much a challenge to staying warm for them as for us. And think how miserable you feel when getting soaked in a windy rain, even in summer. Despite their feathers, getting wet while exposed to wind and low temperatures can be lethal.

But it is good to remember tree roosting when thinking about housing. The fact that some flocks roost in trees—in some cases by preference—reminds us that our birds are pretty tough critters. When thinking about housing, it's important to banish the concept of pampering from the beginning.

One of the most frequent questions I encounter about chickens is, "How do you heat their house in the winter?" In my mid-Atlantic climate (Zone 6B, where winter temperatures may get down into the subteens), I add *no* heat in the winter housing. And I have not installed any artificial insulation, nor doubled the walls of the henhouse.

Flocksters considerably to the north of me should need no artificial heat or insulation either (though I can't advise those keeping fowl up in Alaska, or northern Canada). Indeed, *adding either would probably be more detrimental than beneficial:* A warm, airtight house will be a damp house—both the manure and the chickens' exhalations accumulate moisture in the coop—and dampness encourages both disease pathogens and molds.

—— *from* ——

The Holistic Orchard
Fruit Trees and Berries the Biological Way
Michael Phillips

2011

Following the success of his first Chelsea Green book, The Apple Grower, *author and farmer Michael Phillips began digging deeper into organic thinking. Was it really enough to simply replace chemical sprays with organically approved treatments like sulfur and copper? And what was this doing to life in the orchard ecosystem: the insects, birds, and soil microorganisms? Wasn't there a better alternative, one that would ensure a good crop of orchard fruits and keep pests and diseases in check while at the same time supporting all living things? In* The Holistic Orchard, *which won an American Horticultural Society Book Award, Phillips proves that this is indeed possible by going "beyond organic" and employing deep, mindful, science-based ecological practices.*

ANYONE LOOKING TO GROW FRUIT FACES a good hundred years' worth of chemical obstinacy despite this lengthy rundown of biological advantages. We must make certain our philosophy once and for all to answer that pivotal question with which we began this chapter: Are we going to honor tree wisdom or not?

Our grandparents' generation didn't make the turn toward chemical agriculture so much out of dire necessity as out of uncomprehending enthusiasm. Pest and disease problems are frustrating when you've worked so hard to plant, water, and cultivate, only to see moths gain the upper hand or rot ruin nearly every peach in a particularly wet summer. Blunt chemicals like lead arsenate and Bordeaux copper dealt a blow to mortal pest enemies in the Roaring Twenties. Insidious chemicals like DDT (among the many organochlorine/organophosphate compounds developed as nerve toxins during and after World War II) upped the ante. And what do we really know about the "softer chemicals" like imidacloprid being used today, other than that honeybee populations worldwide have crashed precipitously? Advocates for chemical agriculture make a tantalizing case for labor saved, the certainty that food will come to hand, and the moral imperative that a burgeoning human population must be fed by industrial means. All this can be argued. Health data presented. Refined thinking pursued. I'm not going to engage anyone's beliefs here about what makes for righteous agriculture. I am, however, going to make clear what happens in the orchard ecosystem when chemicals are relied upon as a primary means of growing fruit.

In a sense, pests and disease in the orchard—whatever the scale—should be thought of as symptoms that show up whenever system health is less than optimum. Environmental stress, nutrition imbalance, lack of diversity, input ramifications, and human arrogance all contribute to this broad mandate for trouble. We may want to make big-picture decisions, yet almost invariably we react to a perceived threat in the here and now by seeking a potent medicine to alleviate a crop-threatening situation. Such short-term solutions merely address symptoms and can never be more than a prop for a sick patient . . . although they may seem to do good at the time. Eventually stronger medicine is needed as the system gets weaker from not having relied on its own internal fortitude. Mycorrhizal fungal connections are lost as fungicides used to prevent potential disease up high in the tree (a fairly common orchard strategy) change the hospitality of the living soil below.

Feeder roots limit their reach in favor of the intravenous-like drip provided by soluble nitrogen. Mites and other foliar pests weaken plant vitality as beneficial allies disappear due to the use of broad-acting toxins. Inherent nutrition in the food we eat becomes a degenerative joke when there's little respect for soil biology. The grower, of course, gets a crop. Some say the fruit even looks grand. Next year it's more of the same. Chemicals again prop up a less-than-optimum situation. The next year the grower gets another crop, just as empty of real nutrition as the one before. The beat goes on.

This is not a basis for a happy home orchard where children walk through the grass to pick berries and birds sing. Nor will any fruit grower find joy in contemplating the "-ide side" of conventional thinking: Insecticides, fungicides, herbicides, and soluble fertilizer-ides come with complicated instructions and myriad danger warnings. Perpetuating imbalance takes more effort than some people might wish to admit.

Choosing to go organic is no reason to be smug, however, if we fail to make the connection to health across the board. Utilizing a substitute arsenal of natural toxins does not change the underlying paradigm of how we view food production. Dealing with symptoms—be it codling moth stings or nutrient deficiency or rust defoliation—is not the same as supporting health and biodiversity throughout the orchard ecosystem.

———— *from* ————

The Organic Grain Grower

Small-Scale, Holistic Grain Production for the Home and Market Producer

Jack Lazor

2013

Longtime farmer and organic pioneer Jack Lazor wrote this, the first-ever book on growing organic grains on a market scale, based on his decades of experience growing and storing wheat, barley, oats, corn, dry beans, soybeans, pulse crops, oilseeds, grasses, nutrient-dense forages, and lesser-known cereals in cold and snowy northern Vermont. His book is part agricultural history and part practical guide, with information found nowhere else. To read it is to feel like you're standing at the edge of a wheat field in the sun, breeze rustling the seedheads, listening to Jack spout wisdom as he leans against his tractor.

My own personal farming saga began in the early 1970s. While attending Tufts University in politically turbulent times, I somehow decided that a simple life providing for myself from the earth would be more fulfilling to me than political protest. Books like Helen and Scott Nearing's *Living the Good Life* helped me solidify my plan of action, and I even created my own major focusing on the history of agriculture. Summers found me working as a costumed interpreter on the historical farm at Old Sturbridge Village, a living historical museum located in central Massachusetts close to where I grew up. My first exposure to grain was spending the day riding on an old combine harvesting rye on a neighboring farm in 1961, and at Sturbridge Village I got to harvest rye by hand with a curved reaping sickle. The hand-cut grain was tied off into bundles that were stood up to dry in the field. Later I got to thresh this grain out on the barn floor with a handheld flail.

In 1973, I moved to Warden Farm in Barnet, Vermont, to work on an old-fashioned dairy operation where there was lots of evidence of a once thriving grain culture. One of the farm's outbuildings was a granary that contained many old grain-harvesting tools like reaping sickles, grain cradles, flails, and winnowing pans. My employer, Robert Warden, told me many stories from his earlier days in the 1920s and '30s when they grew oats and flint corn as a matter of common practice. Circumstances took me to rural southern Wisconsin in 1974 and 1975, where I found a culture of dairy farming with farmers growing their own grain as well as hay for their cows. I spent many hours with my friend and mentor John Ace of Oregon, Wisconsin, learning all about oats and ear corn for the dairy. There was also a thriving Amish community around New Glarus, south of Madison. My partner, Anne, and I went to many of their auction sales and began to learn that the Amish grew much of their own wheat for bread using horse-drawn grain drills, grain binders, and belt-powered stationary threshing machines. This was it. I was hooked. I wanted to return to Vermont and grow grain the old-fashioned way for ourselves and our livestock.

Anne and I began our farming careers as back-to-the-land homesteaders on a small farm in Irasburg, Vermont, in May 1975. We were equipped with a lot of idealism and a truckload of old farm antiques we had brought with us from Wisconsin. My first project was to trial six different varieties of heirloom flint corn that I had obtained from the USDA seed bank. (I found out all about how much raccoons like flint corn that first summer.) Anne and I took many trips to the Eastern Townships of Québec that first summer together in northern Vermont, and we were surprised to see so many fields of golden ripening grain during our travels. In August, there were combines everywhere harvesting the oats and barley. The fact that all of this grain was growing quite well only ten miles away across the border was all the proof I needed that I could do this on my side of the border, too. And so we bought our first sixty acres in Westfield, Vermont, in 1976 and grew our first six acres of wheat, corn, and barley in 1977. Planting was done with an antique $25 horse-drawn wooden grain drill pulled by a 1954 John Deere 40 tractor, and we bought a six-foot John Deere grain binder (reaper) and a Dion threshing machine in Coaticook, Québec, for $250. We spent most of the month of July readying the reaper for the upcoming harvest and procuring new canvases from the Amish in Ohio. We ended up buying a second grain binder from Doug MacKinnon of Barnston, Québec, for extra parts. (Doug had used this machine well into the 1960s to reap his and his neighbors' oats.) Beginner's luck was with us, and we successfully reaped and stooked all six acres of our wheat and barley. We powered the stationary thresher with a sixty-foot endless flatbelt attached to the belt pulley of our old Super M Farmall tractor. Five or six old-timers from our area provided us with lots of help, support, and good advice, and the general consensus was that field-cured grain reaped, stooked, and threshed was far superior in taste and color to its modern counterpart direct-cut with a modern combine. The old guys were right—our wheat was quite dry and golden-red in color. Another neighbor, Milton Hammond of Newport Center, let us use his small grain cleaner and burr mill grinder to make whole wheat flour for our first loaf of homegrown whole wheat bread. We thought that we had arrived, but little did we realize that our grain-growing adventure had just begun.

This all happened thirty-four years ago. We tried selling whole wheat flour to our local food co-op but were quite surprised at how little our very special product was worth. No one seemed to give any value to homegrown whole wheat flour except us and the old-timers who had helped us accomplish this modern-day anachronism! But slowly, demand grew, and we have continued to grow wheat and other grains ever since this very humble beginning. We gave up the grain binder and the threshing machine after six years and increasing acreage, and have upgraded to four different combines over the years. I have managed to collect a pile of old and some new machinery for planting, harvesting, storing, and processing our farm-grown grains, and we have gotten mountains of advice from a large group of older farmers in Vermont and Québec, many of whom were French-speaking. Most of these old guys have passed on, but their stories, advice, and goodwill live on with me every day. We have made numerous mistakes and learned many hard lessons over the last thirty-plus years of trying to grow grain in northern Vermont—we have lost crops to bad weather, and flooding has become more prevalent over the last decade. But we have learned a lot about proper grain moisture for long-term storage by watching grain mold because it was harvested too wet and not properly dried. The lessons have been difficult, but the successes have been ever so sweet. Indeed, the feeling and security of producing our own food staples represents true wealth and well-being to us.

Lots of water has passed under the bridge over the last three-plus decades, however, and we are no longer young back-to-the-land types. We remain just as optimistic and idealistic, but we are now commercial organic dairy and grain farmers processing our own milk and growing hay and grain for humans and livestock on four hundred acres of land. Integrating crops, livestock, milk processing, and family into a whole farm organism that restores the earth has become a way of life for us; we still grow just about all of our own food and provide all the grains for our cows, pigs, and chickens. Our crop base has expanded from barley, oats, and wheat to include corn, soybeans, dry beans, field peas, sunflowers, flax, and buckwheat, and in most years we can clean and save seed for just about all of our grain crops. Crop growing continues to be my primary agricultural passion along with grain processing, and I continue to learn about and experiment with elementary farm-based plant breeding of open-pollinated corn and wheat as well as on-farm grain processing of spelt, oats, and emmer. It is my dream that our farm can continue to be a center of hope, innovation, and inspiration for those who want to nurture the earth and grow good food for others. We have certainly held many workshops here at Butterworks Farm over the years and have hosted many visitors who have given us as much as we have given them. As interest in grain growing continues to expand, I feel that it is time for me to chronicle as much of my knowledge and experience as I can muster to further the pursuit of a sustainable and organic culture of grain growing in our region. So many people have been so generous to me with their farming knowledge and wisdom over the years; it is my turn to give a little back.

—— *from* ——

An Unlikely Vineyard
The Education of a Young Farmer and Her Quest for Terroir
Deirdre Heekin

2014

Deirdre Heekin and her husband, chef Caleb Barber, own Osteria Pane e Salute, a farm-to-table restaurant in Woodstock, Vermont. The couple has always been connected to organic gardening and the land, and much of their food comes straight from their own farm and garden. But Heekin is also an expert on wine, spirits, and perfumes, which she wrote about in her previous Chelsea Green book, Libation: A Bitter Alchemy. *So when she got serious about growing grapes and making natural wines, using organic and biodynamic methods, it was only fitting that she write about her education and discoveries. Her Vermont "microwinery," under the name la garagista, is currently making a name for Heekin's expression of her local terroir, in a region not known for producing wines of great distinction.*

I RETURN TO THAT NOTION THAT FERMENTATION and fire are the two hallmarks of civilization. Both take food from its basic and animalistic elements to something more cogent; food goes from its raw state and is transformed into something else that requires contemplation and some skill. From an evolutionary level, cooking by either fermentation or fire means the food is easier for our human bodies to digest, and these processes provide easy access to the energy stored in the food. From an artistic level, they allow us to shape our food in more complex ways, providing intricate and intriguing flavors. Fire and fermentation also provide creature comforts, essentially that of heat. Fire gives off calories in heat, and fermented foods create inner heat. Both fire and fermentation improve our basic, animalistic lots in life.

The fermentation of wine is the complement to photosynthesis in the vines. Photosynthesis is the transformation of heat and light into matter. In the cellar, fermentation is the liberation of heat and gas. Inhalation and exhalation. Birth and death. Transformation of one substance into another. A life cycle.

This is one of the basic reasons that many wine appreciators, growers, producers, and writers believe that wine begins in the vineyard. It begins with the photosynthesis in the leaves and the formation of the flower that turns into the grape and the cluster. Fermentation becomes an extension of the vineyard work, and just as important. The yeast that grows on the fruit is part of the culture of the vineyard. It is dependent on what you use on your plants and fields during the season. Chemicals in the field—insecticides, pesticides, and fertilizers—all kill ambient yeasts as well as suppressing natural biological activity. But if you use minerals, plant teas, and compost, the yeasts of that season thrive. They come onto the fruit and into the cellar, and they ignite the fermentation process if they are allowed to do so. Every year they are slightly different, responding to the nature of that year's weather and growing conditions.

FOOD &
FOOD CULTURE

crock

jars

cooler

mandolin

pickle press

SALT

mixing bowl

timer

cutting board

markers

thermometer

hand grater

masking tape

ELARA TANGUY

—— *from* ——

Whole Foods Companion

*A Guide for Adventurous Cooks, Curious Shoppers,
and Lovers of Natural Foods*

Dianne Onstad

1996; second edition, 2004

*Whole Foods Companion has become the definitive resource guide to the
rapidly expanding world of whole foods, covering fruits, vegetables, grains,
legumes, nuts, seeds, oils, herbs, spices, and other foods. Each entry includes
nutritional value, general information, buying tips, culinary uses, and, when
appropriate, health benefits. No mere collection of dry nutritional information,* Whole Foods Companion *also explains the origins and naming of
different foods and relays some of the legends and traditions with which
they have been associated.*

ALTHOUGH THE EARLY AZTECS OF MEXICO considered the tomato a "health"
food and reverently offered it to their gods of healing, Europeans shunned it
because of its association with known poisonous plants, and because its bright
shiny colors—red, orange, yellow, and white—were highly suspicious. The
turning point for the pro-tomato faction in America, according to time-honored legend, occurred on the steps of the Salem, New Jersey, courthouse on
September 26, 1820. That was the day when Colonel Robert Gibbon Johnson
ate, in public and without ill effect, an entire basketful of tomatoes. Colonel
Johnson, an enthusiastic gardener, had earlier introduced the tomato to the
farmers of Salem after a trip abroad in 1808, and each year offered a prize for
the largest fruit grown. A forceful individualist and notorious eccentric, the
Colonel wanted his introduction to be regarded as more than an ornamental
bush, so when he announced that he would in public eat not one, but a *whole
basket* of "wolf peaches," a large crowd of some two thousand curious people
from miles around gathered to watch him commit certain suicide. Dressed
in his habitual black suit with impeccable white ruffles, a tricorn hat, black
gloves, and gold-topped walking stick, the Colonel made an imposing figure
as he ascended the courthouse steps at high noon to the accompaniment of
a dirgelike tune played by the local fireman's band. Selecting a tomato from
his basket, he held it aloft and launched into his spiel:

The time will come when this luscious, golden apple, right in nutritive value, a delight to the eye, a joy to the palate, whether fried, baked, broiled, or eaten raw, will form the foundation of a great garden industry, and will be recognized, eaten and enjoyed as an edible food . . . And to help speed that enlightened day, to help dispel the tall tales, the fantastic fables that you have been hearing about the thing, to show you that it is not poisonous, that it will not strike you dead, I am going to eat one right now!—Hendrickson, *Foods for Love*, pp. 188–89

Colonel Johnson bit into the tomato, and the juicy bite could be heard through the silence, until he bit again, and again—at least one female spectator screaming and fainting with each successive bite. The crowd was amazed to see the courageous Colonel still on his feet as he devoured tomato after tomato. He soon converted most onlookers, but not until the entire basket was empty did the band strike up a victory march and the crowd begin to chant a cheer. The Colonel's personal physician, Dr. James Van Meeter, had taken a dim view of the proposed tomato-eating and had been quoted as saying, "The foolish colonel will foam and froth at the mouth and double over with appendicitis. All that oxalic acid! One dose and you're dead." Barring immediate effects, it was feared that the tomato skins would stick to the lining of the stomach and eventually cause cancer (tomatoes were generally held to induce cancer until nearly the end of the nineteenth century). Dr. Van Meeter stayed, black bag in hand, until the whole basketful of tomatoes had been devoured, and then quietly slunk away. The Colonel, undaunted, continued to live in undisputed health to the ripe old age of seventy-nine.

—— *from* ——

The Bread Builders

Hearth Loaves and Masonry Ovens

Daniel Wing and Alan Scott

1999

The late Alan Scott was an influential baker in Australia and California—influential because of his design for a practical wood-fired masonry bread oven, which is the subject of The Bread Builders. *Vermont baker and masonry oven expert Dan Wing collaborated on this book with Alan, and years later it is still in print and still regarded as one of the classic works on the subject. The explosion of interest in both good bread and outdoor masonry ovens has fueled sales over the years, and the fact that the book hasn't needed a substantial revision in fifteen years speaks to the careful craftsmanship of the authors as well as the timelessness of this oven-building method.*

THE BEST CURRENT GUESS IS THAT GRAINS were first domesticated ten to twelve thousand years ago in the northern part of the Fertile Crescent, along what is now the border between Syria and southwestern Turkey. Fields of wild einkorn wheat grow there still, probably much like those that drew hunter-gatherers thousands of years ago at harvest time. There are wild wheat stands dense enough to be harvested by hand, and experiments have shown that a few weeks of work could have supplied a family with enough grain for a year. In that bounty of wheat there are a few strains or types that are genetically and physically similar to strains of einkorn still cultivated today in some remote areas. Relatively few differences exist between some of the wild and cultivated stocks.

Archaeologists and agricultural researchers are now exploring how harvesting wild grain may have led to the evolution of the cultivated varieties. Characteristics such as sturdier stems to hold the kernel on the plant longer and thicker kernels with fragile spikes and loose husks may have been selected—inadvertently at first—that permitted the rapid (for so it seems to have been) development of agriculture. The cultivation of grain was soon followed by the domestication of animals and the development of early civilizations. Whether the first grain cultivated was einkorn wheat, emmer wheat, or barley isn't known—these were all domesticated over a fairly short span, and in the Fertile Crescent. What is clear is that the attainment of such a reliable source of food was the major technological breakthrough in human history. Rye was first cultivated later than wheat, and probably in a more northern area with cooler, wetter weather. Rye grass, the precursor and relative of cultivated rye, is widely distributed.

Eating raw grain would have been a real chore, though: people don't have the teeth, the belly, or the gustatory appreciation for it. Plain cooked grains are better but they won't keep long without refrigeration, and the taste is bland. Sprouting the grain first is a good way to make nutrients more available, but the sprouted grain must be eaten when it is ready, or drunk when the beer is sound. Baking fermented grain, though, making bread: this is the way to make grain palatable and nutritionally available. We have been doing it for thousands of years with a variety of grains, ferments, and baking techniques across cultures, continents, and centuries.

Throughout this history, almost everyone was involved with, or at least aware of, the process of making some kind of bread. Baking day has always been a bit of a holiday in rural settings, with most of the village involved. In the cities, citizens visited the baker every day of the week. The Vermont baker/ writer Jules Rabin tells a wonderful story about meeting an elderly baker in New York's Little Italy. He had been visiting with the old man, asking about the big coal-fired oven in the tenement basement where he worked, when the baker asked him to come upstairs to the sidewalk. The baker pointed down the street, indicating about every fourth six-story tenement. "There was a baker there, and there, and there, and there. They are all gone, now, but me." Each group of tenements had been a little village, each with a baker. Each group of tenements probably held five hundred people, and that is the size of the community that a family of bakers can supply. According to Christian Petersen, an English bakery of the middle of the last century used about two hundred and eighty pounds of flour a day to make three hundred and fifty pounds of bread. This served a community of four to six hundred people; village bakeries throughout Europe were the same size, and interestingly, that is the same amount of bread Jules and his wife Helen make today.

----- *from* -----

Wild Fermentation

The Flavor, Nutrition, and Craft of Live-Culture Foods

Sandor Ellix Katz

2003

We first met Sandor Katz when he stopped by our offices in the early 2000s bearing a little self-published pamphlet titled Wild Fermentation *and a canning jar full of homemade "krautchi," which we passed around and ate as we talked. Little did we know at the time that this colorful, passionate advocate of fermentation in all its glorious diversity would be such an incredible dynamo, traveling all over the world to spread the gospel of fermentation and collecting friends and devotees wherever he went. Today this first book of his is still a bestseller, aided by the burgeoning interest in fermented foods and the success of his second Chelsea Green book,* The Art of Fermentation.

PONDERING FERMENTING MEAT REMINDS ME that the distinction between a food that is fermented to perfection and one that is rotten is highly subjective. After a goat slaughter, I fermented some of the meat for a couple of weeks. I placed the meat in a gallon jar, then filled it with a mixture of all the other live ferments I had around: wine, vinegar, miso, yogurt, and sauerkraut juice. I covered the jar and left it in an unobtrusive corner of our basement. It bubbled and smelled good. After two weeks I poured the meat and its marinade into a covered pot and roasted it in the oven.

As it cooked, an overwhelming odor enveloped the kitchen. It smelled like a very strong cheese suited to only the bravest gastronome. There was some swooning and near fainting, and several folks were nauseated and had to leave the room. Lots of people complained about the smell. It was a notorious evening that immediately entered our homegrown folklore.

We had to open the windows, in spite of the December cold. Perhaps a half dozen of us tried the meat. It was quite tender for goat meat, and its taste was much milder than its smell. My fellow communard Mish absolutely loved it. He hovered over the pan for a long time picking at the meat, praising its strong cheesy aroma, and gloating over the rarefied "acquired taste" that only he and a few others could fully appreciate.

Many cultures have favorite fermented dishes with such strong flavors and aromas, or such unusual textures, that they become important symbols of distinctive cultural identity, all the more so because people outside the group generally find them repulsive. My father, an intrepid eater, once spent a Christmas visiting friends in Sweden. Forty years later he still winces when he describes tasting the traditional Swedish Christmas Eve feast of *lutfisk*, fish treated with lye and fermented for several weeks before cooking. Though many Asian soy ferments have gained widespread popularity in the West, slimy Japanese *natto* seems to have more limited appeal; and the Chinese treat known as "hundred-year eggs" actually only need to ferment in horse urine for a couple of months before the egg solidifies, the yolk turns green, and the white turns smoky black.

Food scientists use the word *organoleptic* to describe the qualities of how food feels in the mouth (as well as subjective feels of the other sensory organs). Fermentation often transforms the organoleptic qualities of foods, and sometimes it is an organoleptic quality more than flavor that influences what we like or dislike. One culture's greatest gastronomic pride is another's worst nightmare. "The concept of 'rottenness' therefore belongs to the cultural rather than the biological sphere," notes Annie Hubert, the director of France's National Scientific Research Center in an essay in *Slow*, the magazine of the international Slow Food movement. "The term defines a point where a food becomes unsuitable for consumption according to criteria associated with taste, presentation, and the concept of hygiene in different human societies."

This boundary is fluid, and fermented foods have a way of making boundaries in general somewhat fluid. Take the dualism of life and death. Fermentation is the action of life upon death. Living organisms consume dead food matter, transforming it and in the process freeing nutrients for the further sustenance of life. Many fermentation recipes mysteriously instruct you to ferment "until the flavor is ripe." You will have to be the judge of that. I advocate tasting your ferments at frequent intervals as the process progresses so you can learn about the spectrum of fermentation, discover what degree of ripeness you find most appealing, and experience the flavors of the other side of the elusive and slippery subjective boundary of rottenness.

Sometimes people ask me whether improperly fermented foods can cause food poisoning. I have never experienced this, nor heard any reports of it from other fermentation enthusiasts. In general, the acidic or alcoholic environments created by fermentation are inhospitable to bacteria associated with severe types of food poisoning such as salmonella. However, I cannot state in any absolute or authoritative way that food poisoning could not result from something going wrong in a fermentation process.

If it looks or smells disgusting, feed it to the compost. Usually I find that the funkiness is limited to the top layer, which is in contact with the microbe-rich air. Underneath that, the ferment is fine. If in doubt, trust your nose to be your guide. If you're still in doubt, taste just a little bit. Mix it with your saliva and swish it around your mouth like they do at wine tastings. Trust your taste buds. If it doesn't taste good, don't eat it.

—— *from* ——

Full Moon Feast

Food and the Hunger for Connection

Jessica Prentice

2006

Accomplished chef and passionate food activist Jessica Prentice follows the thirteen lunar cycles of an agrarian year. Each chapter of her book includes recipes that display the richly satisfying flavors of foods tied to the ancient rhythm of the seasons—locally grown, humanely raised, nutrient-rich, and traditionally prepared. Combining the radical nutrition of Sally Fallon's Nourishing Traditions, *keen agri-political acumen, and a spiritual sensibility that draws from indigenous as well as Western traditions,* Full Moon Feast *is a call to reconnect to our food, our land, and one another.*

THE CULINARY TRADITIONS SURROUNDING grain-based staple foods capture something quintessentially human. Though not timeless, they are certainly ancient—as ancient as sowing and reaping. One health-conscious writer warns against eating bread because "there are no bread trees" and bread does not occur in nature. But this argument does not move me.

I learned to bake bread from a French baker who used the large, wood-fired brick oven at the arts center where I was the chef for a number of years. He came twice a week bearing sacks of freshly ground, organic flour and a traditional sourdough starter that he had made a few years before. He built a fire in the oven from the wood stacked in a shed just outside the kitchen, and tended it while he fed his starter, measured out flour and water, minced rosemary, toasted sunflower seeds, and soaked polenta to be added to different loaves. Meanwhile I made dinner.

Sometimes I stayed overnight and met him back in the kitchen at three o'clock in the morning to learn how to mix the dough, knead it by hand, and use the natural leaven to make the loaves rise. He shaped each loaf by hand with a deftness and mastery that I could hardly imitate. He swept the ashes out of the oven and mopped its floor with a wet rag. Then he loaded his loaves into it with a long wooden peel and sprayed water into the oven to create the steam that would give the bread its desirable golden crust. He could fit forty loaves into the oven at a time, and it was a magical moment when we first opened the door and peered into the depths with a flashlight to see all those loaves risen and baking perfectly in the even heat held in the bricks. When it came out of the oven, I was so intoxicated by the smell that it was very hard not to cut into the bread while it was still burning hot. I had to learn to let it cool down and settle a while before having the first slice.

Eventually my friend moved back to France, but he left me some of his hearty starter, and I keep it alive to this day and use it for baking. While writing these words, I have been eating slices of toast from bread that I baked last night using wheat grown, harvested, and milled by one of my favorite local organic farms, and that precious starter I consider an heirloom. . . .

It is perhaps precisely because bread doesn't grow on trees that it carries with it an air of the sacred. Martin Prechtel teaches that among the Tzutujil

Maya, the gifts that people offer to the gods to feed them are precisely the things that only humans can make, using our human hands and our dexterous opposable thumbs. This is the gift the gods find irresistible—the particular beauty that only human hands create.

On the Corn Moon may we remember how to make handmade things too beautiful to be resisted, and offer them back to the divine source of life. May we do this even when we bake bread, or steam *idlis*, or fry *injera*, or roll *tamales*. May we begin to rebuild an agricultural system that respects, honors, and replenishes the Earth, even as we beg forgiveness for all the ways in which we act like we own the place. May we feel wonder for the gift of grain, which through dying is born again, or else gives its life to us.

—— *from* ——

Cheesemonger

A Life on the Wedge

Gordon Edgar

2010

Gordon Edgar (Gordon Zola to his many blog fans) is, to say the least, an unconventional and somewhat reluctant "foodie." As the cheesemonger at Rainbow Grocery Cooperative in San Francisco, he gets to interact with a wide range of people, and in this highly readable memoir Gordon tells many amusing and fascinating stories (exposing some of the embarrassing episodes and pretentious attitudes of the cheese world), while at the same time teaching people a lot about cheese in a down-to-earth way—just as he does at his job every day. His next book for Chelsea Green, on the history and culture of cheddar, is currently in the works.

ONE OF THE MAIN SELLING POINTS OF CHEESE is the popularly conceived notion of the dairy farmer as the salt of the earth. There's something both quaint and powerful about that stereotype. The idea of the dairy farmer conjures images of hard work, passed-down knowledge, no-nonsense work ethic, and skill. And yet, ironically, artisanal cheese typically evokes images of art openings and the parties of the rich.

How is it that knowledge of peasant food enables one to have entrée into the cocktail-party set? The ability to travel to foreign lands is certainly helpful. As I mentioned before, the I've-lived-in-France-ers are their own subset of cheese customers, but admitting a knowledge of cheese, and the desire to eat adventurous varieties, puts one on a particular side of the class war.

I grew up with more privilege than most of my coworkers and went to a fancy college. Maybe that's why I was well positioned to become a cheesemonger, even if I never saw any fancy cheese growing up. My parents had simple tastes, and a block of Cheddar that hadn't been transformed into processed cheese was kind of a special occasion for us. Still, as the buyer for a more yuppie-accessible section of our store, I felt the daily need to keep cheese accessible, both monetarily and through demystification. There is a lot of push—not only for cheesemakers but also for cheese sellers—to become as snooty as the wine industry.

Class positioning can work both ways. Familiarizing oneself with the nuances of cheese, like those of wine, can make one appear to be a member of a different class. Cheese knowledge is cocktail-party knowledge is upper-class knowledge. When I was in college, it seemed the real reason many people attended was so they could learn how to appear smart at business dinners and client parties. Learning to appear knowledgeable about elite foods is one alternative to taking out all those loans.

I once saw a small farmstead cheesemaker at the annual Fancy Food Show (officially called the National Association for the Specialty Food Trade Show) handing out chunks of his new washed-rind, soft-ripened, raw milk cheese. It was such small production that you had to be in the know to get a taste because he didn't have enough cheese to give to everyone. Among the suits, the pretension, and disposable displays, which cost thousands of dollars, he was standing in a T-shirt and dirty boots and offering cheese with a bleeding and bandaged hand, the result of a farm accident the previous day.

Now, we wouldn't let any of our coworkers handle food with a bloody hand, and he certainly wouldn't have worked in his own cheesemaking room like that, but I loved the dose of reality he was injecting into the feeding-frenzy bullshit fest that is the lingua franca of the show. Farmers are meant to be invoked but not seen.

Most of the folks at the show aren't rich. Most of us work for a living. Retailers are not only there to buy products, we are there to learn how to convey authentic, traditional, and sophisticated stories. Nobility, tradition, and suffering are talking-point concepts that evoke the idea to customers that they are purchasing a high-quality product. Tragedy (loss of land, deaths in family, intrafamily betrayal) moves units. Talk of whether a factory is unionized does not. The sales reps stay on message. The world is scoured for peasant food. Farmers are expected to be seen—on promotional materials—and not heard. It is undoubtedly comforting to some end-use consumers that there are still a few places where people know their place, even if it's only on packaging designed by a graphic artist. This kind of tourism-by-dinner offers a glimpse of the past and a nod to cultural roots, sometimes real, but often distorted by nostalgia.

—— *from* ——

Chanterelle Dreams, Amanita Nightmares
The Love, Lore, and Mystique of Mushrooms
Greg A. Marley

2010

Greg Marley has been obsessed with mushrooms, their natural history, and their folklore for more than forty years, ever since he left his native New Mexico and spent a summer in the verdant woods of central New York at the age of fifteen. Neither a field guide nor a cultivation manual, Chanterelle Dreams, Amanita Nightmares *is more like a love letter to the fungus kingdom—one that earned Marley a prestigious International Association of Culinary Professionals (IACP) Jane Grigson Award in 2011.*

THE WEB OF INTERCONNECTEDNESS BETWEEN MUSHROOMS and the rest of nature seems limitless. Consider, for example, an obscure dark gray finger of a mushroom known as the goldenthread cordyceps, *Cordyceps ophioglossoides*. It is a parasite with a yellowish stem and yellow root-like mycelia that connect it to its host, a type of false truffle called *Elaphomyces* that is buried in the soil. The false truffle lives in a complex symbiotic relationship with the roots of the hemlock tree, and those roots also may be connected symbiotically with several other species of fungi, which can include the porcini, *Boletus edulis*, and the destroying angel, *Amanita bisporigera*.

The interrelationships don't end there, however. The northern flying squirrel is a rarely seen nocturnal rodent prone to spending the day in tree cavity nests. It is attracted to the strong scent of the false truffle as the truffle begins to mature and digs up the nut-like fruit in the night. Along with other fungi, truffles make up a dominant part of the squirrel's diet for much of the year. The spores of the false truffle are unusually thick-walled, enabling them to pass unscathed through the digestive tract of the squirrels. The well-nourished rodent then deposits the spores in its feces, where the spores are more likely to find a new host tree than if they were dependent on the truffle alone for dispersal. In short, a common squirrel that we rarely see due to its nocturnal lifestyle feeds primarily on truffles and other underground fungi that we also almost never see unless we spot the elusive parasitic cordyceps easing its obscure head above the forest floor. The truffles rely on animals to unearth and consume their fruit as the only way to distribute their spores, and the forest trees require root associations with fungi like the truffles in order to obtain vital nutrients for growth.

The interrelationships don't end there, either. As the hemlock declines, it becomes prey to fungi that attack and decay the heartwood of the trunk. The rot-softened wood provides an opening to woodpeckers for feeding and nest cavity excavation. Who else, beside the woodpeckers, do you suppose uses these cavities as homes? The shy nocturnal flying squirrel.

This kind of story—and the natural connections it illustrates—brings mushrooms to life for me. Stories make the abstract real, build familiarity, and transform understanding from a vague recognition of separate elements seen on the forest floor to an inkling of the dynamic and intricate web of relationships that move in choreographed dance steps in a natural world we rarely glimpse. These are the kinds of mushroom stories you will find on the pages ahead.

As America travels the path toward embracing mushrooms, toward mycophilia, we will need to develop (or recall) a language and stories about mushrooms as we invite them more deeply into our lives. There are signs that this is already underway.

―――― *from* ――――

Cheese and Culture
A History of Cheese and Its Place in Western Civilization
Paul S. Kindstedt

2012

Paul Kindstedt is a professor at the University of Vermont's Department of Food Science and a widely published authority on cheese. His UVM course "Cheese and Culture" prompted him to spend a sabbatical year finishing his research and writing a remarkably thorough work on how cheese has

shaped Western civilization, and vice versa. In this passage, he highlights
the little-known and even less spoken-of connection between New England
cheesemakers and the Afro-Caribbean slave trade.

NARRAGANSETT OR RHODE ISLAND CHEESE SEEMS to be one of the few examples of a colonial New England cheese identified by its place of origin, no doubt because of its exceptional quality and extensive export to major cities such as Boston and Philadelphia. Other New England cheeses seemed to have been hardly noticed by contemporary writers. What has not been appreciated in the past is that much, if not most, of the famous Rhode Island cheese during the eighteenth century was made by black slave women who served as the dairymaids on the plantations. One of the largest of the plantation dairies reportedly was staffed by twenty-four black dairymaid slaves who produced twelve to twenty-four cheeses a day, each cheese the size of a bushel, probably around 20 to 30 pounds (9 to 14 kg) in weight.

All of the New England colonies except Rhode Island had much higher populations of male slaves than female slaves, the males being generally preferred. Rhode Island, however, with its strong emphasis on the use of female dairymaid slaves, had a singularly high ratio of female to male slaves. Slaves also were used widely on Connecticut farms, though mostly in small numbers (one or two per farm). Interestingly, the gender distribution of slaves varied greatly among counties within Connecticut, with much higher proportions of female slaves occurring in the highly specialized dairying and cheese-making regions of Litchfield, Fairfield, and Windham Counties than elsewhere. This strongly suggests that slave women may have been used widely as dairymaids in those particular counties, though this has yet to be confirmed through archival evidence. If so, slave women must have played an important role in Connecticut cheese making during the eighteenth century, which included considerable exports to the West Indies; some 150,000 pounds (68,000 kg) of cheese were exported annually from Connecticut to the West Indies during the mid-eighteenth century.

In summary, African slaves produced large amounts of cheese in Rhode Island, and probably in Connecticut as well, during the eighteenth century. Much of that cheese was then shipped to the West Indies to feed the slave population there and exchanged for molasses, which was then used to produce rum back in New England. The rum, in turn, was used to purchase slaves in Africa for transport to the West Indies, where they were traded for more molasses . . . and so the cycle continued. Rhode Island became the leader of this so-called triangular trade in the American colonies, but Massachusetts and Connecticut also participated to one extent or another. Indeed, most of the cheese produced in New England for export, whether made by black slave women or white free women, fed into this system from the mid-seventeenth century onward. The great stability and profitably of the Atlantic system encouraged many farmers in Massachusetts, Connecticut, and Rhode Island to specialize in dairy farming. Such was the attraction of the West Indies.

———— *from* ————

The Art of Fermentation

An In-Depth Exploration of Essential Concepts and Processes from Around the World

Sandor Ellix Katz

2012

Sandor Ellix Katz is a self-taught fermentation experimentalist. His first book with Chelsea Green, Wild Fermentation—*which* Newsweek *called "the fermenting bible"—demystified home fermentation and reintroduced an age-old concept to modern food lovers. Over the years Katz has become a globally recognized fermentation expert, and* The Art of Fermentation *is his grand masterpiece, the most comprehensive guide to do-it-yourself home fermentation ever published. A* New York Times *bestseller and winner of the James Beard Award, this book became an instant culinary classic.*

WHAT IS FASCINATING ABOUT THE CONCEPT of coevolution is the recognition that the processes of becoming are infinitely interconnected. As a dynamic between two species, coevolution has been described as "an evolutionary change in a trait in the individuals of one population in response to a trait of the individuals of a second population, followed by an evolutionary response by the second population to the change in the first." Life, however, is never so simple as to be limited to just two interrelated species; coevolution is a complex and multivariable process through which all life is linked.

All the plants our hunter-gatherer ancestors ate, like those our primate ancestors ate, consisted of unique chemical compounds, along with enzymes, bacteria, and other associated microbial forms, to which our ancestors and their microbiota adapted (or not, but they are not here to tell the tale).

The plants' coevolutionary histories do not revolve exclusively around us. For instance, could certain large fruits have evolved to attract the attention and seed-spreading potential of extinct megafauna, to our enduring benefit? Some plants we eventually coevolved with in ways we came to describe as domesticated. "We automatically think of domestication as something we do to other species," writes Michael Pollan in *The Botany of Desire*. "But it makes just as much sense to think of it as something certain plants and animals have done to us, a clever evolutionary strategy for advancing their own interests. The species that have spent the last ten thousand or so years figuring out how best to feed, heal, clothe, intoxicate, and otherwise delight us have made themselves some of nature's greatest success stories."

The influence of coevolution changes all involved. To say that one species is the creation or the master of another is a self-serving oversimplification. What we call "domestication" is a process that exists along a continuum, which ethnobotanist Charles R. Clement describes as running from wild, to "incidentally coevolved," to "incipiently domesticated," to "semi-domesti-cated," to "landraces" and "modern cultivars," representing "a continuum of human investment in selection and environmental manipulation." Like any coevolutionary process, domestication has repercussions for all parties. Coevolutionary success can lead to very specialized relationships. Treeshrews eating the fermenting nectar while pollinating the bertram palms, discussed already, is one vivid example. With the major human food crops, our great investment in selection and environmental manipulation makes us "obligate agents," meaning "sufficiently dependent upon certain plants so that [our] survival, at new densities, is dependent on the survival of the plants."

In that dependence, in all our cultural particulars, we are manifestations of coevolutionary processes with the plants as much as they are manifestations of coevolutionary processes with us. Humans are not the only actors in these relationships. Nor are plants the only other life-forms to benefit from their close association with us. How about *Saccharomyces cerevisiae*, the primary yeast used to produce alcoholic beverages and bread? Yeasts are widespread in nature, but this particular one developed—through its long association with humans and our willingness to grow and process plants, in huge quantities, to its preferred specifications, to feed it generously and cultivate it continuously over the course of the millennia—into the coevo-lutionary partner we now know as *S. cerevisiae*. "Microorganisms are [our] most numerous servants," wrote Carl S. Pederson in a 1979 microbiology textbook, epitomizing a worldview of humans as the supreme creation of evolution, with all other life-forms ours to freely exploit. To view ourselves as masters and microorganisms as our servants denies our mutual inter-dependence. Rather than *Saccharomyces cerevisiae* being the servant of humanity, it could be said that we are its doting fan and servant, much as we are to *Vitis vinifera* (grapes) or *Hordeum vulgare* (barley).

Although we rarely pay much attention to them, we have also consorted with many varied lactic acid bacteria (LAB). By 2007, geneticists could state emphatically: "Every person in the world has contact with lactic acid bacteria. From birth, we are exposed to these species through our food and environment." The LAB's genetic diversity "allows them to inhabit a variety of ecological niches ranging from food matrices such as dairy products, meats, vegetables, sourdough bread, and wine to human mucosal surfaces such as the oral cavity, vagina, and gastrointestinal tract." Comparative genome analysis suggests that in nutrient-rich niches, the LAB specialize efficiency by shedding genes for metabolic pathways they are not using. "The specialized adaptation to milk is particularly interesting," notes the analysis, "because this fermentation environment would not exist without human intervention. The selective pressure came not only from the natural environment, but also from anthropogenic environments created by humans."

Who exactly is the servant of whom? Are the acidifying bacteria in milk or the yeasts in grape juice our servants, or are we doing their bidding by creating the specialized environments in which they can proliferate so wildly? We must stop thinking in such hierarchical terms and recognize that we, like all creation, are participants in infinite interrelated biological feedback loops, simultane-ously unfolding a vast multiplicity of interdependent evolutionary narratives.

—— *from* ——

Taste, Memory

Forgotten Foods, Lost Flavors, and Why They Matter

David Buchanan

2012

Maine farmer David Buchanan is one of a small but closely knit group of people across the United States (and around the world) who are working to promote and preserve our common culinary traditions and the incredible diversity of regional and place-based foods, including heritage fruits, vege-tables, and livestock breeds. He himself has championed varieties like the

Marshall strawberry, once lauded for its phenomenal flavor but ill suited to today's industrial, one-size-fits-all model of agriculture. This fascinating book shows us why we should all care about keeping our foods, and our farms and gardens, as diverse, as tasty, and as interesting as possible.

THE TREND TOWARD UNIFORMITY HAS BEEN a long time in the making, concentrating innovation into ever fewer and more specialized hands. As John Bunker noted in his book *Not Far from the Tree*, for example, back in the 1920s extension agents in the Northeast discouraged planting of all but seven of the most commercially acceptable apples. Their goal was to reduce orchard diversity and standardize fruit quality, production, and marketing. For this they chose a few very old apples like Rhode Island Greening and Gravenstein, plus newer discoveries like Wealthy and Golden Delicious. Some were selected for production potential, others for eating quality, but each offered yield and market appeal designed to guarantee consistent profits. A handful of winners would replace the hundreds of varieties then in common use.

What's wrong with this approach? Within a few years the first signs of trouble appeared. One of their selections, Baldwin, would prove disastrous for growers. Baldwin is good for fresh eating, stores well, cooks into excellent sauce, and makes a fine single-variety hard cider. It was a favorite dating back to 1740 in Massachusetts. Despite many good attributes, however, it has a crippling weakness. It isn't particularly cold-hardy, especially when the trees are stressed by pushing them to produce heavy yields. Several years after farmers began turning land over to the "New England Seven," one of the hardest winters on record struck. The deep freeze that settled over orchards in 1934 killed roughly two-thirds of all apple trees in Maine, and destroyed most of the Baldwins in New England. This marked the end of regional commercial production for the variety, and dealt a substantial blow to the northern apple industry right in the middle of the Great Depression.

You could argue that Baldwin was simply the wrong selection. That's true, but part of the beauty of old plantings was the recognition that no single fruit can meet every need, and that every fruit has its strengths and weaknesses. Cold-hardy apples like Duchess of Oldenburg thrive in northern Maine, in places where most varieties can't survive or produce. Astringent (bittersweet or bittersharp) apples that blend into the best hard ciders aren't good for fresh eating. Sweet summer apples without acidity taste strange to modern palates, but make excellent sauce and pies. Apples serve many purposes beyond fresh eating. They can be boiled to make sauce, fruit butter, and a molasses-like sweetener; pressed for juice, hard cider, and vinegar;

distilled into brandy; dried for long-term storage; baked into pies. Relying on a handful of standardized varieties to deal with every culinary purpose, and to meet endless subtle variations in climate and growing conditions, is a diminished and precarious way to raise food.

———— *from* ————

Rebuilding the Foodshed
How to Create Local, Sustainable, and Secure Food Systems
Philip Ackerman-Leist

2013

In this groundbreaking book, farmer, author, and scholar Philip Acker-man-Leist challenges local food advocates across the nation to take their work to the next level. Forcing us to "to examine assumptions we might not even realize we held," as Deborah Madison writes in the foreword, Ackerman-Leist asks: How far away is local? How do you decide the size and geography of a regional foodshed? How do you tackle tough issues that plague food systems large and small—issues like inefficient transportation, high energy demands, and rampant food waste? How do you grow what you need with minimum environmental impact? And how do you create a foodshed that's resilient enough if fuel grows scarce, weather gets more severe, and traditional supply chains are hampered? Showcasing some of the most promising, replicable models for growing, processing, and distributing sustainably grown food, this book points the reader toward the next stages of the food revolution. This book is the third in the Community Resilience Series, a collaboration between Chelsea Green Publishing and Post Carbon Institute.

Sense of Family
Philosophers, geographers, and psychologists have all pursued the haunting but somewhat ethereal "sense of place" that we humans seem to share in the deeper reaches of our minds. The culmination of sensory experience, memory, and terrain, a sense of place is perhaps most easily conveyed through and contained in the combination of taste and smell, our broadest avenue to a storehouse of memories. Local food marketers and advocates constantly

appeal to our sense of place in order to generate both buying and buy-in. They work hard to convince us that the place in which we live is special and meaningful, and therefore worth investing in. They tantalize and taunt us with the possibility that we can never truly experience a place until we taste a particular fruit, a time-honored dish, a unique spirit, any of which may be replicated elsewhere but diminishes in authenticity with every mile it travels beyond a given boundary. These local specialties convince us that local foods are therapy for our culture's chronic transience.

When we become disillusioned with that transience and try to assess its negative impacts on our psyches, our local communities, and our cherished landscapes, we start to gather around the power of place. It appeals to those of us with long-term associations with a particular place, as well as those of us longing for belonging. Rootedness again takes hold—and supporting our local agricultural economy and caring for the well-being of our community seem to be the perfect manifestation of anchoring ourselves and building a home around the table.

Not only does a sense of place give us a certain comfort in the past and a confidence in the future, it can also serve as a foil against the economic and cultural homogenization so many of us feel in an increasingly globalized world—a world in which our most common links to food simply strengthen highly homogenized chain stores and food-chain clusters. Philosopher E. S. Casey calls the erosion of our sense of place the "thinning of the life world," meaning that our connections and commitment to our immediate surroundings are diminished due to our transience and geographical oblivi-ousness. Geographer Robert Feagan goes so far as to call it the "annihilation of place." Despite the difficulty in fully assessing or definitively naming this modern-day malady, one self-prescribed response seems to be a healthy dose of local foods, an antidote to the anonymity of mass consumerism. Some empiricists undoubtedly shudder at the thought of basing any actions on a concept so amorphous as "sense of place," but there is clearly a cultural malady in need of a prescription here, and local foods might be just what any good doctor would order.

This indulgence can be taken a step further, from a bioregional, eco-logical, or even hedonistic perspective. The oldest new kid on the block in promoting local foods and their link to our sense of place is terroir, a concept most articulately espoused—albeit with an epicurean accent—by the French foodophile. He raises his wine glass to the air, swirls with cen-trifugal confidence, watches the legs of the wine meander down the sweep of glass, sniffs not once but twice, utters an exclamation, sniffs again, sips, swishes, sips more confidently with an erudite grunt, and smiles slightly before twisting off a morsel of rustic bread and casually beginning to chew it with a small cube of artisan cheese that cuts the palate like the peasant's scythe—"Aahhh . . . ça, ça c'est la Provence." Not only does he make it clear that the three merged tastes of wine, cheese, and bread are born of his region's sun, soil, and sweat, but he goes on to name the qualities of the hillside on which the grapes were grown, the molds inherent in the cheese, and the qualities of the local airborne yeasts that invaded the simple mixture of flour, water, sugar, and local sea salt. Then, naturellement, he tells a quick story about the artisans who crafted the foods. That's terroir—the linking of taste, terra, and tradition. It is, as Amy Trubek calls it in the title of her seminal book on the subject, "the taste of place."

Just as a chef can transform a peasant's plate into a signature dish, France has upped the ante with terroir and even taken it up to the next level: patrimonialization, a concept that merges regional authenticity and heritage with the food products themselves, thereby creating a culinary result that cannot be replicated in its truest form elsewhere. It's a strategy of the underdogs in a globalized world. Simply put, patrimonialization creates certain boundaries of authenticity for specific foods and beverages that would otherwise be lost in the bigger mix. A wine, therefore, is not just the product of a specific variety of grape; it is also the melding of tradition, craft, and location. The local food niche just got a little tighter through the precision linking of people and place.

Relationships

Place is first and foremost the intersection between latitude and longitude, but place as it relates to local foods is also the intersection of people and their environs. And it is not just about existing relationships. In fact, one of the most compelling arguments for rebuilding community-based food systems is that it requires us to broker new relationships—relationships that help build local economies, conserve local landscapes, create entrepreneurial collaborations, enhance food security, enlighten and educate, and generate new friendships. The terms and concepts associated with the relational nature of local food systems are as prolific as summer zucchini: shortened food chains, Know Your Farmer (from the USDA, no less!), civic agriculture, community food security, community-supported agriculture, conviviality, and the list goes on.

In some ways, the emphasis on relationships inherent in the local food push is the most exciting aspect of it all: we are consciously making the choice to build new economic relationships, rekindle traditional ways of doing business, support those in need, and even invent new technology-based social networks that can, rather ironically, link neighbors. The narratives of this good work start to drive the numbers. As author and ethnobotanist Gary Paul Nabhan so eloquently puts it, we are "restorying the landscape." It is through these stories that we move the local food agenda forward . . .

—— *from* ——

Life, Liberty, and the Pursuit of Food Rights
The Escalating Battle Over Who Decides What We Eat
David E. Gumpert

2013

Food doesn't come to most people's minds when they think of the fundamental rights granted to American citizens. And yet it has become a battleground on which the tension between personal freedom and the state's so-called obligation to keep people safe is playing out. In a book described by Joel Salatin as having "the storytelling genius of a spy novel," veteran journalist David Gumpert delves into this brave new world of government aggression, citizen resistance, and the larger implications of what this means for our personal freedoms.

To Americans determined to choose what foods to put into their bodies without the government getting in the way, the regulators and agents who are interfering with those choices have taken on the role of the Wild West's outlaws and renegades. Yet to the regulators and agents, these farmers and consumers are the outlaws and renegades.

The struggle has been cast by regulators as one in which food safety must take precedence over "food rights." For those targeted by the authorities, the struggle is more fundamental; it's about expanding government control into ever more areas of our lives versus individual freedoms promised by the American Revolution and the U.S. Constitution that grew out of it.

This struggle over private food rights appears to be unique to America (and its cousin to the north, Canada, on a smaller scale). In no other countries that I am aware of is such a struggle—pitting government authorities against groups of ordinary citizens trying to access farm-fresh food—presently going on, aside from countries like North Korea and Cuba where control of the food supply is part of the totalitarian effort to control the population.

All of which raises some fundamental questions: When did we lose our right to buy whatever food we want directly from farmers and assorted food producers, outside of the regulatory system of permits and inspections? Or stated more fundamentally, when did the custom of people exchanging food—a natural and essential part of community-based life and commerce since nearly the beginning of humankind—become transformed into such an intense source of conflict that it now is being cast as a "right"?

Was it in 1788 when the U.S. Constitution was ratified without making a single mention of the word "food"?

Was it in 1906 when Congress enacted the Pure Food and Drug Act, and the first regulators were hired to watch over our food system?

Was it immediately after World War II, when the memories of the Great Depression and rationing caused by wartime shortages were still fresh in people's minds, and we committed to modernizing and improving our agriculture sector's productivity?

Was it in the 1950s and 1960s, when many states outlawed unpasteurized milk, and in the process outlawed the sale of raw dairy products or confined such sales to farms that obtained special permits?

Was it in the 1970s, when Secretary of Agriculture Earl Butz repeatedly urged farmers to "get big or get out"?

Was it in 1987, when the FDA, in response to a federal court order, enacted a regulation outlawing the interstate shipment of unpasteurized dairy products?

Was it in 1995, when a Seattle product liability lawyer earned $15.6 million in a settlement of a food-borne illness case caused by a fast-food chain's tainted hamburgers, the largest settlement at that time for damages associated with such illness?

Was it in the aftermath of the 9/11 terrorist attacks on the United States, when food security and bioterrorism became big concerns?

Was it in spring 2011, when public health inspectors issued cease-and-desist orders to shut down ForageSF, an underground food market in San Francisco that gathered monthly for producers of everything from kimchi to chocolate cupcakes, selling to members who paid $5 to join each event? A few months later when San Francisco public health officials shut down a nursery school bake sale? Or the Friday night a couple months after that when a Nevada public health inspector tried to halt a farm's private fork-to-plate event just as dozens of guests were preparing to sit down to an elegant dinner of lamb meatballs and fresh vegetables?

Or was it in September 2011, when a judge in Wisconsin, the nation's "Dairy State," in ruling on a case involving the distribution of raw milk by two farmers there, declared that they "do not have a fundamental right to own and use a dairy cow" and "do not have a fundamental right to consume the milk from their own cow"?

Surely it wasn't any single event, but by the end of the first decade of the twenty-first century, the quickening pace of legal and enforcement challenges demonstrated that the once universally accepted custom of farmers, friends, and neighbors exchanging food without regulatory oversight had been so reduced in consciousness that it was actually under official attack—and that the right to privately obtain the foods of one's choice was in jeopardy across the United States and Canada. In the process of simultaneously promoting cheap food and fomenting fear around the dangers of pathogens in food, something strange has occurred. Traditional avenues of private food acquisition have gradually disappeared.

I can remember seemingly endless farm stands as I traveled across the United States in the 1950s and 1960s. I can also recall various produce trucks with vegetables, meats, and eggs that traversed our neighborhood in Chicago during that time. Even after I became a homeowner in suburban Boston in the late 1970s, we had a milk man and a chicken-egg man who came around with farm-fresh food.

Over the last few years, with the growing interest in fresh locally grown food and fears about commercially available food and the presence of genetically modified organisms (GMOs) and processed ingredients, more people have begun trying to re-create these traditional sources of privately obtained food via members-only food clubs and communal ownership of cows and goats. Many of these efforts were originally begun to secure sources of the increasingly popular unpasteurized milk and then expanded to include beef, chicken, eggs, honey, fermented vegetables, and other so-called nutrient-dense foods.

Unfortunately, when groups of ordinary people began organizing themselves to obtain food directly from farms on a private basis, they ran into trouble. Such foods weren't properly labeled, they were told. Such foods weren't safe. The producers required retail licenses. Such foods needed to be inspected by public health and agriculture regulators. The stories of the farmers and organizers entangled in the enforcement crackdown are the basis of this book.

In the big picture of history, the conflict is sadly ironic, since these battles aren't happening in a time of food scarcity or widespread outbreaks of animal or human illness, but rather during a period of seeming abundance and plenty.

ENERGY & SHELTER

DEANNE BEDNAR

—— *from* ——

Wind Power

Renewable Energy for Home, Farm, and Business

Paul Gipe

Originally published as *Wind Power for
Home and Business* in 1993; second edition, 2004

*For decades Paul Gipe has been a leading voice in what is today a boom-
ing worldwide wind energy industry. His books for Chelsea Green, which
include editions of both* Wind Power *and* Wind Energy Basics, *have given
both professional and DIY readers a greater understanding of how and
where wind power makes sense—from the independent homestead to farms
and businesses to a grid-connected utility-wide perspective. Gipe, who writes
and lectures extensively about renewable energy, has received numerous
honors, including the World Wind Energy Award and the American Wind
Energy Association's Person of the Year award—and he has been honored as
a pioneer by the World Renewable Energy Congress.*

WIND WORKS. IT'S RELIABLE. IT'S ECONOMICAL. It makes environmental
sense. And it's here now. Wind machines are not tomorrow's technology.
Whether it's on a giant wind farm in Minnesota, in a small village in
Morocco, or in the backyard of a German farmer, wind energy works today
in a variety of applications around the world. You, too, can put this renewable resource to work. . . .

To use the wind successfully, you must have a good site and select the
right machine. You also need something else—courage. A wind turbine is
not cheap. It represents an investment in the future. And whether you install
it yourself or contract a dealer to do it, the installation of a wind machine—
small or large—is an undertaking fraught with risk and uncertainty. At
some point, after considering all the pros and cons, only you can make the
decision to proceed. You must weigh your choices, then act. The people who
use wind energy are prudent, but they're doers.

People use wind machines for many reasons: economic, environmental,
and philosophical. The knowledge that you're saving money—or earning
it—is often sufficient reward for plunging into wind energy. Yet for many
people there's more to it than that. Windmills have fascinated us for centuries and will continue to do so. Like campfires or falling water, they're

mesmerizing; indeed, entrancing. People respond almost instinctively. Few escape feeling excitement at seeing a sleek turbine whirring in the wind.

Working with the wind is more than just a means to cheap electricity. It becomes a way of life, a way of living in closer harmony with the world around us. Harnessing the wind enables us to regain some sense of responsibility for meeting our own needs and for reducing our impact on the environment. By generating our own electricity cleanly and with a renewable resource, we can reduce the need for distant power plants and their attendant ills. Wind energy can and does make a difference.

If you're fortunate enough to install a wind machine with your own hands, you'll experience sensations few others can share. You'll know what it's like to gaze from the top of your tower at the countryside spread out before you. You'll know the feeling of seeing your wind machine spinning overhead for the first time. You'll rediscover the sense of accomplishment received from a job well done. You and your friends will discover the hearty, backslapping camaraderie that grows among people after several arduous days of working together. There's nothing quite like it.

—— *from* ——

The Straw Bale House

Athena Swentzell Steen, Bill Steen, and David Bainbridge, with David Eisenberg

1994

This book was one of the signal bestsellers for Chelsea Green in the 1990s, partly because it appeared at an opportune time, while interest in sustainable building methods was running very high, and partly because the houses photographed in The Straw Bale House *were just so, well, damn beautiful. Couple that with fire-resistant, super-insulated walls, easy construction, and the appropriate use of a renewable resource (straw, especially rice straw, which used to be burned in the field but has now become a valuable building material), and it's easy to see why this title became such a classic.*

THE THICKNESS AND SUBTLE CURVES of straw bale walls have a special character and beauty. Combined with their high insulation value and breathability, these walls create an overall feeling of comfort not found in the thin flat walls often produced from modern materials. Straw bale walls are similar in appearance to old thick stone and adobe walls, reminiscent of European country cottages, Mediterranean villas, and southwestern adobes. Yet, at the same time, they have an intangible quality all their own.

Sometimes people's personal lives can most easily be read in the walls of their buildings, such as where a deep and softened entryway graciously welcomes one in, where a detailed niche displays precious belongings, where intimate nooks with built-in seats invite quiet repose, or where beautifully beveled window edges frame a treasured view. The thickness of straw bale walls and their ability to be easily modified make it easy to change bale walls according to the needs and creativity of the inhabitants.

The mass and dimensions of straw bale walls can induce physical and psychological feelings of well-being. When combined with a soft adobe or gypsum plaster, the flowing surfaces are not only a pleasure to look at and to touch, but instill a soft sound quality to each room.

When finished with natural plasters and paints, straw bale walls can breathe, resulting in indoor air that feels fresh, invigorating, and clean compared to the low-oxygen, stale, toxic air common to most homes. The high insulation value of bales also helps create a very stable environment that is easy to cool and heat and provides far superior living conditions to that of modern housing.

In the Great Plains, baled homes were preferred because they were extremely quiet and could seal out the howling of the Northers, winds that could torment a person's mind on the open plains. In the city, bale houses could provide a much needed haven in a noisy and chaotic world. Perhaps it is within these silent, sculpted walls, which impart a sense of timeless peace, that a new and better vision of shelter resides.

———— *from* ————

The Independent Builder

Designing and Building a House Your Own Way

Sam Clark

1996

Sam Clark is a designer and home builder based in Vermont, and his book is a comprehensive manual of best practices for owner-builders as well as professional builders and their clients. In addition to presenting specific

building techniques, Clark explains the design principles and planning pro-
cesses that underlie all good building, so that readers can develop their own
exceptional designs.

WHEN I STARTED BUILDING, I HAD a real faith in innovative methods. Like
many owner-builders and self-taught builders who didn't come up through
the trades, I didn't think much of the regular, suburban-looking houses I saw
around me. Illogically, I made the jump to the idea that I could come up with
something better. I looked to architecture for inspiration, and to the stream
of building books put out by professionals, and by other self-taught builders
and owner-builders. Two books were particularly popular, *Your Enlightened
House*, and *The Owner-Built Home*, both of which held standard construction in contempt and promoted completely non-standard building methods.
The Whole Earth Catalog also presented hundreds of alternatives.

Encouraged by such books, I and many other builders around me tried
new approaches and materials every time out. We built domes, A-frames of
recycled timbers, yurts, log houses, and stone houses like Helen and Scott
Nearing's. We roofed with tin, boards, shingles, and sod. We heated with all
sorts of solar systems, most of which we fabricated ourselves. We built with
native materials, particularly stone and locally produced lumber, and used
recycled windows and other materials. We tried everything. This was the
height of the owner-builder movement.

Starting perhaps in the late 1970s, reality—what works and what
doesn't—made some harsh judgments. The traditional approach to building
proved to be right more often than not.

Some clever building systems simply failed to work right. Geodesic domes
were hard to live in, more expensive to build than promised, and prone to
leaks. Other systems, like the Nearings' stone building system, worked, but
added months of extra labor to the process of building a home, and saved
only a little cash. When owner-builders turned professional, as many did,
some of these once-appealing systems were abandoned because they didn't
cost out for our customers and there were too many "callbacks."

Many seemingly clever and economical systems failed more slowly. Board
siding was drafty and subject to rot. Flat-pitched shed roofs were subject to
leaks and ice dams, at least in cold climates. Recycled windows rotted out,
and didn't keep out the wind.

Column foundations are a good example of a system that looks good, but
causes trouble later. Here in New England, the conventional wisdom held that
a full concrete foundation was essential. Rex Roberts and other writers argued

that the basement was expensive and superfluous. Like many people, I built numerous buildings on wood or concrete posts with insulated floors. This approach did save initial costs, and buildings went up fast. The foundation system was kind to the site. But over time it became clear that houses on posts had problems. The floors were cold. Pipes tended to freeze where they came into the house. Sometimes the posts themselves were subject to frost heaves or settling. Animals got under the house, pulled down the fiberglass insulation, and sometimes made nasty smells. These problems are expensive to fix.

Early solar systems were also disaster-prone. Most of these systems were homemade, and put relatively vulnerable materials like glass, plastic, and plumbing outside the protection of the house or roof overhangs. They were subject to direct assaults by sun, wind, water, and cold temperatures. In Vermont, I'd say very few of the earlier sunspaces, solar greenhouses, or active solar systems really worked well. Many were roofed over, insulated under, or "decommissioned."

What I learned from such experiences is that traditional approaches to building were often smarter than they appeared. What seems ordinary at first may prove elegant and wise after a few years. Innovation is important, but even new methods that seem well engineered and brilliant may have hidden costs, maintenance problems, or unintended consequences. I think many builders came to similar conclusions.

Today, traditional building methods, and the people who were practicing them all along, have much more respect. At the same time, standard building has been changed. We have a basic vocabulary of new, good ideas that has become accepted practice. We site houses toward the sun and insulate them better. Many new products and methods have been incorporated into routine practice.

—— *from* ——

Who Owns the Sun?

People, Politics, and the Struggle for a Solar Economy

Daniel M. Berman and John T. O'Connor

1996

Lead author Dan Berman is a passionate progressive who has worked for decades on issues of social justice, occupational health and safety, workers' rights, and renewable energy. He and his friend, the late environmental activist John O'Connor, wrote about the public power movement at a critical time in its history. It's a story that (like many Chelsea Green books) was far ahead of its time and one that is still being written. This thoughtful and detailed work received high praise from Ralph Nader and others, and it still provides an important history of our nation's energy development, as well as a clear plan for what we must do to democratize and decentralize our power grid as renewables gain an ever-greater share of the market.

ONE HUNDRED AND TEN YEARS AGO, when electricity was in its infancy, no one was certain how electric power would be sold and who would buy it. At first, the "dynamo" was thought of "as a kind of appliance, like a hot-water heater, to be installed at any gold mine or grand hotel that wanted to generate current for electric light. . . . No one . . . had thought of the [electric current] coming out of the dynamo as a commodity in its own right, a product that could be made in one central place and then sold to the general public—though gas for gas lamps had been made and piped and sold that way in San Francisco for a quarter of a century." The first large-scale use of electricity was for streetlighting. The new lights were demonstrated and sold at great public spectacles, much like today's manned rocket launches. Charles Brush, an inventor and entrepreneur, promised to make downtown Cleveland "as bright as day" on the evening of April 29, 1879, with twelve of his own electric arc lights powered by a dynamo of his own design. As a crowd of thousands gathered, Brush motioned for his assistant to throw the switch: "The first globe flickered with purplish light. Thundering cheers gave way to astonishment as the other lights came on. In the awed quiet the Cleveland Grays band struck up its brass, and artillery boomed along the shorefront. Cleveland became the first city to light its public square with electricity." A year later in Wabash, Indiana, Brush turned on four 3,000-candlepower lamps atop a 200-foot-high courthouse dome on a moonless night. According to an eyewitness, " 'the strange weird light, exceeded in power only by the sun, rendered the square as light as midday. Men fell on their knees, groans were uttered at the sight, and many were dumb with amazement.' " Despite the success of Brush's light show, Wabash city leaders, repelled by what they knew about the rate-gouging of private power companies, refused to issue a franchise for a privately owned concern controlled by Brush, and eventually established a city-owned system.

Many cities wanted electric streetlights, but it wasn't clear at first whether electricity could be generated and sold for a profit. Thomas Edison, financed at first by J.P. Morgan, the nation's top investment banker, built New York City's first generating plant in 1882, but Morgan was reluctant to rush ahead in building generating capacity. Competition from gaslights was still strong, and the cost of buying and maintaining electrical generating equipment and transmission wires—which remained idle during the day when the lights were turned off—was extraordinarily high. Another problem was that the direct current then in use could not easily be transmitted much farther than a mile. For the time being, Morgan thought, there was more money to be made in buying up electrical equipment patents and manufacturing the equipment.

What changed this picture was the introduction of alternating current (which could be transmitted dozens of miles) and the construction in 1887 of an electric streetcar in Richmond, Virginia, which created a demand for electric power during the day as well. This trolley car (which got its name because it "trolled" for power from an overhead line) proved an instant hit. By 1895, ten thousand miles of track had been laid in over eight hundred cities. Now financiers such as J.P. Morgan and Samuel Insull bought into the generation business in a big way, and Morgan founded General Electric to gobble up electrical equipment manufacturers. Giant financial combines led by Morgan and Insull also battled against municipal utilities over who was to collect the vast sums that industrialists and consumers would soon be spending on electrically powered transportation, lighting, motors, and appliances.

People who believed that electricity, like roads, should be a public responsibility fought bitterly against the power trusts, who sought to keep control of electricity production as a "dividend machine" for private monopolies. In most cases the private monopolies won, yet these private combines were later brought to a stalemate during the New Deal era, when the Tennessee Valley Authority and other federal hydroelectric complexes were built. Promoters fighting for the city streetcar and electrical franchises paid off mayors by the hundreds and aldermen by the thousands. In this welter of headlong expansion and corruption, the electric power business was born, and gigantic fortunes were made and lost.

In San Francisco, the financial battle between gas and electric interests lasted only a decade. Rather than slug it out over lucrative municipal lighting contracts coming up for renewal, the San Francisco Gas Light Company and the Edison Light and Power Company merged into the San Francisco Gas and Electric Company in 1896, capitalized at $20 million. In 1905 SFG&E spearheaded the creation of Pacific Gas & Electric from what were once over five hundred independent companies, and the question of gas versus electricity became a technical rather than a financial issue. Gas continued to be the system of choice for cooking and heating, though some gas streetlamps lingered on until 1930. Today, PG&E is the largest private utility in the United States.

——— *from* ———

The Natural House

A Complete Guide to Healthy, Energy-Efficient, Environmental Homes

Daniel D. Chiras

2000

Dan Chiras is a prolific building writer who was the perfect person to write this book, a sort of cook's tour of the construction, costs, and pros and cons of fourteen natural building methods. Straw bale, rammed earth, cob, cordwood, adobe, earthbags, papercrete, Earthships . . . whatever the method, the common goal is to create a house that is economical, energy-efficient, nontoxic, soothing to the soul, kind to the environment, and pleasing to behold. This sourcebook has proven valuable for many home builders, contractors, and architects.

OUR HOMES PROVIDE REFUGE, and by working carefully with natural materials and design we can make them comforting and nourishing. Many natural materials lend themselves to organic designs that replenish the human spirit. Design strategies that link the inner and outer space of a home create outside living spaces that flow gracefully into the interior of our homes, joining us more firmly with the basis of life, our environment. The pliability of natural materials also leads to greater artistic expression, allowing us to create a personal habitat that expresses our individuality while permitting us to break out of the oppressive influence of the rectilinear world we are imprisoned in. This organic design, often drawn from patterns of nature, permits us to create dramatic structures with curved walls that express our individuality and nourish our spirits. A home is also a defining statement. By turning to sustainable design and natural materials, we express our commitment to environmental stewardship and good health.

Creating a home that will soothe the soul is an extraordinarily complex task. In modern society, convenience tends to dictate unimaginative rectilinear structures. Even some natural homes leave much to be desired. In conventional or natural homes, homeowners who have not designed beauty and grace into their structures often end up spending a fortune trying to decorate a home to give it a soul, often to no avail.

The art of creating a home that feeds the human spirit is the art of creating a house that not only works for people at the most basic levels of convenience, but whose features "are in sync with the psychology and physiology of how people thrive, or don't thrive," according to Sam Clark. This task is not just about creating a visually appealing home. While vision is important, it is only one sense through which we experience a home. We must not forget warmth, comfort, textures, solidity, and the play of sunlight on the floors and walls. We are participants in a structure. When we move from one room to the next, our senses shift. The size and shape of a room, its color, warmth, and light give us a bigger sense of the whole. It is these subtleties and interactions that give a house a soul of its own.

—— *from* ——

The Hand-Sculpted House
A Philosophical and Practical Guide to Building a Cob Cottage

Ianto Evans, Michael G. Smith, and Linda Smiley
Illustrated by Deanne Bednar

2002

Cob has been a traditional building process for millennia in Europe, even in rainy and windy climates like the British Isles, where many cob buildings still serve as family homes after hundreds of years. The technique is relatively new to the Americas, however. As the authors point out, a cob cottage might be the ultimate expression of ecological design, a structure so attuned to its surroundings that its creators refer to it as "an ecstatic house."

BUILDING WITH NATURAL MATERIALS REDUCES the push for resource extraction and for industrial processing. It decreases pollution, deforestation, and energy use.

The construction industry is a major cause of mining and industrial processing, with all their attendant pollution, economical havoc, and social disruption. Modern building materials depend on mining: gypsum for drywall; iron for rebar, hardware, and roofing; lime for cement. And every material used in a typical modern building is the product of energy-intensive processing. The lumber mills, the steel foundries, the factories making plywood and chipboard, the industrial plants using tremendous heat to turn minerals into cement—all consume vast quantities of power, supplied by the combustion of coal and oil, the damming of rivers, or the splitting of atoms.

These manufacturing processes release toxic effluent into the water and hazardous chemicals into the air. The manufacture of Portland cement, for example, accounts for an estimated 4 to 8 percent of greenhouse gases. And even after our building materials are made, modern construction depends on a stream of polluting trucks to deliver them to us, usually from hundreds of miles away. It's no accident, either, that the dumpster is a prominent feature of most construction sites. A major by-product of industrial construction is landfill waste, which comprises up to 25 percent of landfill volume.

Seventy-five percent of all trees cut in North America are used in construction. Here in the Pacific Northwest, the trail from clear-cut to sawmill to building site is easy to follow. Loaded log trucks roar down every county road, and on almost any day Linda and I hear from our house the crashing of trees, the whine of chain saws. When we built our house here only seven years ago, primeval forest, miles of it, still stood within sight of our windows. Now a sorry few remnants remain, a long drive away.

The United States has lost 15/16ths of its original forest, and the lumber industry is trying hard to cut down the last sixteenth. Now Siberia is under attack, and the last great tropical forests, to make cheap plywood for million-dollar wooden houses that will be defunct in half a century.

By substituting earth for wood in the walls, floors, and finishes in a standard 2,000-square-foot house, we can save 60 to 80 percent of the lumber. If as a whole society we switched to earthen buildings, six hundred to eight hundred of every thousand trees currently marked for cutting would be spared. The United States could be completely self-sufficient in timber without ever making another clear-cut.

Earthen building also dramatically reduces the need for extraction and processing of other materials. In cob construction, earth for building is dug locally; generally surplus earth from the building's own footprint is used. Processing is minimal, involving no machinery or chemicals, and can be almost silent. No mile-deep open pit mines, no toxic tailings or effluent ponds, fewer trucks on the road, no company towns. Earthen construction generates no air or water pollution. Excess material goes right back into the ground, effectively unaltered. When an earthen building is no longer wanted, it returns to its original components and grows a garden again.

Of course, it's impossible to build a house with no environmental impact, but it's our responsibility to minimize and localize the damage. Digging a hole in your yard for clay to make a cob house may look ugly at first, but it's a lot less ugly than strip mines, giant factories, and superhighways, and you personally can take control of turning problems into assets. That hole in your yard would make an excellent frog pond.

———— *from* ————

Passive Solar Architecture
Heating, Cooling, Ventilation, Daylighting, and More Using Natural Flows
David A. Bainbridge and Ken Haggard

2011

In this comprehensive overview of passive solar design, David A. Bainbridge and Ken Haggard, two of America's leading solar design pioneers, give home-owners, architects, designers, and builders the keys to successfully harnessing the sun and maximizing climate resources for heating, cooling, ventilation, and daylighting. They draw upon more than three decades of experience to offer overarching principles as well as the details and formulas needed to successfully design a more comfortable, healthy, and secure place in which to live, laugh, dance, and be comfortable. Even if the power goes off.

OUR GOAL IN BUILDING SUSTAINABLE BUILDINGS must always be to improve the comfort, health, and security of people. To do this, we need to rethink our approach to design and operation of the built environment while maximizing use of renewable resources and minimizing life-cycle costs. Improving comfort and health yield the biggest dividends. Energy and water use, waste minimization and recycling, ecosystem protection, and first cost are also important. Integrating systems is critical to meet multiple needs and goals, maximize benefits, and minimize costs. Optimizing design at the earliest stages can often dramatically improve performance at little or no additional cost.

The first step is proper orientation for solar heating and natural cooling. If possible, insulation should be placed outside the thermal mass. The only exception is in hot, humid climates where light frame or open buildings with optimized ventilation are the key to human comfort. Traditional homes in hot, humid areas often were placed on stilts to get more wind for ventilation cooling, or they had very high ceilings and paddle fans to keep air moving and double roofs to keep solar heating to a minimum.

A review of passive buildings using performance simulations showed that annual energy use for heating and cooling dropped from 54,000 BTU to 900 BTU per square foot per year (98 percent) for a super-insulated roof pond in El Centro, California, and from 48,500 BTU to 4,800 BTU (90 percent) for a super-insulated solar building in Denver with appropriate thermal mass.

A building with just good insulation and sufficient thermal mass usually achieves a 50 to 70 percent energy savings, but with good orientation and window placement, it can reach 80 to 90 percent.

The choice of materials also matters. They should be, insofar as possible, local, natural, and renewable. As Arne Naess notes, "The degree of self-reliance for individuals and local communities diminishes in proportion to the extent a technique or technology transcends the abilities and resources of the particular individuals or local communities. Passivity, helplessness and dependence upon 'megasociety' and the world market increase." Self-reliance is critical, as the building challenge is not simply for the developed countries—although their use of resources is disproportionately large—but must also include the billions of people who remain in poverty.

Application of sustainable design principles can improve the lives of people in Geneva, London, Cape Town, Sydney, Los Angeles, and Lima, as well as the favelas and slums of the world's growing megacities. The oldest occupied communities in the United States, the pueblos of New Mexico, reflect the importance of local, sustainable, and understandable materials. Building systems that employ locally available, safe, and easy-to-use materials such as straw bales and earth deserve special recognition because everyone in the community, including kids, can participate in construction. Community building through straw bale building workshops has created added benefits for this very efficient, sustainable building material.

There are many benefits to changing our cultural attitudes to planning and building, but to start, we would emphasize three key concerns: health, security, and economy.

Sustainable buildings are healthier: Fewer sick days, reduced allergies and irritations, fewer doctor visits, reduced medical expenditures, and better sleep—all these add value. Comfort adds quality to life, and comfort and health add to productivity gains in the office or factory. As Ken found in surveys for a state office building design, people are aware of the problems and flaws in buildings. Many related how they hated their current space and were trying to transfer to different units where offices had more daylight and better ventilation.

More sustainable buildings also provide security and freedom from fear. Even if the power goes out in an ice storm, earthquake, hurricane, political dispute, or power-grid failure, homes will remain comfortable and livable. Commercial and industrial buildings remain inhabitable even when the power goes off, and workers can wrap up their work rather than groping their way through a dark and unpleasant building to get to safety outside.

The most important reason for change is for long-term prosperity. Better design can save money now and as long as the building is used. Money can be spent on more productive activities rather than simply going to the utility company. As the California blackouts of 2001 showed, we can't count on nonrenewable energy resources. They will be more expensive in the future— perhaps much more expensive.

Energy costs for operating a sustainable building are low, and will remain low. This can be critical for retired people and institutions and is important for families and most businesses. Heating and cooling costs can be kept below $50 per month, in contrast with the rapidly rising utility bills many people experience today.

Sustainable buildings increase the quality of life. They improve health, speed learning (schools), increase sales (retail), improve patient outcomes (hospitals), and improve productivity (manufacturing and services). In commercial buildings, the return on investment for improvements on air quality alone has been estimated to be 60:1. In central California, the revised design of a tract home led to reduced construction costs and a seasonal energy savings for heating and cooling of 70 percent. Rather than "freezing in the dark," as the fossil-fool-funded opponents of renewable energy have argued, occupants and workers in sustainable buildings will be dancing in the sunlight!

——— *from* ———

Reinventing Fire

Bold Business Solutions for the New Energy Era

Amory B. Lovins and Rocky Mountain Institute

2011

Drawing praise from former president Bill Clinton, former national security advisor Robert McFarlane, and a host of others, the award-winning Reinventing Fire *has piqued the interest of political, business, and world leaders alike. With clarity and mastery, Amory Lovins and Rocky Mountain Institute point out the opportunities for enterprise to create a new energy era and pave the way to more and better jobs, and greater national security, health, and environmental stewardship. This book demonstrates how market-based solutions across the nation's transportation, building, industry, and electricity sectors could get the United States off oil and coal by 2050.*

IMAGINE FUEL WITHOUT FEAR. No climate change. No oil spills, dead coal miners, dirty air, devastated lands, lost wildlife. No energy poverty. No oil-fed wars, tyrannies, or terrorists. Nothing to run out. Nothing to cut off. Nothing to worry about. Just energy abundance, benign and affordable, for all, for ever.

That richer, fairer, cooler, safer world is possible, practical, even profitable—because saving and replacing fossil fuels now works better and costs no more than buying and burning them.

We just need a new fire.

The old fire nurtured our ancestors for the past few million years. As glaciers retreated and woolly mammoths roamed, shaggy fur-clad humans warmed their families and cooked their food at wood-fueled hearths. Later some humans gathered lumps of coal from beaches and outcrops, scooped up oil from natural seeps, and, in China 2,400 years ago, drilled down nearly a mile for natural gas and some liquid hydrocarbons, delivered in bamboo pipes. But nearly all energy in the world came from wood, sun, wind, water, draft animals, and brute-force human toil. Life was short and hard. Winters were cold. Nights were dark.

To varying degrees, nearly half of our fellow human beings still live in that medieval world. One and a half billion have no electricity; they inhabit the vast dark spaces on the satellite photos of Earth at night. Three billion cook over smoky wood, dung, or charcoal fires. But for the more fortunate four billion of us, over the past two centuries fossil fuels have changed everything. Just as fire made us fully human and agriculture made possible cities and states, fossil fuels made us modern. They transformed energy from a preoccupation with personal scavenging to a ubiquitous commodity continuously delivered by extraordinary specialists, esoteric attainments, unthinkably huge machines, the world's largest corporations, and the world's vastest industry.

That industry, invisible to most of us, has become immeasurably skillful and powerful. It delves miles beneath continents and oceans. It inverts mountains. It smoothly delivers sophisticated energy carriers like gasoline, diesel, jet fuel, natural gas, and electricity to our buildings, vehicles, and factories. It is the foundation of our wealth, the bulwark of our might, the unseen metabolic engine of our modern life. Whenever we drive a car, flip a switch, or heat a house, we enjoy its widely affordable potency, convenience, versatility, and reliability. Without fossil fuels, or a similarly capable alternative, most of us would quickly start to experience the struggle for survival that only the world's poorest still suffer daily.

Yet this enabler of our civilization, this magic elixir that has so enriched and extended the lives of billions, has also begun, ever less subtly, to make our lives more fearful, insecure, costly, destructive, and dangerous. Its growing costs and risks erode, and at times may even seem to exceed, its manifest benefits. It puts asthma in our children's lungs and mercury in their lunchbox tuna. Its occasional mishaps can shatter economies.

Its wealth and power buy politicians and dictate to governments. It drives many of the world's rivalries, corruptions, despotisms, and wars. It is changing the composition of our planet's atmosphere faster than it has changed at any time in about the past 60 million years.

In short, our rich legacy of fossil fuels is starting to undermine the very security it built. Military leaders, among our society's most farsighted risk managers, are worried. In February 2010, the lead feature article in *Joint Force Quarterly*, the magazine of the chairman of the Joint Chiefs of Staff, began:

> Energy is the lifeblood of modern societies and a pillar of America's prowess and prosperity. Yet energy is also a major source of global instability, conflict, pollution, and risk. Many of the gravest threats to national security are intimately intertwined with energy, including oil supply interruptions, oil-funded terrorism, oil-fed conflict and instability, nuclear proliferation, domestic critical infrastructure vulnerabilities, and climate change (which changes everything).

A year later, the chairman responded with a call to energy action for security and prosperity—a mission the Pentagon is increasingly helping to lead.

Another threat, too, hangs over the global energy system: the ultimate certainty of fossil fuels' physical and economic depletion. Only its timing is in question. Despite prodigious technological progress in finding and extracting fossil-fuel deposits—exploration geologists now enjoy the digital equivalent of X-ray eyes—the round earth is not getting any bigger. The easy oil is rapidly dwindling and concentrating in fewer countries; the easy coal has only decades left; the huge deposits of U.S. natural gas, trapped in dense shale rock, that are now starting to be exploited are contained in bubbles finer than a human hair. As economists (and some geologists) start to understand how oil-reserve data were widely misinterpreted or misreported, opinions of fossil-fuel abundance are shifting rapidly. In late 2010, the International Energy Agency said world crude-oil output had already peaked in 2006; the Pentagon's Joint Forces Command warned that surplus capacity could disappear by 2012 and urged readiness for an oil-free military by 2040. The same story is emerging even for coal, long thought too abundant to survey carefully. Whether from the perspective of economic geology, affordability, security, or side effects, the Age of Fossil Fuels, viewed in the longer sweep of human civilization, is just a blip about two centuries long.

The fossil-fuel party is drawing to a close. It's time for something completely different.

What might that new fire look like?

The old fire was dug from below. The new fire flows from above. The old fire was scarce. The new fire is bountiful. The old fire was local. The new fire is everywhere. The old fire was transient. The new fire is permanent. And except for a little biofuel, biogas, and biomass, all grown in ways that sustain and endure, the new fire is flameless—providing all the convenient and dependable services of the old fire but with no combustion.

That sounds daunting. Yet, as the reflective Republican secretary of health, education, and welfare John Gardner said when he joined President Lyndon Johnson's Cabinet in 1965, "what we have before us are some breathtaking opportunities, disguised as insoluble problems."

The problems of fossil fuels are not necessary, either technologically or economically. We can avoid them in ways that tend to reduce energy costs—because technological progress has quietly been making fossil fuels obsolete.

About 78 percent of all human activity is fueled by digging up and burning the rotted remains of primeval swamps. But today we have alternatives more modern than sucking up and burning decayed muck hundreds of millions of years old. The same ingenuity and entrepreneurship that now scrape the bottom of the barrel from the ends of the earth can instead energize and enhance our own lives, and enrich the lives of the world's teeming billions, at little or no extra cost and often—even pretty generally—at a profit.

In fact, the new fire will enrich society by many trillions of net dollars in cold, hard cash. These pages will explain how—and what you can do to capture your piece of that once-in-a-civilization opportunity. For at root this is a story not of energy and fear but of energy and hope; not of restrictions and mandates but of choices and enterprise; not of danger and impoverishment but of security and wealth creation.

The new fire described here combines two elements: it uses energy very efficiently, and it gets that energy from diverse and mainly dispersed renewable sources. But this twin transition to efficiency and renewables, already underway and accelerating, isn't just about the old "what"—technology—and the old "how"—public policy. Technology and public policy are important and rich with innovation, so we'll have a lot to say about them: existing ones needing adoption, emerging ones needing refinement, on-the-horizon ones needing development. But they are less than half the story. Today's energy transition is also, often even more, about the new "what"—integrative design that combines technologies in unexpected ways—and the new "how"—novel business models and competitive strategies. In each of these four areas, important innovations are converging to create perhaps the biggest flood of disruptive opportunities ever seen, with effects as pervasive as those of the Information Age but even more fundamental.

——— *from* ———

The Natural Building Companion

A Comprehensive Guide to Integrative Design and Construction

Jacob Deva Racusin and Ace McArleton

2012

Natural buildings not only bring satisfaction to their makers and joy to their occupants, they also leave the gentlest footprint on the environment. In this complete reference to natural building philosophy, design, and technique, builders Jacob Deva Racusin and Ace McArleton offer thorough coverage of straw bale, straw-clay, woodchip-clay, and cellulose wall systems—as well as earthen and stone wall systems. Integrating holistic design and permaculture principles, this illustrated volume informs professionals making the transition from conventional building, homeowners embarking on their own construction, and green builders who want comprehensive guidance on natural building options. The book was created in partnership with the Yestermorrow Design/Build School, where both of the authors teach.

THE BUILDING OF STRUCTURES—FOR LIVING, for working, for storage, for play and gathering—is a practice that has been with us for as long as humans have been on this planet. As the authors of this book and as builders, our goal is to improve and enhance the built environment. In our view, the act of building should promote social and ecological health and well-being while creating structures that perform well in all weather conditions and are comfortable, beautiful, and long-lasting. The flourishing green-building movement is a step in the right direction as more members of the architecture and building communities are clearly starting to take notice that design solutions and building practices focused on reduced energy consumption and improved indoor air quality need to be part of their standard operating procedures.

Green-building practitioners generally hold performance as their approach's highest metric: How much less energy will a given material or building method use than traditional choices? How well will the building perform under temperature, pressure, and moisture stresses? Green building has become more mainstream because the language of performance and energy efficiency is an easily understood and welcome benefit of this type of building strategy. These are undeniably important performance criteria. We need to consume less energy in both building and using our structures to ensure a healthy future on our planet. We need our buildings to maintain the correct levels of temperature and humidity with the minimum amount of resource use to accomplish these goals. We need to know our buildings will perform well when confronted with fire, high winds, excessive rain, or other extreme weather events. We need to know our systems will resist organic threats: mold, mildew, and insect or rodent infestations. We need to understand appropriate materials and systems that work really well for us as builders (and dwellers), and that create not just adequate but excellent shelter.

But what if the performance of our structures is evaluated by other metrics as well? From our standpoint, green-building practitioners' focus on performance that is assessed solely by the structure's level of energy efficiency and durability has resulted in blinders that impede the peripheral vision necessary for the creation of truly ethical and ecologically sound structures. (Note: In referring to "green building" we are speaking of the industry-scale community of design and construction professionals whose standards are largely defined by certifying agencies, such as the United States Green Building Council [USGBC] and its Leadership in Energy and Environmental Design [LEED] program.) While we support the goals imparted by the green-building movement, they are goals that do not dig deeply enough nor span broadly enough to address humanity's ongoing and increasing challenges. For instance, green building has promoted, among other things, the profligate use of foams, which meet performance and efficiency criteria but are toxic, bio-persistent compounds that will be on this planet for an unknown amount of time, harming the ecological systems in which they remain. Already foams, plastics, and other trash items have aggregated in a massive gyre in the North Pacific Ocean and other oceans across the planet, causing serious harm to pelagic ecosystems. These compounds are not bio-degradable, and we must ask ourselves whether using these materials is the best option we have to meet our efficiency and performance goals.

Natural building is broader in its approach and scope than green building. It holds us to a standard that redefines the concept of "high performance" to include consideration of the materials used throughout their entire life stream, including how the materials—and the methodologies with which they are applied—affect the people and communities involved, as well as the broader ecology over time. In addition, natural building is about relationships: we choose to work with natural materials not only because they are "natural" but also because their use helps us develop and sustain as many relationships and connections as possible within the context of the development of a building. People often feel disconnected from their shelter, and natural building—through the use of local materials that are more familiar, a part of the natural world, and less toxic in their manufacture or method of installation—offers a way for more people to connect to the process and practice of creating and maintaining shelter. Natural building is about encouraging access, opening up pathways for involvement, while simultaneously striving for levels of built excellence. Rediscovering how to build high-performance structures with natural materials will take education, research, and investment, but we prefer to strive for this higher level of quality by encouraging more education and by continuing to promote open access to this work, as open-source information and democratic involvement are fundamental principles of natural building.

Natural builders ask such questions as:

- Is a given material toxic in origin, in production, during use, or at the end of its life? For example, the human and nonhuman communities in the Kanawha Valley (nicknamed "Chemical Valley") in West Virginia suffer health risks due to exposure to toxins from plastic and foam manufacturers in their towns. When we do not use a building material such as latex paint made from ingredients synthesized in Chemical Valley and choose instead a natural paint made from local clays and wheat paste, the entirety of these life-cycle conditions and effects are considered. Ideally, building materials should not pose a threat to the health and well-being of the builder and the ecologies of which they are a part for the duration of their life cycles.

- What is the aesthetic and sensory experience for people who live or work with the material? Often those who use natural paints for the first time tell us how surprisingly enjoyable it is not to smell the fumes that accompany the use of industrial paints. Using natural paints can have practical implications as well: the lack of off-gassing of these paints opens up the possibility of painting in the middle of winter, with minimal ventilation—something one could never do with latex or conventional oil-based paint and reside safely and comfortably in the space at the same time.

- Does the material fit with the climatic demands, the local ecology, and the local vernacular building style? Sometimes straw is not available nearby in baled form, and the cost and carbon footprint of transporting it make it not the best choice, so other, more local options may be the more "natural" choice. Additionally, the design detailing relevant to that region—practically and culturally—must at least be considered, with the understanding that the technologies available to us as natural builders can be selected and adapted to support the priorities of regional design.

- Does the material or process connect us to our planet—such as watching the straw that will become the walls of your house grow in your neighboring farmer's fields? And does it connect us to our communities and to each other, such as by acquiring stone or locally grown lumber from a neighbor, or through work parties for a straw bale wall or timber frame raising?

—— *from* ——

The New Net Zero

Leading-Edge Design and Construction of Homes and Buildings for a Renewable Energy Future

William Maclay and Maclay Architects

2014

The New Net Zero has been heralded by The New York Times and others as a masterwork offering the most in-depth information available on designing and constructing net zero buildings, which produce at least as much energy as they consume and are carbon-neutral. Bill Maclay, an award-winning net zero designer whose homes, commercial buildings, and even historic renovations have achieved high-performance goals at affordable costs, makes the case for a net zero future; explains net zero building metrics, integrated design practices, and renewable energy options; shares detailed building plans; and conveys his lessons learned on net zero team building.

IN OUR ONGOING JOURNEY FROM HUNTER-GATHERERS to computer users, energy and settlement patterns have been intertwined. When humans were totally dependent on the wild ecosystem, they continually moved in small groups in search of food. There was little or no settlement, and humans traveled in small family or extended family groups.

With the advent of agriculture and animal husbandry, which were innovations that used the sun's energy to cultivate crops and animal power to work the fields, humans began to stay in one place, first in small tribal settlements and then in large villages with stored food. Later, water mills and windmills allowed for the expansion of industry beyond earlier farm- and animal-based industrial activity. This also fueled the movement of goods, spawned villages catering to increasingly specialized trades, and eventually gave rise to larger urban centers. While the renewable energy was still dispersed, various forms of storage, including crops, water power, firewood, and wind, all allowed for the more concentrated use of energy along with the denser human settlement that accompanied it.

Eventually, in the nineteenth century, coal came on the scene, creating the industrial city and associated urban lifestyle. With coal came trains, large-scale manufacturing, more movement of goods, dense concentrations of housing, and retail trade. This new, inexpensive energy source fueled dramatic wealth and population growth.

The discovery of significant amounts of oil in the late nineteenth century set the stage for the next major transition in daily life and settlement. Since this time oil has become civilization's primary energy source. Oil, similarly to coal, was an intensely concentrated form of energy, which meant it could be transported and used almost anywhere. But because oil in its liquid form was far more easily distributed than coal, energy and settlement no longer needed to be as intimately connected.

Today most of us live in a world shaped by oil, in cities and suburbs strewn with parking lots, shopping malls, and uniform architecture. With people enslaved to their cars, the interaction and cohesiveness of earlier community life has been significantly reduced and lost, and our community structure has been drastically altered.

As anthropologist Joseph Tainter points out, "Energy flow and sociopolitical organization are opposite sides of an equation. Neither can exist, in a human group, without the other, nor can either undergo substantial change without altering both the opposite member and the balance of the equation. Energy flow and sociopolitical organization must evolve in harmony."

There are, however, a few other drivers of human lifestyle that have remained fundamental for as long as we have existed. Everyone from yesterday's hunter-gatherers to today's nine-to-fivers has been concerned with survival (whether physical or emotional), community (whether family, tribe, or Facebook), materiality and economy (whether arrows and food or computers, SUVs, and 401(k)s), and spirit (whether organized religion or simple wonder). The prominence of each of these concerns may have ebbed and flowed over the course of our history, but they have never vanished.

Another constant in our evolving history is the role of beauty. Whether found in nature, art, or the built environment, beauty reminds us that we are just an infinitesimal part of an awesome and inspiring world. We can see it in artifacts dating back to ancient civilizations in Mesopotamia, India, and China. We can find it in the diverse evolving empires of China, Greece, Rome, Egypt, Babylonia, and Mesoamerica. Walking through ancient remains, we can visualize the richness of daily life—of growing and finding food; of prayer with others; of living closely connected within the larger community of families, tribes, city-states, and empires. Additionally, we can see the interconnections with surrounding regions and ecosystems in providing food, resources, energy, and trade.

What was it like living in these beautiful places? What went on in daily life? What did the inhabitants really care about, dream about, or fear? What did they value, and what gave their lives meaning? And how does all this connect to the physical world they created?

There exists a continuous interplay between physical space and human activity that generates and evolves the future. Whether now or thousands of years ago, our quality and way of life gives us purpose and meaning, and our human-built, physical world supports and expresses this way of life.

So how might our needs for survival, community, spirit, beauty, and more come together in a world shaped by renewables? Paul Hawken, Fritjof Capra, David Korten, Ken Wilber, and many other modern thinkers believe we are at a turning point as powerful as the one that occurred between the Middle Ages and Renaissance. There is a growing consensus that our current scientific and technological framework will not get us out of the massive challenges we face on a global scale. As Albert Einstein once said, "The problems that exist in the world today cannot be solved by the level of thinking that created them."

There is great hope that the emerging paradigm—the force that determines how we live and how we design and inhabit our world in the future—will be grounded in an understanding and appreciation of life and living systems and a desire to restore and regenerate them.

Building individual dwellings and communities that can evolve in harmony with ecosystems and restore connections between people and nature is step one in this process. But whether you are a designer, builder, homeowner, or building owner, remembering your connection to this larger shift is key. We should be thinking about net zero communities and infrastructures if we're going to build the world we want to live in.

PERMACULTURE & REGENERATIVE AGRICULTURE

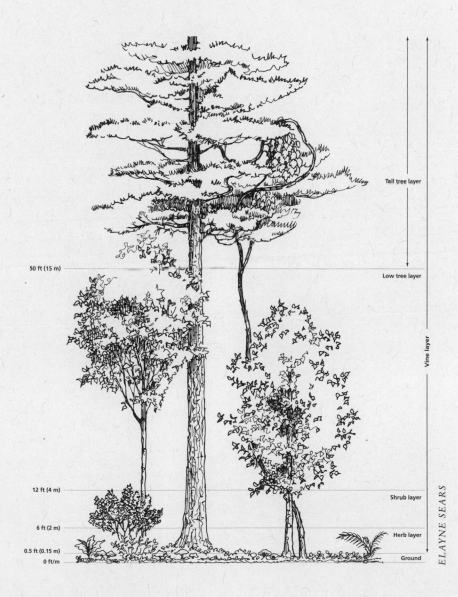

Tall tree layer

50 ft (15 m) — Low tree layer

Vine layer

12 ft (4 m) — Shrub layer

6 ft (2 m) — Herb layer

0.5 ft (0.15 m) —
0 ft/m — Ground

ELAYNE SEARS

Gaia's Garden

A Guide to Home-Scale Permaculture

Toby Hemenway

2000; second edition, 2009

Longtime bestseller and winner of a Nautilus Award, Gaia's Garden *sparked the imagination of America's home gardeners, introducing permaculture's central message: Working with Nature, not against her, results in more beautiful, abundant, and forgiving gardens. Toby Hemenway, a leader in the permaculture community, wrote this book—the first-ever permaculture guide for the home-scale grower—showing that it's fun and easy to create a "backyard ecosystem" by assembling communities of plants that can work cooperatively and perform a variety of functions.*

NO HUMAN DESIGNED AN ALPINE MEADOW, a tropical forest, or a creekside grotto, yet these wild landscapes are never ugly. They follow a larger natural order that seems to ensure beauty. In the previous chapter we began to glimpse a few aspects of nature's order. Now we can use these principles and patterns of nature to design our gardens.

A natural landscape is patterned in ways that harvest the energy (sun, wind, heat) and matter (water and nutrients) that flow through it, casting a living net that collects these resources and shuttles them into myriad cycles that transform them into more life. Nearly everything that enters a natural landscape is captured and used, absorbed and reincarnated into vibrant biodiversity. Anything produced in that landscape, from by-products such as sugary root secretions to "wastes" such as manure and molted insect casings, is recycled, swallowed up again, and reincorporated into new living tissue. And the landscape "learns" as it goes, selecting and improving the patterns that work best. Each captured bit helps build and refine a network that gets better than before at catching what comes its way.

Billions of years of evolution have left few loose ends in nature. One creature's waste is another's food. Nearly every niche is tightly held, every habitat is packed full of interconnected species. Anything faintly resembling a resource will be used: if one species can't use it, another will.

It is this interconnectedness—this linking of one species' "outputs" to another's "inputs"—that we seek to re-create in the ecological garden.

Unfortunately, we don't have billions of years to wait while our gardens evolve to the immense "webiness" of the natural landscape. But we have another tool: our creative minds. We can consciously evaluate the pieces of our landscape and use permaculture principles to design the connections. Observation is the key to good design.

By observing the patterns and cycles that nature uses to solve design problems, we can replicate these forms in our gardens, not as mere static shapes but as dynamic solutions that save labor, resources, and energy. Then our gardens can be almost as interlinked as nature is, producing no waste or pollutants, needing little excess labor, ripe with habitat, yielding abundantly.

—— *from* ——

Edible Forest Gardens

Volume One: Ecological Vision and Theory for Temperate Climate Permaculture

Volume Two: Ecological Design and Practice for Temperate Climate Permaculture

Dave Jacke with Eric Toensmeier

2005

For years during the 1990s at Chelsea Green we followed the growing interest in both permaculture and agroforestry, specifically "forest gardening," as they were being developed in Australia, Great Britain—seemingly everywhere but here in the United States. Our climate is so different from these other regions that it was difficult to find a good, comprehensive reference adapted to our specific conditions in eastern North America. Fortunately, when we met Dave Jacke and his collaborator, Eric Toensmeier, we knew we had found the right guys to do an American book on forest gardening. Several years, many drafts, and two big volumes later, Edible Forest Gardens *appeared in print, winning an award from the Garden Writers Association, and it remains today the definitive work on the subject.*

THE ROLE THAT EDIBLE FOREST GARDENING can play in restoring the ecology of our cultural landscape is large. This arises not only from the potential for low-maintenance productive food systems in people's yards and public spaces and from the wide variety of forest gardens we can create. This powerful role exists because of the interconnections we can create throughout our neighborhoods and towns on an ecosystem scale, and because of the changes of hearts and minds necessary for edible forest gardeners to succeed.

Bill Mollison, cofounder of permaculture, has said that the suburbs represent one of the best opportunities for sustainable design and living. There are more people with a little bit of land in these habitats than in any other. In the cities, people have far fewer opportunities to connect with any semblance of the natural world, much less to be self-supporting in any major way. Rural areas have too few people for high productivity without machinery driven by fossil fuels. We can, however, reunite the shreds of ecological fabric that still exist in the suburbs. We can restore and link natural areas, though humans will manage many, as in precolonial times. More importantly, we can turn the cultural landscape of our communities into an ecosystem that works by designing, planting, and tending our yards in accord with nature's way, overlaying our purposes onto the landscape appropriately. Creating edible and otherwise useful forests, savannas, meadows, thickets, and wetlands in our yards can do this. It can also recreate strands that will help weave the remaining forest fragments back into a more healthy and stable ecosystem. With thoughtful action on the part of thousands, if not millions, this is completely achievable. That's the ecological restoration part. But this can happen only with a deep and ongoing change in the hearts and minds of those who are responsible for the world we have created and can create—and that's all of us. This change of heart is the ecological reformation of which we speak.

Gardening writer Janet Marinelli explores what she calls "gardening in the age of extinction" in her book *Stalking the Wild Amaranth*. After reviewing the history and philosophies of garden styles from Greece to the present day and discussing the ecological realities we humans face in the coming years, she writes:

> What is the place of landscape design in such a world? As William Howard Adams points out in *Nature Perfected*, the presence of massive overpopulation and monstrous cities has raised critical questions about the form, the function, and even the very survival of gardens. "Concocting bogus images of lost paradise," in his view, "only exposes our impoverishment." It seems that we are being forced back to something akin to the "walled gardens of some barbarous medieval town," he writes, "but without any

of the metaphysics to transform our isolation into a civilized, revitalizing environment." Is there any way out of this horticultural—and metaphysical—abyss?

First, there is nothing wrong with exposing our impoverishment. Indeed, such is the first step of any healing or transformational process, as difficult or painful as it might be. The way we think, eat, live, and garden has contributed to this impoverishment. Take it in and own it: *we are all responsible for this*.

Second, there is at least one way out of the abyss: the metaphysics are out there in the Garden itself. Adam and Eve left the Garden of Eden after eating the fruit from the Tree of Knowledge, when they became self-conscious and realized a sense of separateness between themselves and God or Nature. The history of Western civilization is the story of our increasing knowledge, and our application of that knowledge to meet the needs originally met with ease in the Garden of Eden. Meanwhile the natural world became "other," objectified, simply a means to an end, a tool or resource for us to meet our goals, an object with no intrinsic value of its own. We now find our knowledge leading us back to an understanding of unity, and of sacredness.

The boundaries we saw between our world and ourselves are breaking down. Physics shows us that what we thought were particles are also waves, and that the act of observing something changes the observed. Physicists don't mention that it changes the observer too! Ecology shows us that our limiting and false beliefs that we are separate from "nature," and that it is possible to study "pristine" ecosystems in their "natural state," threaten our own survival and that of many other species. We cannot go back to the boundaryless, unself-conscious union of children, to the Garden of Eden we imagined, and possibly experienced, before. Now is the time for us to create the kind of partnership with the natural world that only mature adults can create, based on self-knowledge, humility, and respect. We humans are both particles *and* waves. We are separate individuals *and* we are interacting and interdependent with all of creation at many levels. We have creative power, but not creative dominion. We can take, but we must also give. We cannot go back to the primeval forest we have destroyed, but we can recreate the primal forest, at least metaphorically, in the here and now. We can create a new Garden of Eden, but we can't do it alone. We need nature's help, and she needs ours.

This metaphysics involves envisioning ourselves as part of the natural world and acting in accord with that vision, not in the same way as the native peoples of this continent did before us, but as participants in ways appropriate for our time in history, for our culture, for the ecosystems that exist now. Now is the time to restore ourselves to the ecosystem, and thereby to restore the ecosystem itself. To do that we must reform ourselves: reform our sense of who we are, of what is right and wrong, of how the world works, and how we operate within it socially, economically, ecologically, and spiritually. This radical undercurrent flows through this whole book and whole forest garden idea. Since the word *radical* literally means "of, relating to, or proceeding from a root," it is an appropriate word to use. Let's get to the root of the issue, or the "weed" will still come up.

So, the edible forest garden requires us to be open. To listen and look. To hone our skills of observation and discernment. To use these skills before we intervene in our gardens, and in our world. To act with respect, humility, and as much wisdom as we can muster. To expand our sense of where our gardens begin and end to include the neighbor's yard, the town, the region, and the planet, with all of the inhabitants therein. We must challenge our assumptions and sacred cows. We must be committed to truth. And we must spend time in our hammocks, hanging out in the Garden.

Edible forest gardening requires us to learn ecology, not just theoretically, but with our bodies outside in the field. What principles guide the behavior and design of natural ecosystems? Only by understanding these can we consciously design edible forest gardens that mimic how nature works. Then we must coevolve with these systems. In that process we learn and change. We embody these principles in ourselves; they become part of us. How can we not change the way we think and live as a result?

———— *from* ————

The War on Bugs

Will Allen

2008

Author, farmer, and activist Will Allen has farmed in California and Vermont, served as head of the Sustainable Cotton Project, sits on the board of the Organic Consumers Association, and has been arrested in more protests than any other septuagenarian we know. A passionate advocate for organic agriculture, Allen researched, over many years, the history of agricultural chemicals (fertilizers and pesticides), and found that their roots stretch back much farther in history than anyone suspected. In this fascinating book he reveals that a combination of slick advertising, biased farm journals, and governmental/scientific "experts" persuaded farmers over many years to accept chemical poisons that many never wanted to use. The War on Bugs *offers a glimpse into the history of not only agriculture, but our society.*

POST-WORLD WAR II SALES OF THE CHEMICALS to farm families in the United States were consistently profitable because chemical corporations and magazine editors knew that very few farmers traveled broadly. The advertisers and salesmen knew that farmers didn't know much of what was going on outside their own community. They knew that the rural American public's grasp of history was short, its awareness local and often culturally bound within a relatively small region.

DDT had failed in Europe after four or five years of use. Most U.S. farm families, often parochial by choice or economic circumstance, didn't know about these DDT failures. Most farmers also didn't know there were already concerns about environmental damage from DDT by the mid-1940s, before they ever used a drop. There was no TV yet and reports from Europe on the radio were censored by the networks for the "war effort." Oldest surviving sons and farm fathers were exempt from the military draft so that they could run the farm. Because labor was scarce, they focused most of their attention on the farms, not on national or international events, even though farmers followed the progress of the war as closely as they could. As a result, most were not aware of any problems with the newly released chemicals. And the media affected a hear-no-evil, speak-no-evil, see-no-evil attitude toward the war poisons.

Consequently, a chemical could fail in one place and still remain popular and be considered effective just a few miles away. Often, failures occurred as close as a neighboring state or county—yet, just as often, no one in the adjacent area knew of the problems. The chemical corporations banked on the fact that farmers were not informed about most product failures, dangers, and spills. Most of us *still* are ignorant about the presence, and the dangers, of these chemicals in our environment and on our food.

Manufacturers have depended upon our collective ignorance and isolation and have continued to sell their chemicals and publicly defend them until long after their effectiveness has passed—and until long after they have damaged our health and our communities. The corporations put whatever spin on the failure of each chemical that they could, in order to keep the poisons on the market and derive as much revenue as possible, for as long as possible. They fought, and continue to fight, bitterly with all their time-worn themes—safety, incredible effectiveness, feeding the world, frightening brand names, labor savings, union busting, war, destruction, babies, boxers, beautiful women, violence, and the silver bullet (the techno-fix).

The adaptability of the ads and the ad makers to deal with the safety and product quality concerns of the customers for the last 160 years is capitalism at its finest. Their adaptability emerged in the 1980s after several terrible accidents and deaths involving their products. So, finally, after so much criticism about the accidents with and the dangers of so many chemicals, the corporations shifted their focus and concentrated on the safety of handling and application. Then, while no civilians were looking, during the Gulf War in 1991, these "safe" chemicals (such as Deet and Roundup) morphed into battle-hardened warriors once again. In the late 1990s, advertisers shifted their tactics once more and began selling their chemicals as "environmentally friendly." Such doublethink opportunism punctuates the history of farm-chemical advertising and explains why it is so successful.

Farm magazines today still occasionally laud DDT and lament its loss. There's been noise among some politicians, here and abroad, to bring back DDT to control malaria in Africa, the argument being that banning it amounts to cynicism (even racism) by far-out Birkenstock-wearing environmentalists, who sit in their comfortable American homes and care more for the snail darter than they do for the poor suffering people of Africa.

There is truth to the indictment of spoiled Americans, but this is rhetoric designed to point fingers at well-intentioned people in order to mask the fact that DDT is still widely used in many parts of Asia, Africa, Latin America, and the Middle East. It comes home to your dining room table on a regular basis if you buy nonorganic foreign produce. Proponents argue that it kills mosquitoes in many malaria-infested regions. Environmentalists, toxicologists, and public-health advocates have argued against the use of DDT for malaria everywhere since the 1960s, but they have not been able to stop its use.

—— *from* ——

Holy Shit

Managing Manure to Save Mankind

Gene Logsdon

2010

When we asked Gene Logsdon one day what his next book would be about, he said, "Well, I have a subject that I really want to write about. But the only thing is, you have to use the title I want." Normally in publishing that kind of agreement would be a deal breaker. That is, until we found out that the book would be about manure, and that Logsdon wanted to call it Holy Shit. *We instantly agreed, and published this provocative little book that is occasionally irreverent, to be sure, but deals with a serious subject that all of us should care about: how we can manage manure more effectively and turn it into a valuable asset instead of a solid waste problem.*

THE INVENTION OF THE MANURE SPREADER ought to be hailed as more momentous than that of the plow, or the automobile. Both of these latter cultural icons might be considered destructive, the first by causing erosion and the second by filling the air with carbon monoxide, while the manure spreader eases humans in what was, and is, one of civilization's more onerous tasks—returning to the soil the fertility taken from it. But probably no technological wonder is as ill thought of, or is less publicized, than the manure spreader. Since we have such a low opinion of manure itself, the machine that handles it also suffers from prejudice, or at least from ignorance. Books that trace the early development of farm machinery often ignore the manure spreader. For example, Michael Partridge's wonderful *Early Agricultural Machinery* (Frederick A. Praeger, 1969) does not mention or show even one illustration of a spreader or its predecessor, the muck cart. It is as if the subject were too distasteful to the delicate, civilized mind.

Once, when I was in the company of very advanced students of philosophy and theology, a tractor and an empty manure spreader passed by our view. One of the onlookers, proficient in Greek, Latin, and Thomistic philosophy, asked me what it was. "A marshmallow picker," I said, trying to sound nonchalant.

"Oh," he replied, and then went on discussing Aristotle's theory of hylomorphism. I am not making this up. This brilliant scholar not only did not know what a manure spreader looked like but also could accept the notion that marshmallows grow on plants. Or perhaps he just had his mind on higher matters. To his credit, he came around to me a week later, having thought about what I had said and having checked me out, I presume, and informed me, "You are even a bigger manure spreader than Aristotle."

——— *from* ———

Sowing Seeds in the Desert

Natural Farming, Global Restoration, and Ultimate Food Security

Masanobu Fukuoka

2012

Masanobu Fukuoka's inspiring and international bestselling book, The One-Straw Revolution *(Rodale, 1978), spoke directly to the growing movement of organic farmers and activists seeking a new way of life. For years after its publication, Fukuoka traveled the world spreading his teachings and developing a devoted following of farmers seeking to return to the truth of nature.* Sowing Seeds in the Desert, *a summation of those years of travel and research, is Fukuoka's last major work—and perhaps his most important. It sums up his life's work, to rehabilitate the world's deserts and achieve global food security by using natural farming—letting nature lead, without imposing rigid systems—including practical solutions for feeding a growing human population and providing a deep and renewed understanding of the relationship between human beings and nature.*

SCIENTISTS HAVE HISTORICALLY ASSUMED THAT it is acceptable to control nature using human will. Nature is seen as the "outside world" in opposition to humanity, and this idea forms the basis of modern scientific civilization. But this fictitious "I" of Descartes can never fully comprehend the true state of reality. Just as human beings do not know themselves, they cannot know the other. Human beings may be the children of "Mother Nature," but they are no longer able to see the true form of their mother. Looking for the whole, they only see the parts. Seeing their mother's breast, they mistake it for the mother herself. If someone does not know his mother, he is a child who does not know whose child he is. He is like a monkey, raised in a zoo by humans, who is convinced that the zookeeper is his mother. Similarly, the discriminating and analytical knowledge of scientists may be useful for taking nature apart and looking at its parts, but it is of no use for grasping the reality of pure nature. One day scientists will realize how limiting and misguided it is to hack nature to pieces like that. I sometimes make a brush-and-ink drawing to illustrate this point. I call it "the cave of the intellect." It shows two men toiling in a pit or a cave swinging their pickaxes to loosen the hard earth. The picks represent the human intellect. The more these workers swing their tools, the deeper the pit gets and the more difficult it is for them to escape. Outside the cave, I draw a person who is relaxing in the sunlight. While still working to provide everyday necessities through natural farming, that person is free from the drudgery of trying to understand nature, and is simply enjoying life. Ironically, nature is also being damaged by people who pride themselves on following a path of moderation, who may think they have nature's best interest at heart. These well-meaning people, known for their compassion and practical sense, might say: "Human beings have lived in nature for thousands and thousands of years, sometimes joyfully, sometimes filled with sorrow. Isn't that the essence of the relationship between people and nature? Isn't it simplistic to see nature as only filled with truth, good, and beauty while seeing human beings as insensitive and ignorant?" At first glance, this opinion seems sensible, and appears to be an objective point of view. But these goodhearted people have not escaped the realm of relative thinking. Seen from a nonrelative perspective, nature transcends beauty and ugliness, good and evil. Whether we see this world as filled with contradictions, or as existing in perfect harmony, is determined by whether we analyze it using our intellect, or grasp the entirety of nature without making any distinctions at all. It is only by doing the latter that we can see nature's true form.

No God or Buddha Will Rescue the Human Race

The destruction of nature will lead to the destruction of the human race, but many people seem to be convinced that even if humans should disappear, they will be brought to life again by the hand of their god. This idea, however, is nothing more than fantasy. The human race will not be born again. When the people on the earth have died out, there will be no God or Buddha to rescue them. People do sometimes sense the sacredness of nature, such as when they look closely at a flower, climb high peaks, or journey deep into the mountain. Such aesthetic sense, love, receptivity, and understanding are people's most basic instincts—their true nature. These days, however, humans are flying in a completely different direction to some unknown destination, and they seem to be doing it as rapidly as possible. Perhaps the people who most easily perceive that nature is sacred are a few religious people, artists of great sensitivity, and children. With their compassion they often perceive, at the very least, that nature is something beyond human invention and that it should be revered. The poets who write about nature, the painters who turn it into works of art, the people who compose music, the sculptors . . . I would like to believe that they are the ones drawn to what is truly meaningful. But if an artist's understanding of nature is unclear, no matter how keen his sensitivity, no matter how excellent his power of expression, no matter how refined his technique, he will eventually find himself lost.

The Dragonfly Will Be the Messiah

There has never been a generation like the present where people's hearts are so badly wounded. This is true of every area of society—politics, economics, education, and culture. It is reflected in the degradation of the environment, which comes about through the material path humanity has chosen. Now we have the ugly sight of industry, government, and the military joining forces in the struggle for ultimate power. In the present age of disintegration the various religions of the world, old and new, large and small, are becoming very active. Indeed, whenever the world has fallen into disorder, religious movements have flourished. Let me give one example of a religion that promises wealth and good fortune. A young man who was worshiped as the founder of a new religion in Kobe came to my farm with ten or so of his disciples. This fellow told me that he had received special training to transform him from an ordinary religious person to the founder of this new religion. He learned such things as physiognomy, mind-reading, fortune-telling, palmistry, divination, hypnotism for healing disease, exorcism, and various ways of communicating divine messages, such as writing in sand. He told me in great detail about the schemes he had used to get believers into the palm of his hand, starting with tricks for determining potential believer's character flaws and problems. This, he said, would help him attract new followers. This is only one type of many religious imposters who hold both the deities and the people captive and run around acquiring believers in order to make money and gain power. But many of them are popular and well-regarded, and would not seem to be the stereotypical image of an imposter. This paradox leads me to reflect how human beings are nothing more than animals dancing to a tune piped by their own ideas. I look forward to the day when there is no need for sacred scriptures or sutras. The dragonfly will be the messiah.

A Life of Natural Culture

When I mention that human society is on the wrong path, I often hear the retort, "Then show me a better one." Because it does not have a name yet, I will refer to it as "natural culture and community." Natural culture is simply a way of life in which people enjoy the truth and beauty of nature, a life in which people, with freedom in their hearts, climb mountains, play in meadows, bathe in the warm rays of sunlight, breathe pure air, drink crystalline water, and experience the true joy of life.

Sowing Seeds in the Desert

The society I am describing is one in which people will create a free and generous community. Once the primal source of nature is destroyed, however, it will no longer be able to restore itself, and this image of a natural culture will become obsolete. Indeed, many species of plants and animals become extinct each day, and the meaning of the disappearance of one bird or one plant is not just the death of that bird or that plant. It is of grave significance to us all. It is connected with the destruction of the harmony of all living things. If humanity can regain its original kinship with nature, we should be able to live in peace and abundance. Seen through the eyes of modern civilization, however, this life of natural culture must appear to be monotonous and primitive, but not to me. There are many other people besides me who question the path of modern society. They are filled with foreboding, wondering whether or not we can solve, or somehow evade, the current environmental crisis. There are even many scientists who believe that the long-term sustainability of life on earth, from the standpoint of the natural environment and its resources, will be decided in the next twenty or thirty years. It is these people to whom I speak directly. We must realize that both in the past and today, there is only one "sustainable" course available to us. We must find our way back to true nature. We must set ourselves to the task of revitalizing the earth. Regreening the earth, sowing seeds in the desert—that is the path society must follow. My travels around the world have convinced me of that.

—— *from* ——

The Seed Underground

A Growing Revolution to Save Food

Janisse Ray

2012

In The Seed Underground, *Janisse Ray—whose signature lyricism once prompted a* New York Times *writer to proclaim her the Rachel Carson of the South—tells the stories of the impassioned gardeners around the country who are saving time-honored open-pollinated seed varieties like 'Old Time Tennessee' muskmelon and 'Long County Longhorn' okra, lest they be lost forever. "There's no despair in a seed," she writes, meditating not only on the massive threats that our food supply faces, but on life's ultimate resilience. This brilliant and moving manifesto garnered numerous awards, including two Garden Writers Association awards, an American Horticultural Society Book Award, and the ASJA Arlene Eisenberg Award for Writing That Makes a Difference.*

ALL MY LIFE I DREAMED OF BEING A FARMER. My mother had been glad to leave the farm, where I spent many Saturdays with my grandparents Arthur and Beulah, whose children one by one had moved away to the big Southern cities of Jacksonville, Orlando, Chattanooga. Deep in my psyche are my grandfather's mules, my grandmother's chickens, fields of vegetables and sprawling watermelon vines, full corncribs. During my preschool years, my grandmother milked a cow. Then there was the Farmall-A tractor and bird guano fertilizer, and after my grandfather died, when I was six, subsidized tobacco and Roundup weedkiller, monster combines and terrible erosion and the invasion of privet. The cane grinder was sold, the smokehouses fell, the last hen wasn't even eaten. Grandmama sent the milch cow to the livestock auction. I remember her final pea-patch.

On that same farm, the one I roamed as a child eating crabapples and muscadines, pomegranates and sand pears, now the story is Roundup-resistant pigweed growing among rows of genetically modified (GM) soybeans in fields leased to chemical cultivators. The fencerows are bulldozed, demolishing the plantings of wax myrtle and wild cherry accomplished by mockingbirds and cardinals. Fences are yanked out and the farmers are crowding right up to the road, since the field has to get bigger at all costs.

The sassafras tree my grandfather so carefully skirted with his harrows is dead and gone.

Any one of us middle-aged Americans could be the poster child for the story of agriculture in the United States, one that began with working farms; farm animals; seed saving; land-based, subsistence economies; farming children. And, poof, all that was gone, brushed aside casually.

It happened so quickly. It left me doodling pitchforks in college astronomy and world civ notebooks.

I'm back. Not on my grandmother's farm, but somebody's grandmother's farm. It has forty-six acres in pasture, field, and woods. It has a house built in 1850 by a man whose brother operated a sawmill on Slaughter Creek, which collects water off the fields of Reidsville, Georgia's prison farm, and delivers it to the Altamaha River.

Our gardens are gridworks of raggedly rectangular raised beds. The gardens are fenced to keep the barnyard fowl—including the crazy guineas, which scuttle around like boats on legs hollering their mad, prehistoric calls—from scratching up every seed we plant. We have a pig or two, a few goats and sheep, some chickens, some turkeys and ducks.

Many people still alive today have seen the entire process of American ag: the function, the falling apart, the rise of big chemical, and now the coming back. We are witnessing in agriculture a revolution, a full circle.

Except it's not a circle. We are not returning to where we were. With some of the old knowledge intact and armed with fresh knowledge, we are looping forward to a new place. And we're coming there different. We are coming better prepared. We're coming educated. Girls as well as boys are coming. We're coming as greenhorns, but we're coming together.

We're coming knowing that failure is not possible. To not fail, we desire to understand everything we can about the cycle of life. We plumb the depths of industrial empire. We can no longer believe in false magic, that whatever we hanker for will be available to us, as it has been for most of our lives, whenever we wanted it, that it will appear magically in stores and restaurants as long as we have money wadded in our pockets.

At no time in our history more than now have Americans been more knowledgeable and more concerned about what we eat. We have watched our food systems deconstructed in front of our eyes. In a way, the farmer in all of us has roused. We understand organic, that food grown without chemicals is healthier for us and the earth. We understand local, that food grown closer to home is healthier and helps solve the climate crisis as well. Now we come to the landscape of American agriculture with a fresh realization: We do not have control of seeds, which are the crux of our food supply. When we dig deeper, we realize that our seed supply is in crisis and therefore our food is in crisis. A tragedy of corporate robbery is being acted out on a world stage, except this is not a drama with us in the audience getting to go home afterward. This is real.

The time has come to understand food at its most elemental.

——— *from* ———

Paradise Lot

Two Plant Geeks, One-Tenth of an Acre, and the Making of an Edible Garden Oasis in the City

Eric Toensmeier with contributions from Jonathan Bates

2013

Eric Toensmeier is known throughout the permaculture community for his brilliant teaching and for contributing some of the most in-depth and rigorous research available on perennial crops and their uses. In Paradise Lot, *Toensmeier set out to do something entirely different—to tell the immensely funny and charming story of transforming one-tenth of an acre of blighted urban land into an edible paradise. Along with his friend and collaborator Jonathan Bates, Toensmeier shares the adventures, mistakes, and do-overs, along with the many successes of their twelve-year project.*

As a budding ecologist in the 1970s and 1980s, I learned that the best we can possibly do as environmentalists is to minimize our impact on nature. The ideal footprint would be no footprint at all. That doesn't really give us a lot of room to breathe, and with that as its model, it's easy to see why the environmental movement has not won wider acceptance. The most profound thing I have learned from indigenous land management traditions is that human impact can be positive—even necessary—for the environment. Indeed it seems to me that the goal of an environmental community should be not to reduce our impact on the landscape but to maximize our impact and make it a positive one, or at the very least to optimize our effect on the landscape and acknowledge that we can have a positive role to play.

I began to see that Jonathan and I had stumbled across many indigenous management techniques in our efforts to care for and learn from our backyard agroecosystem. I started to think about how we might apply some of these ancient practices more intentionally in our backyard. Frequent burns were definitely out of the question, but we can and do use disturbance to keep all the patches in our garden from being uniform. Our tools are the broadfork, sheet mulch, pruning, and tillage. We have taken many native species from our region into cultivation and are part of broader efforts to domesticate some. Certainly we get an A for transporting species beyond their native regions, and I enjoy thinking of this as a practice with thousands of years of history on this continent.

It's around the area of regenerative harvests—harvests that maintain or improve the productivity of crops in future seasons—that I have most been trying to wrap my brain. Jonathan and I had already learned that some of our perennial root crops need to be harvested every year. This annual thinning reduces competition among sunchoke plants, for example, which actually stop forming tubers if left to their own devices for long enough. Our efforts to implement a coppiced leaf crop system will be another reflection of regenerative harvest.

At this point most of our weeds are the offspring of species we planted here on purpose. In some cases this can make the acts of weeding and harvesting become one and the same. Sweet cicely seeded itself more than we wanted in several areas of our garden. When I learned that the roots are edible, I ran right out and dug up a year-old seedling. At the base was a taproot like a midsized white carrot. When Jonathan and I cooked some up, we were thrilled to discover that they tasted like sweet licorice. Suddenly the annoying chore of weeding sweet cicely was a lot more fun, to the point that by now they are getting pretty hard to find.

Groundnut is another interesting example. It runs and spreads underground throughout the garden and makes kind of a nuisance of itself, climbing on small trees and shrubs. But when I sit back and think about it, the foliage can be cut and laid down as a nitrogen-rich mulch, and the tubers are always ripe and can be eaten any time of the year. I may not be happy to find groundnut in any particular bed, but knowing that I can mash some up like refried beans for a snack makes it hard to be too upset.

My fantasy is that in decades or centuries to come, almost every interaction with one's garden could be a form of harvest, guiding succession gently to an ever more productive future. Some farmers I know have taken this to a markedly elegant level. Steve Breyer of Tripple Brook Farm, my plant mentor, envisions a landscape of fruit and nut trees, with an understory of berries, perennial vegetables, native wildflowers, and dense, long-lived groundcovers.

One of the obstacles he quickly encountered in his efforts to implement this strategy was that squirrels were taking his nuts. Steve introduced me to the idea of employing squirrels as a labor force. He has a big old butternut tree with a hollow trunk. Squirrels pick out the best nuts (no hollow or worm-infested specimens allowed) and stuff them into the hollow trunk of this tree for storage. Steve often collects nuts there and introduced me to the idea of trading nuts for corn. This is an idea with indigenous roots that may go back thousands of years as well, with hog peanut and sunchoke recorded as being among the species so traded. I recently met a northwestern hazelnut grower named Rick Valley who does just this. One day he had left out some five-gallon buckets full of sawdust near his hazelnut stand and discovered the squirrels had filled them with nuts. Now he sets out many sawdust buckets every year and allows the squirrels (usually the dreaded enemy of hazel farmers) to select the finest nuts and harvest and store them for him. He provides corn for their wages.

For me, this kind of practice is a tiny window into the complex and diverse edible landscapes that could surround our homes. Jonathan and I already have some beneficial interactions with neighborhood wildlife. Birds eat some of the fruit, but they eat insects, too. Opossums eat rotten fruit drops that would otherwise harbor pests and diseases. Even our squirrels, which are at times annoying, eat thousands of Norway maple seedlings every year. Without their efforts, Jonathan and I would be so stiff we could barely stand from the effort of weeding all those trees. Perhaps someday we'll find a way to harness the digging behavior of skunks or even "farm" Japanese beetles and convert more garden enemies into partners.

—— *from* ——

Growing Food in a Hotter, Drier Land

Lessons from Desert Farmers on Adapting to Climate Uncertainty

Gary Paul Nabhan

2013

Many of ethnobotanist Gary Nabhan's two dozen or so books deal with edible plants, but in recent years he has added the unpredictable nature of a changing global climate ("global weirding" as he calls it) to his other his-

torical, cultural, and culinary studies. In this book Nabhan draws upon his extensive travels through the world's desert regions, and his own experience gardening in the Sonoran Desert of southern Arizona, to reveal time-tested methods used by desert farmers, who have always had to adapt to a shifting and uncertain climate. These are lessons we can employ on our own gardens and farms, in terms of conserving water, selecting the best plants to grow, and other issues that have become increasingly important in times of extreme weather or drought. This book offers both parables and practical advice, and brings a positive approach to dealing with the challenges that many food producers will soon be facing, if they aren't already.

OVER HALF OF MY LIFE, I have gained considerable comfort and insight from the wisdom of the desert offered in the parables and proverbs of the monks, nuns, and hermits who left the comforts of civilization for the deserts of the Sceti and Nitria in Egypt. Even today, a thriving rural economy based on desert-adapted sustainable agriculture exists in Wadi al-Natrun in the heart of the Sahara Desert in North Africa. It is focused around monasteries rebuilt on the sites of ruins left behind by the first Desert Fathers in the fourth century AD. Whenever I have visited Wadi al-Natrun, I have come away elated by the fact that an ancient *desert-adapted* contemplative tradition has been revived there. More specifically, it has guided the emergence of an alternative food production and distribution network that now feeds hundreds of monks, as well as thousands of the food-insecure poor dwelling in Cairo and the upper reaches of the Aswan region.

It is clear that the desert hermits who historically lived near Wadi al-Natrun—the Dry River of Nitrate Salts—observed significant changes in climate and land conditions even in their day, and that they anticipated more to come. In a rather ominous story that is perhaps more pertinent today than it may have seemed 14 centuries ago, Abba Macarius the Great explains to the monks how to read the signs that will tell them whether their own desert is being devastated:

> When you realize that someone can come and build on dry ground right where you knew we once had a tiny marshland around a spring, know that the devastation of the Desert of Scetis is near. When you see a different kind of tree encroaching on the desert itself, know that dramatic changes have already arrived at our door. And when you see young children arriving as orphans and refugees in our midst, take up your sheepskin bed mats and flee . . .

I have been particularly moved by this story, because the monk who has twice shown me around Wadi al-Natrun is also named Macarius. When he first came to dwell in the desert, he adopted the name of that ancient camel-driver-turned-hermit in an act of inspiration. But monks like Macarius the Great—those who initially established the contemplative tradition in Wadi al-Natrun between AD 285 and 330—surely did not expect everyone to be able to live with the austerity of a truly desert-adapted life. Their admonitions remind us that not all of us may be mentally or emotionally equipped—at least at present—to patiently practice the kinds of desert survival strategies that got them through, but we can all metaphorically learn from their tradition nonetheless. One story told by the Coptic Christian monks of Wadi al-Natrun today offers all of us a way to learn from their desert experience:

There was once in our monastery a newcomer called Abba Gelasius who was often stricken by fear with just the mere thought of going to the desert to live the hermit's life. Disappointed with himself, he finally worked up the nerve to tell his brothers that he needed to do a trial run of desert living, but wanted to first practice the desert hermit's discipline within the confines of the monastery's walls. So he told the other monks not to bother him for a while if they saw him walking around this cloistered space in silence.

Abba Gelasius then began his mini-pilgrimage through the small patch of desert held within the monastery's walls. Although the other monks did not speak directly to him, he soon realized that his head was full of his own talk and fear. As he kept on talking to himself in his head, he pretended that he had actually ventured out into the surrounding desert.

He would proclaim to himself, "He who walks in the desert does not partake of oven-baked bread, but instead relies on wild desert herbs. So when one gets hungry and weary in the absence of bread, one must feel free to eat the sparsely-populated vegetables on the desert floor."

Abba Gelasius then ate the desert herbs and vegetables until he was no longer hungry, but his weariness persisted. And so he spoke to himself again, saying:

"He who becomes one with the desert has no need to lie in a bed, but should give up the fear of sleeping in the open air on the barren ground."

So he lay down and slept in the bare spaces within the monastery walls, as if he were truly out in the desert. He continued on his imaginary pilgrimage into the desert for three days more, constantly circling around within the walls of the monastery, eating desert chicory leaves wherever he found them and then sleeping in the open air whenever weariness took over.

Finally he realized what the matter was, and got to the root of what had troubled him and kept him from being a true desert hermit. It was not that every faithful soul should go out into the true desert to eke out a living, but that they should find a desert-like space and overcome their fear of it wherever they may already be dwelling. If he was not able to practice the way of the desert in his very own home place, there was no reason for him to venture out past the limits of his own capacities. He need not wander away into the Desert of the Sceti to become an ascetic. Instead, he needed to learn patience and tenacity in his everyday environs, humbly adapting to the place where his own lot had already been cast.

Perhaps Gelasius eventually learned a kind of patience exhibited by the most diligent of the Desert Fathers; that patience may also be the key trait that we need to cultivate in the face of climatic uncertainty.

—— *from* ——

The Resilient Farm and Homestead
An Innovative Permaculture and Whole Systems Design Approach
Ben Falk

2013

Winner of an American Horticultural Society Book Award, The Resilient Farm and Homestead *is a manual for developing durable, beautiful, and highly functional human habitat systems fit to handle an age of rapid transition. Author Ben Falk is a land designer and site developer whose permaculture-research farm has drawn national attention. The site is a terraced paradise on a hillside in Vermont that would otherwise be overlooked by conventional farmers as unworthy farmland. Falk's wide array of fruit trees, rice paddies (relatively unheard of in the Northeast), ducks, nuts, and earth-inspired buildings is a hopeful image for the future of regenerative agriculture and modern home- steading, and pushes forward the conversation of permaculture design and small-scale farming that can weather the storms to come.*

WHY ARE TREES—ESPECIALLY NUT TREES—at the basis of these regenerative land-use systems and highly adapted human cultures? In the simplest terms it has to do with inputs and outputs. A nut tree is simply more effective *and* efficient at converting sunlight and precipitation into value, over the long term, than any other technology humans have yet designed. This becomes clear when comparing biological systems in general with nonliving technol- ogies. Consider a photovoltaic panel or wind turbine, for example. Each requires large and damaging inputs to generate single outputs. What are the inputs for a photovoltaic panel? For one thing, bauxite from which to smelt the aluminum frame, as well as silicon and numerous other minerals (many only found in a dwindling number of difficult-to-access places on the planet). These all must be mined, transported, refined, transported again, then fabricated, then shipped again. All for one output: electricity.

What are the inputs required for a nut tree? At most an exchange between breeder and planter, transporting of the seed or seedling, some wood chip mulch, rain, and sunshine. And *time*. What are its yields? Oxygen, soil, wildlife habitat, moisture retention, carbon sequestration, air and water enhancement, human food, stock feed, building materials, shade, windbreak, and beauty, to name a few. The former resource path of the photovoltaic panel—the abiotic—provides us with a practical service at great cost. The latter, biological (or "soft") path creates an enduring and generative legacy of positive value. And whereas a solar panel, wind turbine, or green building offers diminishing yields over time, a nut tree's output actually increases, for at least the first century or two of its lifetime.

Such is the power—and imperative—of biological systems: They are the only means we have of sidestepping entropy, at least for significant periods of time, on this planet. That's what tips the balance; it all comes down to capture, storage, and transfer. The most functional human-land arrangement is the one that can harvest the most sunlight, moisture, atmospheric fertility, and biological energies, then accrue that value for the longest period of time while converting some of it into products and services that other living things, such as humans, can feed on. Biological systems do this very well, while nonliving mechanical systems cannot.

In the modern era enough research has been done to quantify the advantage of cropping with trees over annual crops. Accepted yields for chestnut, for example, are eight hundred to fifteen hundred pounds per acre. That rivals modern corn production on deep-soil land. However, corn only produces such a crop with constant labor and fertility inputs each year, while reducing the land's capacity to produce because of its erosive forces on the soil. A chestnut orchard, on the other hand, actually improves the land's (and climate's) capacity from year to year *while* it yields; it requires no bare soil or off-site fertility inputs, and it produces hundreds of crops from each plant on marginal, shallow-soiled land (far more of the earth's cover type than deep-soiled land), while taking up less space than corn. And you can crop the same area with other species simultaneously; for example, a chestnut orchard is *also* a pasture, *also* a game preserve/farm, *also* a place for understory berries and medicinal crops.

All in all, you can grow three to eight times the product value (protein, fat, carbohydrate, Btus and other nutrients/values) via a tree crop system than with an annual, input-dependent crop such as corn, and you can do so while improving the land from decade to decade. Indeed, tree cropping and ecological restoration can be performed simultaneously. Annual cropping the same land, year after year, however, usually leads to a ruined soil and culture, even on flat lands (and always on steep lands unless it's rice). Mesopotamia, much of Greece, and many other empires were once forested; now, they are deserts.

Despite abundant human cleverness, we haven't invented a better way to store energy than a stack of firewood. We haven't yet devised a more effective means of capturing solar energy than by putting up a cow and hay in a barn through the winter. Biological energy harvesting and storage is what has allowed us to survive to this point, and our experiments of replacing biological systems with mechanical and chemical systems have at best been delayed catastrophes. We must rely on some nonbiological aspects (the barn in the previous example), but wherever we do we compromise the system and our own returns in the long term. The minute a barn is built, it begins to decay. The famous comparison of a tractor with a draft horse highlights the entropy principle at work here: A tractor and horse are comparable in the amount of work they can achieve on a small piece of land, yet after a time the tractor dies and the horse makes another horse. Only life processes are regenerative. Hence, our prospects for thriving on this planet depend on our ability to partner with life forces.

—— *from* ——

Organic Mushroom Farming and Mycoremediation

Simple to Advanced and Experimental Techniques for Indoor and Outdoor Cultivation

Tradd Cotter

2014

Organic Mushroom Farming and Mycoremediation is an ambitious book, one that sets out to do far more than teach readers how to successfully grow a range of mushrooms. Although he does provide the foundation for successful cultivation, what makes Tradd Cotter's work so unique is that he approaches it with a spirit of constant innovation and experimentation, so that on any given day he might be testing out different kinds of mushroom-infused beers, growing oysters on old blue jeans, thinking through the practicalities of growing mushrooms in space, and testing the potential of mushrooms for use as a low-cost source of food and environmental cleanup in the wake of natural or manmade disasters. He not only shares his ideas and research results but also helps readers understand fungi so that they can independently, and successfully, pursue their own goals and experimentation.

ALTHOUGH THE ANCIENT EGYPTIANS are credited with pioneering the use of yeasts to create beer, wine, and bread, and historical records indicate that cultivation of many edible and medicinal mushroom species dates back over four thousand years in Japan and China, humans are not the only—or even the first—fungal cultivators on the planet. Recent discoveries have estimated that South American leaf-cutting ants have been actively culturing fungi for forty-five to fifty-five million years. In their colonies, specialized worker ants harvest and shred leaves to make a fungal growing medium. The larvae feed on the fungi; the mycelium is rich in protein and provides the ants with a natural antibiotic that helps them combat a dangerous pathogen. When a new queen rises to start a fresh colony, she carries with her a pellet of mycelium, much like a starter culture, stored in an infrabuccal pouch (a cavity in her mouth). Like this new ant queen, guardian of the mushroom spores and thus of the capacity for perpetual food production, humans too have been bestowed with the gift of mushrooms. We just need to learn to use it.

Although fungi are often somewhat neglected as a kingdom—perhaps in part because they tend to be less visible than plants and animals—they have critical ecological roles, and they interact with their environments in compelling and sometimes surprising ways. Mycorrhizal fungal relationships, for example, are obligate partnerships between plants and fungi at the root interface underground. Some examples of mycorrhizal mushrooms include truffles (*Tuber* spp.), chanterelles (*Cantharellus* spp.), and porcini (*Boletus edulis*). This specialized relationship allows fungi to thread into and around cell walls in the root tips, increasing the surface area within the cell and in the surrounding soil, where nutrients are absorbed and transported to the plant roots. I call this the original carbon trading scheme, where the mycelium collects a resource that the plant has a difficult time procuring and trades it for sugar, which the plant produces as a product of photosynthesis. Within these soil interfaces are countless layers of interkingdom interactions that connect bacteria, fungi, plants, and animals to maintain a dynamic microcosm of constant nutrient exchange and balance.

Not all fungal relationships are mutually beneficial, however. Some types of fungi are capable of attacking other living organisms, such as *Cordyceps* spp., which attack and mummify many kinds of insects and then fruit out of the insects' body. Some molds, including some *Trichoderma* spp., are considered mycoparasites, or fungal pathogens. They possess the enzyme chitinase, which breaks down chitin, a compound found in the cell walls of fungi and various insects and soil organisms. In short, they are designed to attack and digest their fellow fungi. Many strains of *Trichoderma* in my collection are now being used in trials at a local vineyard investigating their ability to help grapevines combat leaf, trunk, and root pathogens. The growers inoculate the vines with *Trichoderma*, and the mold imparts an immune response to the plants, which then synthesize their own compounds designed for targeting a wide spectrum of fungal pathogens.

Eumycota, or "true fungi"—as opposed to slime and water molds, which are not technically part of the fungi kingdom—share many common characteristics, including reproduction by means of spores, a lack of chlorophyll, and the presence of chitin—a hard natural substance that provides structure and protection—in their cell walls. Fungi produce and secrete many different kinds of extracellular enzymes, such as lignin peroxidase, manganese peroxidase, laccases, amylases, and cellulases. Think of these enzymes as "chemical scissors" or "molecular keys" that cut or unlock the bonds of large molecules, such as lignin, embedded in woody plant tissue. As the mushroom's enzymes break down its growing substrate, the smaller, essential chemical units in the substrate, such as carbon, organic nitrogen, minerals, and other trace elements, are released and are transported through the fungi's cell walls for use as energy sources and for metabolic function.

In this process, fungal cells first stream outward into the environment—the "infantry cells," as I like to think of them—and communicate back to the body of the mycelium, instructing it to produce enzymes specific to the kind of food available and what will be needed to break down those particular compounds. Fungi sweat these "cell-free" enzymes, meaning that the enzymes are able to saturate and move freely into the environment to degrade the organic substances before the actual fungal filaments reach them. Bacteria, by contrast, must contact their food source directly, making use of surface receptors that disassemble and transport their food source directly across their membranes. Fungi's amazing chemical consciousness and profound ability to adapt and react quickly to the environment are part of what makes them so captivating.

—— *from* ——

Integrated Forest Gardening

The Complete Guide to Polycultures and Plant Guilds in Permaculture Systems

Wayne Weisman, Daniel Halsey, and Bryce Ruddock

2014

Permaculture as a movement is coming into its own, and one of its essential practices is to develop perennial agricultural systems that thrive over several decades without expensive and harmful inputs: perennial plant guilds, food forests, agroforestry, and mixed animal and woody species polycultures. The guild concept often used in permaculture is one of "functional relationships" among plants—beneficial groupings of plants that share functions in order to bring health and stability to a plant regime and create an abundant yield for our utilization. In other words, it is the integration of species that creates a balanced, healthy, and thriving ecosystem. Integrated Forest Gardening covers in detail both what guilds are and how to design and construct them.

PERMACULTURE DESIGN MUST ADDRESS CHANGES in our climate over years or decades. We cannot resist the change or facilitate these changes, at least in our environment concerning plants and animals. Still, we can build more resilient ecosystems that have the ability to adapt over time. The speed at which climate change happens will fluctuate with increases and decreases in temperature. So if you consider that water freezes at 32°F (0°C) and condenses in the air at the dew point, that insects need a certain number of degree-days to emerge, and that plants need a certain amount of light and warmth for maturity, you see that 1°F (0.5°C) can make the difference between snow and rain and the loss of a crop. Our design work must reflect change over time. This can be best accomplished by incorporating as diverse a palette of plants in the landscape as possible, sculpted to retain resources and buffer extremes.

Diversity buffers the extremes in long-term change. A diversity of plants will build a resilient ecosystem, though some plants respond more slowly than others. The canopy shields and takes the brunt of the external conditions, supported by the understory, but a few years of drought can decimate an unprotected stand of trees (one with very little understory). Should this happen in a well-designed plan, the canopy will open, other plants will advance, and the old trees will fall and become organic matter on the forest floor, thus increasing the available water capacity for the other plants shooting up in their wake. It becomes a self-supporting and adaptive system no matter what the future brings.

It would also be fruitful for us to adapt our expectations to changing resource availability, limiting our consumption and developing an attitude of intermittent abundance. For example, all summer our landscapes stockpile organic material and nutrients on and above the soil. While most of us are getting our food needs met based on seasonal availability, this abundance is coming to an end very quickly. Eventually we will have to change our diet and lifestyle to conform to a whole new set of environmental conditions. Perhaps we will need to become more like the plants and animals, less about on-demand resource availability and more about a catch-and-store, pick-and-preserve, cut-and-dry pattern of living.

We often get asked the question: How does the scale of climate change affect guild design? The answer is that it totally depends upon the design and its components. In one orchard, for example, you might have alpine strawberries, tiny little fruiting perennials that seem insignificant in comparison with the five apple trees and plethora of ground cover species. These strawberry plants—which have established themselves without any intervention on your part—make a lot of seed. You will undoubtedly notice over time that a small alpine strawberry is growing hundreds of feet away from the original planting, probably the result of a seed cast by some bird or chipmunk. Although many of the original strawberry plants may be gone as a result of the apple trees' crowding and shade, they continue to cast an influence throughout your property. In a similar fashion, it is also possible that a volunteer apple tree sprouts and sets fruit on the opposite side of your house from the orchard. When you bring in any plant, if it can establish itself it has a one in ten chance of continued propagation.

Investment in research and development of ecological systems has focused primarily on highly controlled niches in the temperate climate and uncontrolled niches in severe climates. One of the goals of this book is to raise interest and research into ecologically sound and sustainable food production in the uncontrolled niche.

If we till up a backyard and plant a garden for one season and do not plant it again, it's pretty easy to see that the garden will be taken back by grass and weeds, and if mown will probably look like the rest of the yard within a few years.

When you think about it, all we are doing as designers is moving things around. It's much like redesigning our living room using the same furniture, or perhaps bringing some in from another room. By planting polycultures we are developing functional living systems that are self-supporting and enhance available ecological services. We influence the structure of the niche and the patch, allowing for the cycling of nutrients as we buffer environmental changes. Whether that landscape design will last for years or centuries is up to the next occupant, but for the most part, if the landscape design is ecologically sound, it's less likely to be disturbed by humans and more likely resilient enough to adapt to new circumstances.

Over time the species in our guilds may change—some come in, some go out—but the structure will still support whatever plants occupy the space, when it's designed well. Hopefully, with maintenance provided by animals as they harvest the nutrients and contribute their services, the design will expand and transition into other spaces, and additional plants and animals will benefit. The designed plot of land is influencing external ecological spaces as it is dependent upon them for genetic diversity and ecological integrity.

Climate disruption and climate change have accelerated to the point that a new issue has arisen: At this rate of change, plants and animals will not be able to reproduce and sustain the generations required in order to adapt. Although a great amount of genetic material exists in the world, with many possibilities for mutation, the process needs time. Intermittent disturbances that stress plants and ecological systems accelerate the genetic mutations that aid in this process. Fast and extreme changes, however, may not allow for natural adaptation by native plants over time; thus natural selection favors more resilient opportunistic species that may not be endemic to a particular bioregion.

As a result of rapid change, researchers are planting trees in the Boundary Waters Canoe Area of Minnesota to see what happens to hardwood trees over the next twenty years and how this affects the ecosystem compared with areas where sudden changes have not taken place. We need to continue such research to gain a macro perspective across a wide landscape. If you can imagine what the ecosystem in your region looked like five hundred years ago and then think of how it might have been able to adapt to changes in climate, you will realize that many of the related ecological services do not exist anymore—the grazers that controlled so-called invasive species and plant life have been exterminated; rivers have been moved and deepened; huge spaces of wetlands and trees have been leveled and filled. On the other hand, whatever happens, something will be here eventually that is adapted to the new conditions. There may be a time of great change, but if the soil is stable and organic material is present with its myriad microorganisms, a new ecosystem will emerge; over time, so will wildlife adapted to it.

We have seen areas where alien, non-native species seem to just pop up and take over. Are these invasive? What is an invasive species? It has been said that the only invasive species on earth is the human being. The dandelion has been in the United States for upward of eight hundred years. Is this thriving lawn plant any more or less "native" to this country than, say, a bur oak tree? The movement of peoples all over the face of the planet necessitates the movement of all species, plant, animal, and human. The horse was endemic to this country until it was made extinct in ancient times. It was reintroduced to this continent by the Spanish in the 1500s. Is it native or alien? This shift in biological populations is inevitable and has happened throughout time. Opportunistic species fill niches and thrive where others cannot. The natural succession of a forest may begin with "alien" plants and mature into a stately forest in the long term. Invasive? Good or bad? If we step back, take in a wider perspective, and attempt to understand the broader cycles of evolution and growth of the natural world, we may find that the so-called invasives are simply doing their job: setting up the infrastructure and building healthy soil for another ecosystem to come to fruition in all its richness and diversity.

SCIENCE &
ENVIRONMENTAL
POLICY

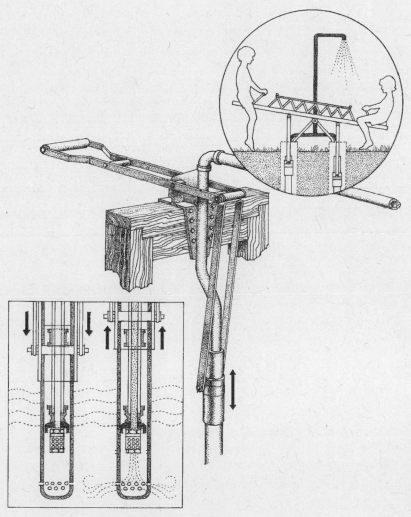

Gaviotas Manual Sleeve Pump

MICHAEL MIDDLETON

End of the Road

From World Car Crisis and How We Can Solve It

Wolfgang Zuckermann

1991

In this 1991 book Wolfgang Zuckermann, a Paris-based researcher for EcoPlan International, confronts our love affair with our automobiles in a thorough and well-reasoned argument. Though a few details have changed slightly in recent years (hybrid and solar electric cars come to mind), the author's prescriptions about redesigning cities, suburbs, and our transportation systems still ring true. However, he also offers smaller steps we all could take to reduce our environmental and carbon footprints.

ALL OF THIS HAPPENED IN ONE CENTURY, a split second of geological time. In that period we have changed the face of the globe from that of a rosy-cheeked young boy to the shriveled face depicted in the picture of Dorian Gray. We have covered the earth with asphalt scars and wrinkles where once were beckoning earth lanes, grassy tracks, and color- and texture-rich paving stones.

What we lost in this process of change is what the American forester and planner Benton MacKaye sixty years ago called "connectedness," our direct link to the earth and its landscapes, three of which—city, country, and wilderness—he considered to be essential for the maintenance of our psychic health and well-being.

Gradually, and without our ever being aware of it, the car has literally disconnected us from the ground we walk on by putting us in a closed metal container with four wheels. One might argue that the post chaise did the same; but, as so often in car-related issues, better is worse. The car encloses us more fully, drives us more smoothly, and speeds us faster through the landscape and in vastly greater numbers than the horse-drawn cart, making our isolation considerably more complete.

MacKaye wrote about the effect that making or breaking daily landscape connections has on the lives of large populations. He held that our lives are diminished whenever our connections with any one "elemental environment" are blurred or broken.

"Together," he wrote, the three environments we need "seem to form . . . a complete and rounded external world adapted to man's psychological needs.

Depletion in any one of them means a corresponding depletion in man's life." MacKaye considered that the personality of a place evaporates when development covers an area with "structures whose individual hideousness and collective haphazardness present that unmistakable environment we call . . . the slum of commerce." The car's contribution to such landscape deterioration is threefold: first, it is largely responsible for this "individual hideousness and collective haphazardness" that MacKaye talks about by allowing structures to be scattered about in no particular order with a sea of parked vehicles around them; secondly, and more surreptitiously, it isolates us and speeds us through these very same landscapes so that we lose our distaste for them and they bother us less; and finally, having created the nondescript landscape and having isolated us from it, the car then gives us the means to leave such an area behind and embark on a search for an unspoiled landscape eventually to be blighted in its turn.

—— *from* ——

Limits to Growth

The 30-Year Update

Donella Meadows, Jorgen Randers, and Dennis Meadows

Originally published as *Beyond the Limits* in 1992; second edition, 2004

In 1972 three scientists from MIT created a computer model that analyzed global resource consumption and production. Their results shocked the world and created conversation about global "overshoot," or resource use beyond the carrying capacity of the planet. Three decades later the same pre-eminent environmental scientists—Donella Meadows, Jorgen Randers, and Dennis Meadows—teamed up again to update and expand their original findings in Limits to Growth: The 30-Year Update. *Citing climate change as the most tangible example of our current overshoot, the authors offer a plan to reduce our needs to meet the carrying capacity of the planet.*

The Next Revolution: Sustainability

It is as impossible now for anyone to describe the world that could evolve from a sustainability revolution as it would have been for the farmers of 6000 BC to foresee the corn and soybean fields of modern Iowa, or for an English coal miner of AD 1800 to imagine an automated Toyota assembly line. Like the other great revolutions, the coming sustainability revolution will also change the face of the land and the foundations of human identities, institutions, and cultures. Like the previous revolutions, it will take centuries to unfold fully—though it is already underway.

Of course no one knows how to bring about such a revolution. There is not a checklist: "To accomplish a global paradigm shift, follow these 20 steps." Like the great revolutions that came before, this one can't be planned or dictated. It won't follow a list of fiats from government or a proclamation from computer modelers. The sustainability revolution will be organic. It will arise from the visions, insights, experiments, and actions of billions of people. The burden of making it happen is not on the shoulders of any one person or group. No one will get the credit, but everyone can contribute.

Our systems training and our own work in the world have affirmed for us two properties of complex systems germane to the sort of profound revolution we are discussing here.

First, information is the key to transformation. That does not necessarily mean *more* information, better statistics, bigger databases, or the World Wide Web, though all of these may play a part. It means *relevant, compelling, select, powerful, timely, accurate* information flowing in new ways to new recipients, carrying new content, suggesting new rules and goals (rules and goals that are themselves information). When its information flows are changed, any system will behave differently. The policy of *glasnost*, for example—the simple opening of information channels that had long been closed in the Soviet Union—guaranteed the rapid transformation of Eastern Europe beyond anyone's expectations. The old system had been held in place by tight control of information. Letting go of that control triggered total system restructuring (turbulent and unpredictable, but inevitable).

Second, systems strongly resist changes in their information flows, especially in their rules and goals. It is not surprising that those who benefit from the current system actively oppose such revision. Entrenched political, economic, and religious cliques can constrain almost entirely the attempts of an individual or small group to operate by different rules or to attain goals different from those sanctioned by the system. Innovators can be ignored, marginalized, ridiculed, denied promotions or resources or public voices. They can be literally or figuratively snuffed out.

Only innovators, however—by perceiving the need for new information, rules, and goals, communicating about them, and trying them out—can make the changes that transform systems. This important point is expressed clearly in a quote that is widely attributed to Margaret Mead, "Never deny the power of a small group of committed individuals to change the world. Indeed that is the only thing that ever has."

We have learned the hard way that it is difficult to live a life of material moderation within a system that expects, exhorts, and rewards consumption. But one can move a long way in the direction of moderation. It is not easy to use energy efficiently in an economy that produces energy-inefficient products. But one can search out, or if necessary invent, more efficient ways of doing things, and in the process make those ways more accessible to others.

Above all, it is difficult to put forth new information in a system that is structured to hear only old information. Just try, sometime, to question in public the value of more growth, or even to make a distinction between growth and development, and you will see what we mean. It takes courage and clarity to challenge an established system. But it can be done.

In our own search for ways to encourage the peaceful restructuring of a system that naturally resists its own transformation, we have tried many tools. The obvious ones are displayed through this book—rational analysis, data gathering, systems thinking, computer modeling, and the clearest words we can find. Those are tools that anyone trained in science and economics would automatically grasp. Like recycling, they are useful, necessary, and they are not enough.

We don't know what will be enough. But we would like to conclude by mentioning five other tools we have found *helpful*. We introduced and discussed this list for the first time in our 1992 book [*Beyond the Limits*]. Our experience since then has affirmed that these five tools are not optional; they are essential characteristics for any society that hopes to survive over the long term. We present them here again in our concluding chapter "not as *the* ways to work toward sustainability, but as *some* ways."

"We are a bit hesitant to discuss them," we said in 1992, "because we are not experts in their use and because they require the use of words that do not come easily from the mouths or word processors of scientists. They are considered too 'unscientific' to be taken seriously in the cynical public arena."

What are the tools we approached so cautiously? They are: visioning, networking, truth-telling, learning, and loving. It seems like a feeble list, given the enormity of the changes required.

But each of these exists within a web of positive loops. Thus their persistent and consistent application initially by a relatively small group of people would have the potential to produce enormous change—even to challenge the present system, perhaps helping to produce a revolution.

"The transition to a sustainable society might be helped," we said in 1992, "by the simple use of words like these more often, with sincerity and without apology, in the information streams of the world." But we used them with apology ourselves, knowing how most people would receive them.

Many of us feel uneasy about relying on such "soft" tools when the future of our civilization is at stake, particularly since we do not know how to summon them up, in ourselves or in others. So we dismiss them and turn the conversation to recycling or emission trading or wildlife preserves or some other necessary but insufficient part of the sustainability revolution—but at least a part we know how to handle.

——— *from* ———

Gaviotas

A Village to Reinvent the World

Alan Weisman

1998

Author Alan Weisman, who went on to write the international bestseller The World Without Us *(2007), tells the story of the Colombian architect and visionary Paolo Lugari, who created a small community of like-minded scientists and engineers in Colombia's remote and barren eastern savanna (llano) in the 1970s and 1980s. The community, Gaviotas, became one of the world's most celebrated examples of the possibilities for sustainable technology and development in an unforgiving Third World environment. In the 1990s UN and other government funding dried up and the Gaviotans had to become self-sufficient. This excerpt tells the story of how this amazing community accomplished the feat.*

PAOLO HAD BROUGHT THE IDEA BACK from Venezuela, where he'd heard an agronomist mention the hardiness of *Pinus caribaea*, the tropical pine that grew in a variety of soils throughout Central America. Zethelius obtained seedlings from Guatemala, Nicaragua, Belize, and Honduras. So far, everything was still alive and even getting taller, with the Hondurensis variety still performing the best. Sven's little plot of foot-high, long-needle pines became a Gaviotas curiosity.

"What will we do with pine trees?" an engineer asked him.

"Who knows? At the very least, we'll learn something from them. What did we do with your five-meter solar engine?"

Like Pompilio Arciniegas, Otoniel Carreno had been a government forester who was lent to Gaviotas for a year and then never left. When he first arrived, eight years earlier, they weren't dunking the roots in dissolved clay or pruning seedlings before transplanting, because nobody was doing that. At Gaviotas, however, people were prone to fiddle and experiment, and so he was doing nearly everything the opposite from what he'd been taught. Everybody else transported seedlings between nursery and plantation with their roots protected in black polyethylene bags, but the Gaviotans had reasoned that in the tropics, plastic bags get hot inside. Switching to clay had lowered seedling mortality below five percent—a third of what the forestry literature predicted—and saved them the expense and pollution of the plastic.

Likewise, they'd noticed that unpruned roots often got bent when transplanted, and they figured that this might slow a young tree's development. No one could be sure if this were so, but eight-year-old trees in the Gaviotas forest were already taller than fifty feet.

Otoniel led Gonzalo to a bed of three-year-old seedlings, left unharvested at the nursery's southern edge during an old experiment, to show him the latest infraction of conventional forestry wisdom. It was a scattering of brown puffball mushrooms, barely more than an inch across. Underground, fungi such as these form a relationship with the roots of baby pine trees, a bond as vital to the growth of the forest as a neural synapse is to the execution of a thought. Their scientific designation is *Pizolithus tinctorius*, but Otoniel and every schoolchild in Gaviotas referred to them by the name of a natural symbiotic exchange that allowed the pines—and their community—to survive. "Those," he announced proudly, "are mycorrhiza."

"Here?" said Gonzalo. "You're kidding."

Back in 1982, Sven Zethelius had suspected that Caribbean pines would require the help of mycorrhiza to digest the *llanos* soil, and had obtained and injected dashes of desiccated fungi around the roots of the first experimental seedlings. When Otoniel and Henry Moya went to Venezuela to study commercial pine cultivation a few years later, foresters there confirmed that without a mycorrhiza fungus, their plantation would fail—and that the one they needed didn't occur naturally in the *llanos*.

While they were there, a Caracas company donated three kilos of *Pizolithus tinctorius* from the United States to Gaviotas, worth nearly two thousand dollars, enough to get their project underway. They'd learned to apply it, dosing month-old trees with water mixed with fine brown powder made from crushed mushroom caps. Soon, little white chains of mycorrhiza fungus formed on the roots, creating the biochemistry needed for them to absorb whatever nutrients were available.

Then, something unexpected occurred. The foresters who ran the pine plantations in the Venezuelan *llanos* needed to reapply the mixture repeatedly. But once trees in Gaviotas were inoculated with mycorrhiza mixture, they never seemed to require more. Each time Pompilio or Otoniel dug up a specimen, the roots were webbed with thriving, healthy fungus—so healthy, it turned out, that now, after a few years, the mushrooms had begun to reproduce in Gaviotas. As Oto and Gonzalo picked their way along the long bed of pines, they found the little brown caps popping up everywhere. "We have our own mycorrhiza bank," Otoniel said. "This wasn't supposed to happen."

"Wonderful! Any idea why?"

The biggest difference between them and the Venezuelans, Oto speculated, was that Gaviotas wasn't using herbicide to eradicate extraneous foliage that inevitable sprang up in the pine rows. As in weeding a garden, routine forestry practice requires cleaning underbrush that might compete with or actually displace the cash crop. Partly to avoid chemical sprays, partly due to cost and labor, partly out of curiosity, Gaviotas hadn't bothered to eliminate the other growth in one of their earliest experimental stands of pine. Since they weren't adding fertilizer, they reasoned that the surrounding savanna grasses might contribute some nourishment to the meager, two-centimeter-thick soils. As the pines grew surprisingly fast, there seemed no need to weed subsequent plantings, even when all kinds of vines, shrubs, and woody plants began emerging in the moist, cool shade of the spreading pine boughs.

Several years later, they would realize how monumental this casual decision to let nature take its course would prove to be.

Once it had been established that Caribbean pines would thrive in the *llanos* where nothing else seemed to, the question facing Gaviotas was what to do with them. Mill lumber? Produce wood pulp? Maybe one day there would be a demand in the *llanos* for these, but so far, masses weren't streaming over the Andes into the savanna, in need of construction materials for new homes. Paper companies in Cali already produced plenty of pulp-wood, and soft timber that had to be hauled sixteen hours over horrendous roads and steep mountains wouldn't be very competitive. It was Paolo Lugari who'd spotted a newspaper article that mentioned a scarcity in Europe of natural gum and colophony, the resinous ooze found under the surface of pine bark. Production in traditional sources such as Portugal and Spain had fallen as labor-intensive resin collection became too expensive in the European community, and as petroleum-based substitutes became available. Nevertheless, demand was growing for the natural stuff, especially for use in quality paints, glues, cosmetics, perfume, and medicines.

From the Venezuelans, they learned that tapping into the resin of Caribbean pines was viable, but the trees needed first to mature for at least twenty years. Nevertheless, by 1990 their eight-year-old pines, still sprouting vigorously from an increasingly tangled understory, were already 20 percent taller than the predicted heights for trees their age. Once again, Gaviotas set to experimenting.

They scraped away outer bark and pruned the branches two meters up the trunk of their oldest pines, as they'd been instructed. Using a Portuguese hand tool that was part hatchet, part hammer, they made incisions in the exposed bark and stapled thick plastic bags, also imported from Portugal, to the trees and let them fill with the sticky amber fluid. Every twelve days they made a new cut, slightly higher than the last, and applied a sulfurous black paste they'd purchased from the Venezuelans to keep the incision from closing. At the end of thirty-six days, their yield of golden resin was, according to the manuals, what they should be getting from trees twenty-five years old.

In Colombia alone, companies making paints and varnishes had been importing four million dollars' worth of pine resin a year. "Not any more," Lugari told a meeting of all the Gaviotans. Their Caribbean pines had turned out to be veritable nutrient pumps, machines that processed light and water into a forest product for which he had already identified a willing clientele. "Gaviotas will still be in the solar energy business," Paolo announced. "Whether we do it with solar collectors or with trees, our future is to transform sunlight into energy."

Best of all, like solar energy, the resin was renewable. Otoniel explained that it wasn't the sap they were drawing, but a fluid produced by the bark that acted like a natural insecticide, protecting the tree from wood-boring ants and other pests. They could safely tap a pine for at least eight years, working their way up the trunk on all four sides, two years to a side, then resting the tree for another eight years, then beginning again. This would mean never having to chop their forest down in order to make a living from it. And, like an extra bonus for finding a way to have their resource and profit from it too, when they heated raw resin to purify it, the residue they extracted was another marketable by-product: clear turpentine.

—— *from* ——

Exposed

The Toxic Chemistry of Everyday Products and What's at Stake for American Power

Mark Schapiro

2007

When award-winning investigative journalist Mark Schapiro wrote Exposed, *Americans were waking up to the fact that many of their household products and cosmetics were exposing them to an array of hazards—including rising rates of infertility, endocrine system disruptions, neurological disorders, and cancer. But they weren't aware, for the most part, that citizens in Europe were being protected from these threats as the EU countries actively legislated away dangerous ingredients like Bisphenol A (BPA) and plastic-softening phthalates. Nor were they aware that the environmental progress under way in Europe was prompting innovation and enabling their firms to beat American companies in the global competition for markets. This eloquent and hard-hitting narrative explores the intersection of environment, economics, and politics and warns of the market loss American companies would suffer if they focused more on lobbying to keep toxic products legal than on creating nontoxic alternatives that could compete in the global arena.*

EVERY MORNING ACROSS AMERICA, tens of millions of women apply from twelve to twenty "personal-care" products to themselves, according to the Cosmetic, Toiletry and Fragrance Association (CTFA). From tubes and bottles and delicate brushes come the tools of beauty, hygiene, and self-preservation known as cosmetics. American women might assume that somebody has been watching to ensure that potential toxins in those ingredients are kept away from intimate contact with the body's largest organ, the skin. They would be wrong. The FDA provides oversight and monitoring of over-the-counter and prescription drugs, as well as food additives, but it has minimal authority to regulate the ingredients in cosmetics.

"Women believe that the government which they think is there is actually there," comments Charlotte Brody, a registered nurse and executive director of Commonweal, an environmental-health organization. "But it's not there."

Back in 1938, when the mandate of the Food and Drug Administration was expanded by Congress to give it authority over drugs and food additives, industry lobbying succeeded in blocking the agency from requiring testing of cosmetics. That hasn't changed for seventy years. Procter & Gamble and other industry giants—like Revlon, Unilever, Estée Lauder, and others—have successfully opposed every effort to broaden the FDA's mandate to include cosmetics. Since the governing principles of the FDA were established some seventy years ago, entirely new disciplines of science have emerged to study the long-term effects of chemicals on the human body. But the FDA's authority over these substances has changed little. This vacuum at the heart of America's regulatory apparatus is not difficult to discover: it's right on the agency's web site. "FDA's legal authority over cosmetics is different from other products regulated by the agency, such as drugs, biologics, and medical devices," reads a statement by the agency's Bureau of Colors and Cosmetics. "Cosmetic products and ingredients are not subject to FDA pre-market approval authority. . . . Cosmetic firms are responsible for substantiating the safety of their products and ingredients before marketing." The FDA makes one exception to this open door: it does require premarketing review for color additives.

The closest U.S. equivalent to the EU's "scientific committees" comes not from government, but from the industry's lobbying and public-relations arm. In 1976, as Congress debated strengthening the mandate of the FDA, the CTFA argued to maintain its exemption from scrutiny and promised to police itself. The trade group created a Cosmetics Ingredient Review (CIR) board, a panel of scientists that convenes three times a year in Washington to review the literature on chemicals used in cosmetics. The panel is financed entirely by the CTFA's member companies. Their recommendations to the industry are only that—and are not necessarily listened to in any case. The CIR's opinions are available on the Web; they list several ingredients that the board identified as substances of concern that have yet to be removed from U.S. cosmetics. These include coal tar, a black hair dye that the University of Southern California School of Medicine says may be linked to bladder cancer among hairdressers and is still used in many low-cost beauty salons; and sodium borate, sometimes called boric acid, which has been linked to testicular development problems and which the CIR recommended "should not be used on infant or injured skin," and is an ingredient in Desitin diaper-rash lotion for infants, according to a Household Products Database maintained by the U.S. National Library of Medicine.

By contrast, in Europe the scientific committees deliver their findings to the Health and Consumer Protection Directorate, the EU body charged with overseeing consumer-product safety, which determines what if any action to take if a risk has been identified. The critical distinction between the U.S. and European systems, according to David Vogel, the University of California–Berkeley economist who has compared the approaches to cosmetic regulation, is that in Europe scientists act independently of the government or industry, and politicians, operating under the precautionary principle, may take action on potential risks even before an absolute scientific consensus has been reached.

In the United States, however, there is no disinterested party assessing a product's potential toxicity before it is sold and ultimately applied to your skin. That doesn't mean that a product is unsafe, but neither is there any independent affirmation that it is safe. One FDA rule, for example, requires that warning labels be put on products that contain ingredients "whose safety has not been determined." But it is the cosmetic companies, not the FDA, that make that determination. While the cosmetic companies assert that their products are safe, 89 percent of the ingredients used in cosmetics today have not been assessed by either the FDA or by industry. Nor are there clear guidelines defining what is meant by "safe." When it comes to chemicals in food, for example, the Environmental Protection Agency is mandated to impose restrictions on pesticides to ensure that the danger of getting cancer from exposure to a carcinogenic pesticide is limited to one in one million. No such standards are applied to cosmetics. Jane Houlihan, an environmental engineer and research director at the Environmental Working Group, a Washington, D.C.–based NGO, characterizes the ingredient-review board's focus as emphasizing acute symptoms, rather than more chronic, accumulative health effects. "The [CIR] boards look at things like eye and skin irritation, factors which most directly affect what people buy, and not what the long-term implications might be."

John Bailey, a chemist and former director of the FDA's Office of Cosmetics and Colors, who is now executive vice president for science at the CTFA, disputes that description. In a telephone interview in April 2007, he told me that the CIR's seven members—three dermatologists, two toxicologists, a nutritional scientist, and a veterinarian—"are knowledgeable about risk and risk assessments. If you have a checklist, you don't need experts. Experts apply their expert knowledge, and their findings are disseminated to the world."

The seventh amendment to the EU's Cosmetics Directive spoiled the laissez-faire party that the cosmetic industry had enjoyed around the world for the better part of a century. Those ingredient reviews never conducted by the FDA in Washington are now being conducted by the "scientific committees," overseen by the Health and Consumer Protection Directorate in Brussels. Their results are posted publicly on the Web. You can take a look yourself and check the ingredient lists on the tubes and bottles on your own bathroom shelf against the toxicity reviews conducted by the European Union.

When the Environmental Working Group (EWG) compared the ingredient lists in over fourteen thousand personal-care products to lists of potential chemical hazards compiled by the EPA, FDA, the International Agency for Research on Cancer, the European Chemicals Bureau, and thirty other scientific and regulatory institutions around the world, their discoveries were a revelation. The EWG found hundreds of varieties of skin and tanning lotions, nail polish and mascara and other personal-care products that contain known or possible carcinogens, mutagens, and reproductive toxins. Ninety-nine percent of the products on the market contained one or more ingredients that had "never been publicly assessed for safety." Sixty percent of the products tested contained potential endocrine disrupters, and a third had ingredients that "limited evidence" suggested could be carcinogens. No one before had even looked.

———— *from* ————

Notes from the Holocene

A Brief History of the Future

Dorion Sagan

2007

Operating on the precept that the universe is far weirder than we might imagine, Dorion Sagan—son of acclaimed scientists Carl Sagan and Lynn Margulis—uses his knowledge of philosophy, science, sleight-of-hand magic, and the fantastical writings of Philip K. Dick to explore some of the deepest questions we face on Earth. He provides fresh insights as to why we are here, the nature of technology, the prognosis for humanity, and the living nature of our planet, along with a reasoned explanation why our universe is probably just one of an infinite number.

THE WORLD IS A STRANGE AND BEAUTIFUL PLACE. And magical. The same reality admits of multiple perspectives. We can see it from the front of the stage, like spectators at a magic show. Or from the back, like scientists figuring it out. But science learning the secret—such as the strange correspondence between mathematics and phenomena—may lead to further mysteries. "The most beautiful experience we can have is the mysterious," wrote Albert Einstein, perhaps the greatest scientist of the twentieth century. "It is the fundamental emotion which stands at the cradle of true art and true science." "Perhaps the only real thing about him was his innate conviction that everything that had been created in the world of art, science or sentiment, was only a more or less clever trick," wrote Vladimir Nabokov, perhaps the greatest writer of the twentieth century. Illusion is the first of all pleasures, wrote Oscar Wilde, perhaps the greatest wit in the history of the English language. But as quantum physicist David Bohm says, science is about finding the truth *whether we like it or not*. Sometimes we don't want to know. The whittling down of something wondrous to something mechanical can be disappointing. The ultimate example of potential disillusionment leading to depression is the knowledge that we may die. A lot of people don't like science because it doesn't tell them what they want to hear. Like a new bride, they want to hear that they are special, but science says no, we're not. The situation reminds me of a Groucho Marx joke from the time when he was a narrator on the quiz show *You Bet Your Life*. A husband came back to see how his wife answered the question, *From which direction does the sun rise?* She said west and of course her husband was chagrined.

She saw his expression and heard his disparaging, "The sun always rises in the east."

"Not in our neighborhood it doesn't, honey."

Like the disappointed newlywed, we are chagrined to confront the scientific litany of our cosmic ordinariness. The Earth is not the center of the universe. We share 99 percent of our genes with chimps. The atoms of our bodies are mostly hydrogen—the most common atom in the cosmos. The other main atoms, carbon, oxygen, nitrogen, sulfur, and phosphorus, are also common. The element used to treat manic depression, lithium, is the third lightest atom and one of the first to appear, according to cosmologists, after the Big Bang. Perhaps God knew manic depression was coming and wanted to get a head start preparing the medicaments. We did not fall from the sky but came out of the cosmos with its mélanges of matter; we are not pure but latter-day taints, the progeny of microbial miscegenation and skulking apes. And as suggested above, and detailed below, even the energetic processes in which we are involved are not original. Our energy-garnering ways are shared with other matter-cycling manifestations of the second law; not only are we organic dreck, cosmic debris as Frank Zappa once put it, but we are, in our swirling operations, our backing and filling to acquire the resources necessary to preserve our system of cyclical resource acquisition, typical. We may just be another natural form of growing thermodynamic system. Not just the stuff of our bodies, in other words, but the processes in which we are involved may be frightfully common.

The temptation to consider ourselves special is overwhelming. Even my father, in his Gifford Lectures, after titling one "The Retreat from Copernicus: A Modern Loss of Nerve," retreats into the siren-like sanctuary of human specialness, assuring his readers (his listeners) that humans are the dominant species. With which most people of course would be as quick to agree as would the ladies' man to tell his lover *de nuit* that she is the most beautiful woman in the world. We may not be special but, well, we are special. The temptation is tenacious, like the spiral eyes of some secret Narcissus beckoning an adolescent to gaze again into the bathroom mirror.

Yet as that same adolescent we all were may have heard, "Consider the source": When the species in question is judging itself, despite all the careful scientific qualifications, to be the latest, the greatest, the most evolutionarily significant thing since sliced bread, we need to take a step back. Is it possible, perhaps, that we are not the dominant species?

In fact the focused ways in which we seek food, shelter, mates, money, and safety for our children are all ways to maintain our particular form of cyclical material organization. We may well be, despite the creative audacity of our delusions of grandeur, just one more nonequilibrium system that produces more entropy than would be the case were it not to exist—were it to be replaced by a mere random collection of particles. In a quote sometimes credited to Mae West, "Life is not one thing after another; it's the same damn thing, over and over again." Our cycling of matter to preserve our particular form, I would wager, partakes of a universal process. Call it the dilemma of the loose species. We would like to think we are virginal and pure—a level below the angels in the great video game of traditional religious cosmology. But the reality is more like the Madonna song: We are *like* a virgin. This isn't that bad because it is ultimately more fun—and, I would say, more religious—to own up to our cosmic promiscuity. *Religion* comes from the Latin words for "relinking." Noticing the extent to which we are part of, rather than apart from, the cosmos gives us new fortitude to withstand those well-noted feelings of alienation, the existential malaise that the German philosopher Martin Heidegger called "thrownness."

In other words, not only the stuff of life but also its process—including its purposeful behavior to seek food and energy sources, and our own tendencies to do so—is not special. The world isn't all it's cracked up to be. We did not come out of the cosmos like a virgin birth. We are different in particulars but general in type. Despite the widespread acceptance of evolution among educated people, there is a sort of atavistic cultural mechanism by which we try to insist that we are in some way special. If not our spirits then our opposable thumbs, our ability to speak and write, our culture, our technology, our brains or brain-to-body ratio, whales excepted. What is amusing about this ad-libbing, this hemming and hawing to find something, anything, special about *us*, is its desperation. We protest too much. Indeed, the need to separate ourselves in some final way from natural phenomena runs counter to the spirit of evolution itself: Charles Darwin's connection of humans to other life-forms through common descent is a movement of connection, just as Copernicus's placement of the sun at the solar system's center, far from sending us to our room, crying about how the universe doesn't like us, should make us jump for joy that we truly belong to the biggest, greatest club there is. Woody Allen said he always put his wife under a pedestal. We do not need to be manic-depressive. We are neither gods nor beasts but tribal nomads on an increasingly crowded planet that remains, nonetheless, full of potential.

The loss of our theological virginity, our would-be divinity, is an illusory catastrophe. We never were virgins. As that brilliant American wit and daughter of a southern senator Tallulah Bankhead put it: "I am as pure as the driven slush." Let us take the epigram of the Alabama socialite to heart. We, too, are as pure as driven slush.

And this, I submit, is a good thing.

—— *from* ——

Thinking in Systems

A Primer

Donella H. Meadows,
edited by Diana Wright, Sustainability Institute

2008

When Donella Meadows suffered an untimely death in 2001, the famous systems scientist and popular voice for sustainability had an important work nearly complete, one she hoped would distill systems thinking and make it easy for anyone to implement—in corporations and institutions, in government, and even in everyday life. Her assistant, Diana Wright, supplied the finishing touches, and Thinking in Systems *has since become a go-to guide for problem solving, translated into numerous languages. When the book was finished, Peter Senge, author of the systems thinking classic* The Fifth Discipline, *wrote, "Few matched Dana Meadows' remarkable blend of eloquence and clarity in making systems thinking understandable. When Dana began her career, the field was esoteric and academic. Today it is the sine qua non for intelligent action in business and society. The publication of Meadows' previously unfinished manuscript is a gift for leaders of all sorts and at all levels."*

EARLY ON IN TEACHING ABOUT SYSTEMS, I often bring out a Slinky. In case you grew up without one, a Slinky is a toy—a long, loose spring that can be made to bounce up and down, or pour back and forth from hand to hand, or walk itself downstairs.

I perch the Slinky on one upturned palm. With the fingers of the other hand, I grasp it from the top, partway down its coils. Then I pull the bottom hand away. The lower end of the Slinky drops, bounces back up again, yo-yos up and down, suspended from my fingers above.

"What made the Slinky bounce up and down like that?" I ask students. "Your hand. You took away your hand," they say. So I pick up the box the Slinky came in and hold it the same way, poised on a flattened palm, held from above by the fingers of the other hand. With as much dramatic flourish as I can muster, I pull the lower hand away.

Nothing happens. The box just hangs there, of course. "Now once again. What made the Slinky bounce up and down?" The answer clearly lies within the Slinky itself. The hands that manipulate it suppress or release some behavior that is latent within the structure of the spring.

That is a central insight of systems theory.

Once we see the relationship between structure and behavior, we can begin to understand how systems work, what makes them produce poor results, and how to shift them into better behavior patterns. As our world continues to change rapidly and become more complex, systems thinking will help us manage, adapt, and see the wide range of choices we have before us. It is a way of thinking that gives us the freedom to identify root causes of problems and see new opportunities.

So, what is a system? A system is a set of things—people, cells, molecules, or whatever—interconnected in such a way that they produce their own pattern of behavior over time. The system may be buffeted, constricted, triggered, or driven by outside forces. But the system's response to these forces is characteristic of itself, and that response is seldom simple in the real world.

When it comes to Slinkies, this idea is easy enough to understand. When it comes to individuals, companies, cities, or economies, it can be heretical. The system, to a large extent, causes its own behavior! An outside event may unleash that behavior, but the same outside event applied to a different system is likely to produce a different result.

Think for a moment about the implications of that idea:

Political leaders don't cause recessions or economic booms. Ups and downs are inherent in the structure of the market economy. Competitors rarely cause a company to lose market share. They may be there to scoop up the advantage, but the losing company creates its losses at least in part through its own business policies.

The oil-exporting nations are not solely responsible for oil-price rises. Their actions alone could not trigger global price rises and economic chaos if the oil consumption, pricing, and investment policies of the oil-importing nations had not built economies that are vulnerable to supply interruptions.

The flu virus does not attack you; you set up the conditions for it to flourish within you. Drug addiction is not the failing of an individual and no one person, no matter how tough, no matter how loving, can cure a drug addict— not even the addict. It is only through understanding addiction as part of a larger set of influences and societal issues that one can begin to address it.

Something about statements like these is deeply unsettling. Something else is purest common sense. I submit that those two somethings—a resistance to and a recognition of systems principles—come from two kinds of human experience, both of which are familiar to everyone.

On the one hand, we have been taught to analyze, to use our rational ability, to trace direct paths from cause to effect, to look at things in small and understandable pieces, to solve problems by acting on or controlling the world around us. That training, the source of much personal and societal power, leads us to see presidents and competitors, OPEC and the flu and drugs as the causes of our problems.

On the other hand, long before we were educated in rational analysis, we all dealt with complex systems. We are complex systems—our own bodies are magnificent examples of integrated, interconnected, self-maintaining complexity. Every person we encounter, every organization, every animal, garden, tree, and forest is a complex system. We have built up intuitively, without analysis, often without words, a practical understanding of how these systems work, and how to work with them.

Modern systems theory, bound up with computers and equations, hides the fact that it traffics in truths known at some level by everyone. It is often possible, therefore, to make a direct translation from systems jargon to traditional wisdom.

—— *from* ——

Not One Drop

Betrayal and Courage in the Wake of the Exxon Valdez Oil Spill

Riki Ott

2008

Dr. Riki Ott, a commercial salmon "fisherma'am" and PhD marine biologist, describes firsthand the ongoing impacts of oil companies' broken promises after the Exxon Valdez *oil spill that despoiled hundreds of miles of Alaskan shoreline and devastated the fishing community of Cordova. In vivid detail, she describes the human trauma coupled inextricably with that of Prince William Sound's wildlife and its long road to recovery.* Not One Drop *is as much a story of how too many corporate owners and political leaders betray everyday citizens as it is one of the universal struggle to maintain heart, to find the courage to overcome disaster, and to forge a new path from despair to hope.*

ALASKANS FROM OILED COMMUNITIES FLOCKED in droves to the oil spill symposium. So did Exxon scientists who had declined to participate in the conference, claiming that their papers were not yet ready to present. Exxon scientists aggressively courted the media and Exxon public relations specialists videotaped every session of the three-day symposium, giving an air of siege to the event.

Sitting up front in one session and taking notes, I noticed a couple dozen friends from Cordova and other communities, standing all clumped together at the back. I sensed their discomfort in a room full of scientists and media. In a sudden shock of connection, I felt their wild, dark fear of the future and intense love of the Sound. I felt their desperate need to understand what was happening to our environment, to our lives. I swallowed a lump of frustrated anger and forced myself to focus on the unemotional—dispassionate—droning—scientific presentations.

Slowly the mystery of what was happening in the Sound revealed itself in charts, graphs, and slides. A picture began to emerge of lingering harm to beaches, birds, mammals, and fish like a puzzle revealing its design when key pieces are assembled. The trouble seemed to center around oiled beaches. In study after study, the killing did not stop in 1989.

Scientists reported that oil trapped under thick mats of mussels did not break down as expected in 1989, but was still poisonous four years after the spill. Mussels soaked up the highly toxic oil like sponges and passed it on, poisoning wildlife that ate them. Local stocks of shellfish eaters like harlequin ducks, black oystercatchers, and young sea otters had crashed in oiled areas of the Sound. Even wildlife that only occasionally snacked on mussels, like river otters and pigeon guillemots, were not doing well on oiled beaches relative to those that lived on unoiled beaches.

Scientists reported herring and pink salmon that spawned on beaches and grew to adults in bays were also having problems. Almost all of the herring eggs spawned in 1989 along oiled beaches in the Sound had died, and a high portion of the oiled wild pink salmon eggs had died as well. Slides of pink salmon larvae from oiled streams showed tiny bodies twisted and hideously deformed. Ominously, a progressively higher portion of salmon eggs in oiled streams died each year through 1992, causing scientists to scramble for answers. Oil stunted growth of young wild and hatchery pink salmon in oiled nursery bays. These effects all added up to fewer adult wild pink salmon than anticipated by state biologists despite the two years of record hatchery returns.

I thought the new information linked the spill to the 1992 wild and hatchery pink salmon collapse. It was possible that juvenile pink salmon in 1989 had been damaged by their oil bath and were unable to produce offspring, resulting in the collapse. Cordova fishermen drew similar conclusions and asked simple questions: Had oil damaged pink salmon's ability to reproduce or survive? How many generations might be affected? These questions hung unanswered in a room thick with apprehension.

Scientists did not know as much about the early lives of herring—what happened between eggs and adults—but they warned that if oil had similar devastating effects on these young fish, the consequences for the Sound would be disastrous. Herring are a "cornerstone species," one explained, a species that holds the entire ecosystem together. A crash in the herring population could delay recovery from spill losses of birds and mammals that fed on these schooling fish. I turned to look at my friends. Unspoken worry deeply etched their faces. We all knew that the herring born into the spill were supposed to return as adults this year. Now we wondered if they would.

I stared at my pages of notes. The findings pointed to lingering damage from oil—something scientists had said in 1989 would not happen. The studies contradicted what I had been taught in my field of study: Oil does not cause long-term harm. The findings were also at odds with the glowing predictions of record returns of hatchery pink salmon and herring for the upcoming season—134,000 tons of herring and a pink return triple that of the previous year's prediction. Years later, I would learn that the mathematical models used for predictions did not take into account any possible impacts from oil like higher death rates. In other words, predictions based on these models were practically worthless.

I started to think of this new reality presented by the scientists as "Sound Truth." It was as if the Sound was trying to tell us something, yet no one could fully understand it. At the time, it did not occur to me that what I had been taught might be wrong, because it was a function of what scientists knew at the time and time had moved on. The old knowledge could be bowled over like tenpins by more sophisticated science that allowed greater understanding of complex systems.

——— *from* ———

Waiting on a Train

The Embattled Future of Passenger Rail Service

James McCommons

2009

During 2008 journalist James McCommons rode America's passenger rail lines, meeting both travelers and workers along much of Amtrak's system. Partly he just loved traveling by train, but partly, too, he set out to talk to politicians, railroad executives, and other rail enthusiasts, to try to find out why our country has turned its back on passenger rail, and what if anything it will take to restore it to some semblance of its past glory.

WHEN THE ZEPHYR WITH MY SON and me aboard crossed the Mississippi at Burlington that night, it was snowing hard. For a time in central Iowa, we paralleled Route 34, and I peered over to see cars spun out in ditches and tractor trailers creeping along. On a portable radio, Kelly tuned in the AP news, and we heard that airports in Chicago, Detroit, Minneapolis, and Des Moines were closed, thousands of passengers sprawled in the concourses, and the effects on air traffic were rippling across the nation.

It mattered not at all to the Zephyr. The tenor of the locomotives seemed to deepen. It built up speed and sliced into the storm. That evening, we turned out the cabin lights and gazed out at snowdrifts piling up in the empty main streets of small towns. Pickup trucks sat in driveways and television lights flickered from the windows of passing farmhouses.

All evening, our train braked into stations right on time. The conductors and attendants hustled folks aboard and we sped away into the countryside. This was how a train was supposed to run—on time, efficient, and with only enough "dwell" in the stations to get folks off and on. The countryside reeled past. We were making progress.

Kelly changed into his pajamas, boosted himself into the upper bunk, and I latched the safety netting to catch him if the train made a sudden jerk. He was tired and giddy. A few hours out of Omaha, the train punched through the back side of the storm and into the clear skies of the Great Plains. Muted light of a full moon filled the cabin, and I sat up to see black, treeless land rolling away and the red line of dawn on the eastern horizon. The attendant had a coffee pot going and a fresh stack of the *Omaha World Herald*.

In the empty lounge car, I read, drank coffee, and watched the day come to light on the plains. Mornings are always magical on a train—going to sleep in one town and waking up hundreds of miles down the line. When the Zephyr pulled into Denver that morning, we were five minutes early.

Day two also went well. The train climbed the Front Range and plunged into black tunnels that emptied into magnificent snowy valleys. Along the Colorado River, we watched deer and elk bound away from the tracks. A historian gave short lectures over the speakers about characters like Doc Holliday, the tubercular dentist, gambler, and gunslinger who succumbed in a Glenwood Springs sanitarium. In the evening, the train descended the western slope, running along arroyos and beneath red buttes saturated by the setting sun.

But that night, in the Union Pacific yards outside of Salt Lake City, troubles began. While most passengers slept, the train idled for nearly four hours blocked by freight trains and hampered by switching problems. Behind schedule and out of sync with oncoming traffic, the Zephyr was at the whim of Union Pacific dispatchers in Omaha. Time and again the next day we were shunted onto sidings to make room for eastbound freights that rolled past laden with shipping containers off the docks of the West Coast.

"Get out of the way because here come all your Game Boys, microwaves, and cheap Wal-Mart crap," a conductor grumbled.

We'd gotten jammed up in a supply line that stretched all the way back to Asia. The big railroads love this "hook and haul" business, in which goods coming off container ships are put on trains and hauled cross-country. At the time, before the great economic downturn in the late months of 2008, this stream of stuff produced by cheap labor abroad, sold by big box stores, and fueled by consumer credit seemed endless. The shipping containers sported logos in Chinese characters and English—Maersk, China Shipping, and Cosco. Other trains pulled triple-decker car carriers loaded with Daewoos, Nissans, and Toyotas.

No matter what these trains hauled, the Zephyr—filled with nearly three hundred people—pulled over to let them pass, sometimes waiting at a lonely siding for thirty minutes. Such stops mystify the Europeans who ride the trains.

"We're stopped because of a bloody freight train?" one told me. "Unbelievable."

In 1971 when Union Pacific and other freight railroads turned their passenger operations over to Amtrak, they agreed to give passenger trains preference over freights. It frequently doesn't happen that way—sometimes because dispatchers purposefully sideline passenger trains, but more often because the existing infrastructure is just overwhelmed by too many trains. The truth in America is freight matters more than people, and nearly all the track belongs to the big railroads, not to Amtrak.

Amtrak pays incentives to the freight railroads to deliver its passenger trains on time, but those payments are miniscule as compared to the profits earned by hauling freight. In other words, the incentives don't provide much incentive.

In 2007, the Zephyr arrived in California on schedule only about 20 percent of the time, the next-to-worst performance in the Amtrak system. By summer 2009, when the recession cut freight traffic by nearly 25 percent, thus loosening some of the bottlenecks, and the big railroads made a political decision to do a better job of delivering Amtrak trains, the on-time performance of the Zephyr improved to nearly 60 percent.

——— *from* ———

Confronting Collapse

The Crisis of Energy and Money in a Post Peak Oil World

Michael C. Ruppert

2009

Michael Ruppert, an LAPD narcotics detective who left his profession to become a fearless investigative reporter, wrote one of the most celebrated exposés of the 9/11 attacks in 2004, Crossing the Rubicon. *After his legendary 1996 confrontation with then CIA director John Deutch over the CIA's role in drug trafficking in South Los Angeles, Ruppert went on to found the internationally influential alternative news website fromTheWilderness. com. In 2005 he turned his attention nearly full-time to the problem of peak oil and the collapse of industrial civilization. In 2009 the award-winning documentary filmmaker Chris Smith filmed Ruppert in* Collapse—*released in tandem with Chelsea Green's publication of* Confronting Collapse. *Ruppert argues that economic growth depends first and foremost on cheap and abundant fossil fuels. Without these, collapse will not be avoided short of drastic governmental actions. In this book he provides an emergency twen-ty-five-point plan for action.*

ENERGY, NOT MONEY, IS THE ROOT of all economic activity. Money represents only the ability to do work. By itself a dollar bill can do nothing. You cannot put it in your gas tank and expect your car to run. Energy is that which money symbolizes, whether it is the slave labor of centuries past which built civilizations that later perished, the food that comes to your table today, or the gasoline that goes into your car or the electricity that comes into your home. Cheap energy has always been the equivalent of free slave labor for industrial civilization.

There is one other essential difference between money and energy. Money can grow infinitely. Energy, i.e., the slaves necessary to give money value, cannot.

What happens when the "slaves" disappear?

In the first decade of the twenty-first century it has become clear that a major crisis confronts the human race. For the United States it will be, and is, a crisis as great as any we have ever faced as a nation. It will be greater than World War II, greater than the Civil War, and much more devastating to American life than the Great Depression of the 1930s.

This crisis will be different from all others that came before it. In the past America faced all of its great challenges by marshalling and applying our ingenuity to use the one advantage America had over all other nations, our vast and largely untapped base of natural resources. In the Great Depression, America responded with a New Deal. It drew upon seemingly endless reserves of energy and raw materials to build its way out of economic collapse with massive public works projects and preparation for war. In World War II the Manhattan Project took advantage of seemingly unlimited reserves of energy, hydroelectric power, and minerals to enrich uranium and unleash the power of the atom. When President John Kennedy challenged America to put men on the moon and bring them home safely by the end of the 1960s, every commodity needed to achieve that task was cheap, plentiful, and close at hand.

We live in a different world now. The crisis we face is itself a crisis of shortages (not just energy), and if America is to meet the test successfully, we will have to use a different approach. It is not possible to use enormous amounts of resources to address a resource shortage.

In our two greatest historical challenges, the Civil War and the Great Depression, Presidents Abraham Lincoln—a Republican, and Franklin D. Roosevelt—a Democrat, found it necessary to exceed the powers granted them by our Constitution. History has judged that both men acted wisely, and it has well recorded their emotional agony as they gave their health and their lives to protect the Union they loved so dearly.

Barack Obama and the presidents who follow him will be faced with a greater crisis, requiring decisions which will try their minds and souls as no other challenge has tried an American president. They will have to make choices that will be difficult and cannot please all of the people all of the time. They will have to set priorities that cannot give everyone an equal seat at our great table. They will have to eject some from long-held seats to make room for new ones who can help America and mankind move to a new post-industrial paradigm. And they will have to do all of this holding one standard above all others: do what is best for the American people as a united whole. Do what is best for mankind.

What is happening is not just an American crisis. It is a global crisis. It is an emergency for every human being alive today and especially for those as yet unborn. That crisis is a combination of two factors which are converging like a giant claw around all of us. One half of the claw is an exponentially surging rise in human population and its need for food, energy, goods and services. The other half is a rapidly declining supply of cheap, affordable energy in all its forms with which to manufacture, transport, and power those things, whether they are automobiles, TV sets, cell phones, clothing, computers—or, most especially, food.

This is not a Conservative or Liberal issue. The high cost of gasoline, food, electricity, and everything else today impacts everyone, regardless of their beliefs. This policy is not designed to reflect any political philosophy. In fact it is an argument that all pre-existing political philosophies be thrown out. This policy is based upon science: mathematics (in most cases high school- or middle school-level mathematics), geology, and simple chemistry. Numbers are impersonal and apolitical. They can be—and especially when it comes to energy have been—manipulated and misused both intentionally and ignorantly. There is too little clarity and too much confusion when it comes to how much energy there is and what alternative sources are available—and what we can realistically expect to accomplish with them.

Yet one thing is frighteningly clear to everyone regardless of their beliefs: the Age of Oil is coming to an end. Whether you are someone who believes that the United States must somehow wean itself from dependency on foreign oil or you are someone who understands that the human race has failed to plan and prepare for this crisis in time to make a stable transition to some other regime (or combination of regimes), the objective and the urgency remain the same.

——— *from* ———

2052

A Global Forecast for the Next 40 Years

Jorgen Randers

2012

Forty years after Jorgen Randers and colleagues Dennis and Donella Meadows and William Behrens III published The Limits to Growth, *a report to the Club of Rome, Randers found himself more worried than ever. Limits and decades of scientific research had clearly shown the dire consequences of overexploiting the planet's finite resources, yet the world still seemed to be hurtling toward collapse. He wanted to know: Would humanity be able to act fast enough to reverse the trend and avoid looming threats like runaway climate change? So Randers, an internationally recognized sustainability expert and climate analyst, decided to make a forecast for the next forty years. To do this, he asked dozens of experts to weigh in with their best predictions on how our economies, energy supplies, natural resources, climate, food, fisheries, militaries, political divisions, cities, psyches, and more will take shape in the coming decades. He then synthesized those scenarios into a global forecast of how life in the years ahead will most likely look. What he found, and his advice on how to prepare for it, has captivated readers from New York to Munich to Beijing. And his candid approach—steeped in heart, fact, and wisdom—has made the book, also a report to the Club of Rome, an international bestseller, winning awards at home and abroad.*

So what will the future look like? The simplest way to get an answer is of course to ask someone who knows. But if you want a reliable forecast for the future of the world over the next forty years, it is difficult—simply because there is no one who really knows. There are even fewer who pretend to know. And if you also insist that the scenario shall be complete and consistent, there is, as far as I know, nowhere to go. It is relatively easy to find prescriptions on how the world ought to develop (for example, the World Business Council for Sustainable Development Vision 2050, which describes what must be done in order for us to have a sustainable world in 2050). But I do not know of a well-considered forecast of what will actually happen at a global level to 2052.

In the past, there were research groups working on broad-scope computer models of global development, seeking to produce consistent scenarios of the long-term future. But this fad peaked in the 1970s and early 1980s and then died out. Today, long-term models of the world are largely limited to macroeconomics and energy, with 2030 as the longest commonly used time horizon and with important variables (like population and productivity growth) kept exogenous. Of course there exist special-purpose models of the global climate with much longer time horizons, but these do not include socioeconomic variables. So the best offer available is sector perspectives on global development. The full picture is missing.

This lack of a complete picture of the future is the basic reason for my uncertainty and worrying. After a long life in the sustainability movement, and as a builder of world models, I know full well what ought to be done in order to have (what I see as) an attractive world by 2052. But at the same time, I am convinced that humanity will not put in place the full work program necessary to create an attractive world by 2052. So the real challenge is to estimate how much (or how little) of what needs to be done actually will be done.

Luckily it is simple to sketch the big picture of global physical development over the last three hundred years. Before the 1700s, the world was thinly populated, largely agricultural, and using very little energy. This was a world run by slaves, horses, oxen, and some firewood—to use headline language. The advent of steam engines running on coal began the industrial revolution. The transition to the industrial age was characterized by a huge increase in the use of energy. Over the last 250 years this use of energy made the industrialized countries rich in material goods and ensured a less strenuous life for the masses. The less industrialized countries of today are following suit as fast as they can. The recent emergence of China is a vivid illustration of what industrialization of a country means. The rest of the world strives to follow suit.

By 2052, the industrial revolution will be complete in rich countries, like the agricultural revolution before it. The transfer of workers from agriculture to manufacturing will be complete as well, and the workforce will move onward to services and care. Only a few will remain in physical production. From then on, the focus will be on steady improvement in the supply of services and care to the common folk.

But there is another reason why the past focus on industrialization will wane. We know already (deep in our hearts) that there is little increased satisfaction in never-ending growth in the per capita consumption of food and manufactured goods. Once well fed, warm, safe, and comfortable, most humans yearn for more abstract satisfaction. Never-ending growth in material consumption and energy use may generate marginal improvements for some individuals but will be easily overwhelmed by the negative side effects for the masses when everyone tries to emulate the rich—because we live on a finite planet. Thus sooner or later, the industrial revolution will be followed by the sustainability revolution. This is the era when the main objective of nations will be to evolve a national society that can be sustained in the long run both physically and mentally. It will start in the rich countries and spread to the rest of the world later in this century. I can't tell you exactly what this future society will look like. But I am willing to bet that the overriding ambition will not be "fossil-fueled economic growth" but rather "sustainable well-being."

These two words—sustainability and well-being—carry meaning without being sharply defined. We don't know in minute detail what such a shift will involve. But we do know some main parameters. The future world will not have an expanding population. It will still use much energy per person, but that energy will be used wisely and be of the renewable sort. In the end the world will run on energy from the sun—either directly as solar heat or solar electricity, or indirectly via wind, hydro, and biomass. It will be a world that focuses on human well-being, not only on its material component.

The big question is how fast the transition to sustainability will happen. The sustainability revolution has already begun, that is for sure. The new paradigm already emerged forty years ago, or perhaps even fifty (with Rachel Carson in 1962). It has spread since, but it is still far from mainstream. We have evolved an increased understanding of the need to replace fossil energy, but we have not really embarked on the challenge. And some—even in high places—have started to talk seriously about the need to replace GDP growth with growth in well-being as the overriding societal goal. The best recent example is the report by Joseph Stiglitz, Amartya Sen, and Jean-Paul Fitoussi to President Sarkozy of France in 2009, in which these macroeconomists broke rank with traditional theory and started advocating an accelerated shift of emphasis from GDP to well-being.

So the sustainability revolution has started but is still in its infancy. When will it be completed? I am sure that by the year 2100 we will have a world that is much more sustainable than the current one—for the simple reason that "unsustainability is unsustainable," to use the wonderful phrase of corporate sustainability expert Alan Knight. Current unsustainable ways—by definition of the word unsustainable—cannot be continued indefinitely; they will have to be replaced with systems and behaviors that can be maintained in the longer run. Whether the new sustainable world will be attractive or one with much lower well-being than today is hard to tell. It depends on what humanity chooses to do during the rest of the twenty-first century. As you will see from my forecast in this book, I believe the transition to sustainability will be only half complete by 2052, and may run into serious difficulties in the second half of the century. Global society will have to perform a miracle after 2052 if it is to end the century in a desirable and durable situation.

------ *from* ------

Cows Save the Planet

And Other Improbable Ways of Restoring Soil to Heal the Earth

Judith D. Schwartz

2013

Praised by Gretel Ehrlich, Elizabeth Kolbert, and Michael Pollan, this original, hopeful, and courageous book by veteran journalist Judith Schwartz turns environmental orthodoxy on its head. For too long people have felt paralyzing despair over environmental problems, all the more tragic when that despair is based on incomplete or incorrect information. Using soil as a crucible for our many overlapping environmental, economic, and social crises, Schwartz reveals that many of these problems—climate change, desertification, biodiversity loss, droughts, floods, wildfires, rural poverty, malnutrition, and obesity—can be turned into opportunities (and the opportunities are plenty) depending on how we treat the soil.

DRYLANDS—THE ARID, SEMI-ARID, AND SUB-HUMID areas with seasonal, often unpredictable rains—are complex, delicate ecosystems that though resilient are vulnerable when land and water are not sustainably managed. Drylands account for 41.3 percent of the world's landmass, including 44 percent of land under cultivation. Each year upward of twelve million hectares (thirty million acres) of productive land are lost to desertification; this means an area the size of South Africa is slipping away each decade. With two billion people living in drylands, mostly in the developing world, the loss of arable land is pushing large populations trying to eke out a marginal living into poverty, starvation, and migration. Today 1.5 billion people depend for their food and livelihoods on land that is losing its capacity to sustain vegetation. It's estimated that half of armed conflicts can be at least in part attributed to environmental strains associated with dryland degradation. Desertification has contributed to the downfall of civilizations: think Carthage, Mesopotamia, ancient Greece and Rome.

Desertification is not a "natural" development—the result, say, of dune movement or shifting sands. It is a man-made process, driven by actions that disturb the life cycles of many plant and animal species that have adapted to dryland conditions. These endeavors include overcultivation, deforestation, poor irrigation design, poor livestock management, and the use of technology ill suited to the landscape. Land degradation is not unique to drylands; actually, most land deterioration occurs in areas you wouldn't consider dry. The problem is that in drylands the margins that determine adequate rainfall or water scarcity, a good harvest or crop failure, are exceedingly thin. Which means that if you're in England or the U.S. North Atlantic coast, you can get away with messing things up somewhat without facing immediate consequences; residents of Australia or North Africa lack that luxury. Weather-related events like droughts and floods do not in themselves cause but can intensify and hasten the decline to desert—land that becomes "dirt" with life neither on nor within it.

It's ironic that desertification might, global-crisis-wise, need to compete for airtime with climate change and biodiversity loss—because they're all connected. Here's a hypothetical snapshot of how it plays out: Degraded soils in arid lands lack the capacity to store carbon; whatever carbon is in the soil oxidizes to form carbon dioxide, contributing to climate change. Absent plant cover and moisture, bare ground absorbs heat (if you've scorched your feet on hot sand, you'll know what I mean). If you remove plant cover and litter over one square yard, the soil heats up and the microclimate is altered. Do that over the whole of North Africa or most of Australia, and you've changed the macroclimate. The added heat makes any moisture present more prone to evaporate, and want of moisture leaves the soil less than welcoming to microorganisms, the absence of which deprives plants of nutrients and other beneficial exchanges. With the habitat unfriendly for growth, the range of plants that can survive is limited, which then limits the birds and insects that might pollinate or spread seeds. Sparse vegetation means little protection from winds or heavy rains, so these occurrences lead to more soil blowing or streaming away, more carbon oxidizing.

So intertwined are these three—desertification, climate change, and biodiversity loss—that we can consider them manifestations of the same problem: The biological cycles underlying life on earth have been thrown out of whack. We can't hope to make inroads on any one of them without addressing all of them. However, this is not how it's usually discussed.

The word desertification and its association with droughts and barren landscapes makes us think that we're dealing with a "just add water" situation: that all those benighted regions need is a good dose of rain and the land would burst into tulips and daffodils. But if we were to reduce the problem to its essence, desertification is really about soil: soil losing its "aliveness," the wherewithal to sustain life.

One reason desertification does not rank higher in our awareness is that it's often thought of as a third-world problem. It happens over there, in regions we're unlikely to visit, places many of us haven't heard of, let alone be able to pronounce. It's the kind of thing we'd read about on what used to be called "the Africa page" in the newspapers, shake our heads in momentary pity, and think Thank God I don't live there, assured that something like that could never happen where we live. In fact, the continent with the highest proportion of its dryland areas classified as severe or moderately desertified is North America, at 74 percent. In the European Union, another region you might think immune, thirteen countries suffer some degree of desertification.

While working in the United States in the early 1990s Allan Savory, the African wildlife biologist and rancher who developed the planned grazing framework called Holistic Management (its application is generally called "Holistic Planned Grazing"), made this observation: Most experts on desertification attribute its development to overpopulation, overstocking of livestock, cutting down too many trees, poverty, war, lack of education and/ or technology, and the overexploitation of shared resources. In West Texas, where Savory was working, none of these factors was present. The rural population was declining, as were livestock numbers, while mesquite trees grew undisturbed. There was no war, no dearth of money, technology, or education. Nor could one blame the "tragedy of the commons," since all the land was privately owned. Yet West Texas was desertifying as rapidly as anything he'd seen in Africa: Sand dunes were forming, rivers were drying up, and the water table was dwindling.

Clearly something else was going on.

——— *from* ———

The Zero Waste Solution

Untrashing the Planet One Community at a Time

Paul Connett

2013

As Bill McKibben wrote, "Paul Connett's heroic drive to trim our culture's crazy waste" is "an inspiration to us all." For years, Connett, a retired professor of chemistry and founder of two environmental action groups, has gone around the world, giving more than two thousand presentations in forty-nine states and fifty-two countries urging communities to embrace a zero waste goal. The Zero Waste Solution *profiles the most successful zero waste initiatives around the world, showing activists, planners, and entrepreneurs how to re-envision their community's waste-handling processes. It also exposes the greenwashing behind renewed efforts to promote waste incinerators as safe, nontoxic energy suppliers. A leading international figure in the decades-long battles to fight pollution, Connett has championed efforts to curtail overconsumption and keep industrial toxins out of our air, drinking water, and bodies. But he's best known around the world for leading efforts to help communities sustainably eliminate and reuse waste rather than burn it or stow it away in landfills.*

What Is the Zero Waste Strategy?

The zero waste strategy says no to incinerators, no to mega-landfills, no to the throwaway society, and yes to a sustainable society. While it may sound like an idealistic goal, we can put it into a realistic time frame. We do not expect to reach zero waste next year, but we can anticipate that some communities could be very close to eliminating most of their waste by 2020.

People will quibble about how close we can get to producing zero waste, but the point is that by aiming for zero we make our intentions very clear— and we're more likely to get closer to that goal than if we set ourselves a lesser target. Put another way, those in the zero waste movement pose this question: Bearing in mind the needs of future generations, how much waste do you think is acceptable? In short, how much waste are you *for*?

California-based zero waste advocate Gary Liss once explained the zero waste goal this way: "Every day, more than 100 million citizens do the right thing . . . they recycle. Now it is time to set our sights higher and start planning for the end to wasting resources and to our reliance on landfills, incinerators and other waste facilities. Zero waste is a policy, a path, a direction, a target; it's a process, a way of thinking, a vision."

For me, more than anything else zero waste is a new direction. We have to move from the back-end of waste disposal to the front-end of resource management, better industrial design, and a post-consumerist way of life. In both industry and our daily lives we have to get waste out of the system. As Mary Lou Van Deventer and her husband, Daniel Knapp (two entrepreneurs that have turned waste reduction into a business), say, "Discarded materials are not waste until they are wasted. Waste is a verb, not a noun."

In 2004 the Zero Waste International Alliance (ZWIA) established the only peer-reviewed definition of zero waste to date:

Zero Waste is a goal that is ethical, economical, efficient and visionary, to guide people in changing their lifestyles and practices to emulate sustainable natural cycles, where all discarded materials are designed to become resources for others to use.

Zero Waste means designing and managing products and processes to systematically avoid and eliminate the volume and toxicity of waste and materials, conserve and recover all resources, and not burn or bury them.

Implementing Zero Waste will eliminate all discharges to land, water, or air that are a threat to planetary, human, animal, or plant health.

The Four Rs

In my talks to communities fighting incinerators I have had some fun at the expense of high-paid consultants who push incinerators and landfills. I say that they are thinking with the wrong end of their bodies. They are what I call "back-end thinkers." The back-end thinker comes home and finds the bathtub is overflowing so he (and it usually is a *he*) quickly grabs a cup to empty it. That doesn't work, so he grabs a bucket, then a foot pump, and then an electric pump—all in a vain effort to empty the bathtub before it damages the floor. Then his wife comes home and switches off the tap. She is a "front-end thinker"!

Many front-end thinkers have long embraced what have come to be known as the three Rs (reduce, reuse, recycle)—but when it comes to waste, which is ultimately a design problem, we need to add another R to the lexicon: *redesign*. In fact, one of the first Italians to talk about "zero waste" was the greatest designer of all time—Leonardo da Vinci. In his writings he said that there was no such thing as waste. Like nature, each producer's waste product should be another producer's starting material.

Redesign is important in making the fundamental transition from the back-end to the front-end of the waste-resource problem as well as grappling with the larger issue of sustainability. To make this transition we need all sectors of society to accept some responsibility. We need individual responsibility, community responsibility, industrial responsibility, professional responsibility, and political responsibility. We need community responsibility at the back-end of the problem, industrial responsibility at the front-end, and we need responsible political leadership to bring these two together. Moreover, because this issue is too important to leave to the narrow focus of waste disposal experts, we need every sector of the society and economy involved. We need to integrate zero waste planning with farmers, doctors, artists, educators, communicators, philosophers, scientists, engineers, economists, environmentalists, industrial workers, architects, community developers, social activists, and children! In short, we need everyone involved in this massive effort.

But even as a massive effort is contemplated, it's critical to remember that communities recycle—not countries. While national, state, and regional governments can pass helpful legislation—and sadly unhelpful legislation (for example, giant subsidies to incinerators)—the key issue is what your local community can do. The best way a new zero waste advocate can take action is by finding out what other communities of similar size and demography have been able to achieve, then choose the best model and try to copy and improve on it. . . .

When we are looking at what has contributed to the best examples of zero waste to date, I would say that the single most important factor is the willingness of decision makers to work with citizens (and corporate decision makers with their employees) to find solutions we can all live with. Citizens are certainly going to be the enemy when decision makers opt for resource-destroying and polluting landfills and incinerators, but they are the key allies when decision makers seek genuine solutions that move us in a sustainable direction. Similarly, when corporate leaders add two more Ps to *profit* (*people* and the *planet*), they will get huge support from their workers. Such solutions are not only better for the local community and the corporation, but better for the planet as whole. We all need a larger meaning to our work and our lives. Money is not enough.

—— *from* ——

Grass, Soil, Hope

A Journey Through Carbon Country

Courtney White

2014

Courtney White's book tackles an increasingly crucial question: What can we do about the seemingly intractable global challenges of climate change, hunger, water scarcity, environmental stress, and economic instability? The answer involves carbon. Scientists say that increasing carbon in our soils by 2 percent could offset a great deal of the carbon that is currently going into our atmosphere and oceans. In Grass, Soil, Hope *the author explains how efforts by innovative farmers, ranchers, and gardeners around the world could yield cumulative positive effects for humanity, and for all living things.*

CARBON IS THE GRAPHITE IN OUR PENCILS, the diamond in our rings, the oil in our cars, the sugar in our coffee, the DNA in our cells, the air in our lungs, the food on our plates, the cattle in our fields, the forest in our parks, the cement in our sidewalks, the steel in our skyscrapers, the charcoal in our grills, the fizz in our sodas, the foam in our fire extinguishers, the ink in our pens, the plastic in our toys, the wood in our chairs, the leather in our jackets, the battery in our cars, the rubber in our tires, the coal in our power plants, the *nano* in our nanotechnology, and the life in our soils.

. . . And what carbon does is cycle—a process essential to life on Earth. It's a carefully regulated process too, so that the planet can maintain critical balances. Call it the Goldilocks Principle: not too much carbon, not too little, but just the right amount. For instance, without CO_2 and other greenhouse gases, Earth would be a frozen ball of rock. With too many greenhouse gases, however, Earth would be an inferno like Venus. "Just right" means balancing between the two extremes, which helps to keep the planet's temperature relatively stable. It's like the thermostat in your house. If it gets too warm, the cycle works to cool things off, and vice versa. Of course, the planet's thermostat gets overwhelmed at times, resulting in periods of rapid warming or cooling (think ice ages). No matter what happens, the miraculous carbon cycle keeps working, scrubbing excess CO_2 out of the atmosphere, or adding more if necessary. The carbon cycle never sleeps.

Who does all this regulatory work? Two quick answers: green growing plants and evolution. Photosynthesis is the rapid process by which carbon is transferred from sky to soil. It's what makes the Goldilocks Principle tick. Evolution is the methodical process by which life changes over succeeding generations—what lives, what dies, which population expands, which one contracts. It keeps the Goldilocks Principle ticking over time—long periods of time. The two work in concert. The quantity of carbon in the environment influences the course of evolution, and vice versa. The effects of an excessive buildup of CO_2 in the atmosphere, for example, will impact the fate of generations of living things. Carbon and evolution interact and adjust to one another, regulating and responding in a sophisticated dance. Carbon chooses the music, if you will, while evolution dictates the steps in a planetwide choreography. It is a dance with a profound effect on audience members.

Carbon is not the only dance on the planet, of course. Our world is full of cycles—water, energy, nutrients, nitrogen, phosphorus, and many more—each interacting with the others in complicated ways. Some cycles are short, like a song, while others are long, like a symphony or a mass. Carbon has it both ways. Its short, or fast, cycle revolves around green plants and photosynthesis—the process by which carbon is separated from oxygen, stored in roots and soils, and released back into the atmosphere via death and decomposition. Its long, or slow, cycle is geologic—what happens when carbon is released after being trapped or frozen in layers of rock for millions of years. In the case of the slow cycle, the symphony is *really* long—carbon can take between one hundred and two hundred million years to rotate fully through rocks, soil, ocean, and atmosphere.

Luckily, it is the fast carbon cycle—photosynthesis—where our hope can be found.

The process by which atmospheric CO_2 gets converted into soil carbon has been going on for at least a billion years, and all it requires is sunlight, green plants, water, nutrients, and soil microbes. It's an equation: healthy soil + healthy carbon cycle = storage of atmospheric CO_2.

—— *from* ——

Carbon Shock

A Tale of Risk and Calculus on the Front Lines of a Disrupted Global Economy

Mark Schapiro

2014

For almost two decades before journalist Mark Schapiro wrote Carbon Shock, *global climate talks had focused on how to make polluters pay for the carbon they emit. Yet as the book reveals, pricing carbon remains a financial mystery: What are the costs? Who will pay for them? Whom do you pay? How do you pay? And what are the potential impacts? These are the questions that propelled Schapiro on a multi-year investigation into the economic disruption caused by climate change. To find answers, he delved deep into a new kind of chaos—one where carbon, the stand-in for all greenhouse gases, rules and where the axis points of economic power are shifting. Schapiro probes the stories behind the headlines, unveils new understandings of financial risk, and shows readers the costs of carbon in their everyday lives.*

CHAOS AND UNCERTAINTY. THOSE ARE THE CHARACTERISTICS of the natural world under the pressures being wrought by climate change. Normal patterns of rainfall, temperature, and extreme weather are changing so rapidly that past baselines for these primordial forces are less and less relevant.

Scientists have a word for this state of flux. They call it "the end of stationarity," a term with a powerful meaning: We can no longer rely on past events to predict future probabilities. The ground is shifting beneath our feet.

Now it's becoming increasingly clear that the volatility we're seeing in our natural world is reshaping our financial world, too. While we try to hold onto our bearings in the status quo and conduct business as usual, new risks are entering into the equation, and new costs are creeping onto the balance sheets of corporations and nations. Just as chaotically as climate change is altering conditions here on earth, it is changing our understanding of the actual costs of just about everything.

In the financial realm, as in the natural realm, the past provides fewer and fewer clues to our future. Like the migration patterns of songbirds that no longer correlate to the hatching patterns of their insect prey, or the mountain snowpacks that no longer store water for the dry summer months, the economy is facing similar miscues borne of the interactive loop between tumult in the atmosphere and tumult on the earth. Economic calculations are being upended in ways that are similar to how the digital revolution transformed financial decision making—though on a far more monumental scale. In early 2014, a report by the Intergovernmental Panel on Climate Change (IPCC), produced and reviewed by more than a thousand scientists and approved by 194 governments, identified the economic impact of the enormous changes underway: slowing the rate of greenhouse gases into the atmosphere would not have devastating impacts on the economy, as is often feared, but would require a fundamental rethinking of our priorities and our existing business models. Unstated but clearly implied: new forces will rise and others will fall as the true costs of carbon become an increasingly potent economic factor that no longer can be ignored. In 2013, an insurance industry research association called for an entirely new paradigm for assessing risk, because rapid-fire changes in weather and temperature are outpacing traditional actuarial calculations.

In other words, we are on the threshold of carbon shock.

POLITICS, ECONOMY & SOCIAL POLICY

MIKE CUSTODE

—— *from* ——

The Vermont Papers

Recreating Democracy on a Human Scale

Frank Bryan and John McClaughry

1989

The first political book ever published by Chelsea Green, written by two dyed-in-the-wool Vermonters: Frank Bryan, a writer and professor at the University of Vermont, and John McClaughry, a writer and local/statewide politician. Their audacious idea, to create a system of government organized around small-scale bioregional clusters of towns (shires), remains an intriguing, if largely unrealized proposition. Yet the book is well worth reading today, as a way to possibly address, or at least circumvent, our increasingly partisan, gridlocked, and dysfunctional national government.

BACK AT THE GRASS ROOTS THE PEOPLE have barricaded themselves in interest groups as insurance against defeat in the one or two areas where government action is most important to them. Political parties, once healthy, decentralized, and citizen-based, have become too weak to provide coherence and direction. Congress stumbles along, deferring decisions right and left to the courts and the bureaucracy. The president faces incessant attacks by the electronic media, which are more interested in scoring points than in informing the public on key matters for governance. Washington seems more and more remote and irrelevant. The danger is that it is remote but not irrelevant.

National political leaders seem to have a sense that something is amiss, but they lack the understanding to identify the solution or do anything about it if they could identify it. For the solution must push up from below, like wild violets through the dark earth in springtime.

Historian Barry D. Karl puts our condition in brilliant perspective. Centralism may have been necessary at a point in our history, he concedes, but now it has "severed our contacts with the more familiar state and local governments" and has "threatened our sense of ourselves as citizens." No one has better expressed the paradox of politics of the post-modern period: "At a moment in history when the technology of communications is improving by quantum leaps, our suspicions of the truth of what we are told and what we know are greater than they ever have been. These suspicions have their source in the oldest and most profound need: our need to govern ourselves."

The collapse of the American center is a manifestation of a vanishing democracy in the heartland. Jefferson, as Hannah Arendt pointed out, had a "foreboding of how dangerous it might be to allow a people a share in public power without providing them at the same time with more public space than the ballot box and more opportunity to make their own voice heard in public than election day." Jefferson's fears were justified. As the watersheds of community democracy are sucked dry, the rivers of citizenship that fed our great national institutions grow ever more shallow, and the American republic is withering away.

In short the republic cannot survive without representative bodies that are credible and competent. Representation is founded on citizenship. But citizens cannot be factory built or found in electronic villages. They must be raised at home. That rearing takes place in real polities: places where community and politics meet, where individuals learn the *habit* of democracy face to face, where decision making takes place in the context of communal interdependence.

This then is the great American challenge of the twenty-first century: saving the center by shoring up its parts, preserving union by emphasizing disunion, making cosmopolitanism possible by making parochialism necessary, restoring the representative republic by rebuilding direct democracy, strengthening the national character through a rebirth of local citizenship.

—— *from* ——

Walking on Water
Reading, Writing, and Revolution
Derrick Jensen
2004

Derrick Jensen, radical environmentalist, prizewinning author, and finalist for the 2003 J. Anthony Lukas Book Prize, takes a startling and provocative look at teaching, writing, creativity, and life. He reveals how schools perpetuate the great illusion that happiness lies outside of ourselves, and that learning to please and submit to those in power makes us into lifelong clock-watchers. Jensen's great gift as a teacher and writer is to bring us fully alive at the same moment he is making us confront our losses and count our defeats.

IT'S NOT POSSIBLE TO TALK ABOUT SCHOOLING without talking about social-ization. It's not possible to talk about socialization without talking about society, and what society values. We hear a lot of talk—a lot of meaningless talk, really—about how terrible it is that high school students cannot locate the United States on a map of the world (which should be easy enough: just look in the center), give the century in which the American Civil War was fought, or name any members of the president's cabinet. We are told that standardized testing must be imposed to make sure students meet a set of standardized criteria so they will later be able to fit into a world that is itself increasingly standardized. Never are we asked, of course, whether it's a good thing to standardize children (sorry, I mean students), knowledge, or the larger world. But none of this—not maps, not dates, not names, not tests—is really the point at all, and to believe so is to fall into the fallacy that school is about learning information, not behaviors.

We hear, more or less constantly, that schools are failing in their mandate. Nothing could be more wrong. Schools are succeeding all too well, accom-plishing precisely their purpose. And what is their primary purpose? To answer this, ask yourself first what society values most. We don't talk about it much, but the truth is that our society values money above all else, in part because it represents power, and in part because, as is also true of power, it gives us the illusion that we can get what we want. But one of the costs of fol-lowing money is that in order to acquire it we so often have to give ourselves away to whomever has money to give in return. Bosses, corporations, men with nice cars, women with power suits. Teachers. Not that teachers have money, but in the classroom they have what money elsewhere represents: power. We live in a culture that is based on the illusion—and schooling is central to the creation and perpetuation of this illusion—that happiness lies outside of us, and specifically in the hands of those who have power.

Throughout our adult lives, most of us are expected to get to work on time, to do our boss's bidding (as she does hers, and he his, all the way up the line), and not to leave till the final bell has rung. It is expected that we will watch the clock, counting seconds till five o'clock, till Friday, till payday, till retirement, when at last our time will again be our own, as it was before we began kindergarten, or preschool, or daycare. Where do we learn to do all of this waiting?

Also expected is that we will be good citizens, good boys and girls all. We won't question country, god, capitalism, science, economics, history, the rule of law, but in all those areas we will defer—and continue to defer—to experts, just as we were taught. And the experts themselves? It is expected that they will be exquisitely sensitive self-censors, knowing always what or whom to question, what questions to leave unexamined, and most of all which asses to kiss. And none of us, if all goes well, will ever question how these areas—religion, capitalism, science, history, law—trick out in our own lives, even as we give our lives away.

Pretend you wish to make a nation of slaves. Or, to put it another way, you wish to procure for your nation's commercial interests a steady supply of workers, and a population pacified enough to not resist the expropriation of their resources. The crudest and probably most common means of facilitating such production is through direct force. Simply capture the workers and haul them to your factories and fields in chains. A slightly more sophisticated approach is to dispossess them, once again usually at gun-point, then give them the choice of starvation or wage slavery. Alternatively, you can force them to pay taxes or purchase your products, thereby guaranteeing they'll enter the cash economy, meaning, ultimately, that they've got to work in your factories or fields to gain the cash.

The primary drawback of each of these approaches is that the slaves still know they're enslaved, and the last thing you want is to have to put down a rebellion. Far better for them to believe they're free, because then if they're unhappy the fault lies not with you but with themselves.

It all starts with the children. If you don't start young enough, you'll never be able to acculturate them sufficiently so that they disbelieve in alternatives. And if they honestly believe in alternatives—those not delineated by you—they may attempt to actualize them. And then where would you be?

———— *from* ————

The ALL NEW Don't Think of an Elephant!
Know Your Values and Frame the Debate
George Lakoff

Originally published as *Don't Think of an Elephant!* in 2004;
second edition, 2014

Since it became an international bestseller in 2004, George Lakoff's classic has been the essential guide for progressives who want to articulate their goals and values to voters, understand how conservatives think and why people often vote against their best interests, and frame the political debate. Put out in a flurry just before the 2004 elections, the book made publishing history with its record-breaking writing and production time. Completely revised and updated in 2014, The ALL NEW Don't Think of an Elephant! *reveals why, after a brief stint of winning the framing wars in the 2008 elections, the Democrats went back to losing them, and what can be done about it. Lakoff—one of the world's most renowned linguists and cognitive scientists—also delves into the complex issues that face Americans today, urging in-depth public discourse on climate change, the wealth gap, immigration, education, abortion, marriage, health care, national security, energy, and more.*

FRAMES ARE MENTAL STRUCTURES THAT SHAPE the way we see the world. As a result, they shape the goals we seek, the plans we make, the way we act, and what counts as a good or bad outcome of our actions. In politics our frames shape our social policies and the institutions we form to carry out policies. To change our frames is to change all of this. Reframing is social change.

You can't see or hear frames. They are part of what we cognitive scientists call the "cognitive unconscious"—structures in our brains that we cannot consciously access, but know by their consequences. What we call "common sense" is made up of unconscious, automatic, effortless inferences that follow from our unconscious frames.

We also know frames through language. All words are defined relative to conceptual frames. When you hear a word, its frame is activated in your brain.

Yes, in your brain. As the title of this book shows, even when you negate a frame, you activate the frame. If I tell you, "Don't think of an elephant!," you'll think of an elephant.

Though I found this out first in the study of cognitive linguistics, it has begun to be confirmed by neuroscience. When a macaque monkey grasps an object, a certain group of neurons in the monkey's ventral premotor cortex (which choreographs actions, but does not directly move the body) are activated. When the monkey is trained not to grasp the object, most of those neurons are inhibited (they turn off), but a portion of the same neurons used in grasping still turn on. That is, to actively not grasp requires thinking of what grasping would be.

Not only does negating a frame activate that frame, but the more it is activated, the stronger it gets. The moral for political discourse is clear: When you argue against someone on the other side using their language and their frames, you are activating their frames, strengthening their frames in those who hear you, and undermining your own views. For progressives, this means avoiding the use of conservative language and the frames that the language activates. It means that you should say what you believe using your language not theirs.

Reframing

When we successfully reframe public discourse, we change the way the public sees the world. We change what counts as common sense. Because language activates frames, new language is required for new frames. Thinking differently requires speaking differently.

Reframing is not easy or simple. It is not a matter of finding some magic words. Frames are ideas, not slogans. Reframing is more a matter of accessing what we and like-minded others already believe unconsciously, making it conscious, and repeating it till it enters normal public discourse. It doesn't happen overnight. It is an ongoing process. It requires repetition and focus and dedication.

To achieve social change, reframing requires a change in public discourse, and that requires a communication system. Conservatives in America have developed a very extensive and sophisticated communication system that progressives have not yet developed. Fox News is only the tip of the iceberg. Progressives need to understand what an effective communication system is and develop one. Reframing without a system of communication accomplishes nothing.

Reframing is about honesty and integrity. It is the opposite of spin and manipulation. It is about bringing to consciousness the deepest of our beliefs and our modes of understanding. It is about learning to express what we really believe in a way that will allow those who share our beliefs to understand what they most deeply believe and to act on those beliefs.

Framing is also about understanding those we disagree with most. Tens of millions of Americans vote conservative. For the most part they are not bad people or stupid people. They are people who understand the world differently and have a different view of what is right.

All Politics Is Moral

When a political leader puts forth a policy or suggests how we should act, the implicit assumption is that the policy or action is right, not wrong. No political leader says, "Here's what you should do. Do it because it is wrong—pure evil, but do it." No political leader puts forth policies on the grounds that the policies don't matter. Political prescriptions are assumed to be right. The problem is that different political leaders have different ideas about what is right.

All politics is moral, but not everybody operates from the same view of morality. Moreover, much of moral belief is unconscious. We are often not even aware of our own most deeply held moral views.

The political divide in America is a moral divide. We need to understand that moral divide and understand what the progressive and conservative moral systems are.

Most importantly, a great many people operate on different—and inconsistent—moral systems in different areas of their lives. The technical term is "biconceptualism."

Here the brain matters even more. Each moral system is, in the brain, a system of neural circuitry. How can inconsistent systems function smoothly in the same brain? The answer is twofold: (1) mutual inhibition (when one system is turned on the other is turned off); and (2) neural binding to different issues (when each system operates on different concerns).

Biconceptualism is central to our politics, and it is vital to understand how it works.

What Is Rationality?

The brain and cognitive sciences have radically changed our understanding of what reason is and what it means to be rational. Unfortunately, all too many progressives have been taught a false and outdated theory of reason itself, one in which framing, metaphorical thought, and emotion play no role in rationality. This has led many progressives to the view that the facts—alone—will set you free. Progressives are constantly giving lists of facts.

Facts matter enormously, but to be meaningful they must be framed in terms of their moral importance. Remember, you can only understand what the frames in your brain allow you to understand. If the facts don't fit the frames in your brain, the frames in your brain stay and the facts are ignored or challenged or belittled.

—— *from* ——

Unembedded

Four Independent Photojournalists on the War in Iraq

Ghaith Abdul-Ahad, Kael Alford, Thorne Anderson,
and Rita Leistner

2005

In their unflinching look at war-ravaged Iraq, four freelance photojournal-
ists bear witness to the enduring power of independent journalism. Working
outside the US military's official "embedding" program, the authors bring us
face-to-face with the people of Iraq. They combine photographs and essays
with excerpts from two years of personal letters, journal entries, and feature
stories to take us across the front lines and cultural barriers into the lives of
a nation in crisis. This essay, "Hazardous Terrain," is by Rita Leistner.

I INTENDED TO ENTER IRAQ IN MID-MARCH via the Turkish border, which
seemed an obvious and relatively easy plan. As an independent freelancer, if
I wanted to get in I had few other options. I didn't consider the possibility
of not going. Like many people, I had seen images of war in the media, but I
felt compelled to witness this one for myself and to record its effect on those
on both sides of the conflict.

At the time it seemed Turkey would allow the American forces passage
to Iraq. But as it happened, the border never opened, and I found myself
stranded in Turkey as coalition forces advanced from Baghdad to Kuwait.
Some journalists who had been counting on Turkey returned home. Others
got on planes to Kuwait or Jordan to try other means of access. To save
money, I decided to walk to Iraq. Despite the threat of Turkish border guards
who had shoot-to-kill orders, I paid smugglers to lead me on foot through
what I'd been told would be a one-day hike. The trip turned into a harrow-
ing three days. A full moon, which made it more difficult to move undetected
at night, and a sudden unanticipated increase in border patrols meant we
had to change the route through exceptionally steep and often treacherous
mountains in Syria and Iran before reaching Iraq. Halfway, in the pitch dark
as we scaled a cliff high above the Tigris, I slipped, narrowly escaping a
deadly fall. I was lucky and only sprained my knee, but every step thereafter
was agonizing. Stoned on painkillers, I scrambled up snow-covered pitches

with the aid of a stick. Sometimes we could see the garlands of guard tower lights on the cliffs above in plain view. When we finally arrived in Iraq on April 13, it was just in time to watch the fall of Tikrit on television—an event being hailed as the end of the "high intensity phase" of the war. While embedded journalists were preparing to leave their troops and go home, I headed south to Baghdad to see what stories the war had left behind.

I'd given most of the money I had to the smugglers, so when I got to Baghdad I worked for newspapers for cash because there was no way of accessing funds from Iraq. The Turkish press corps put me up and fed me for free. Finally, by late April I had a story of my own. I'd befriended the soldiers of C Troop, 3-7 Cavalry, 3rd ID, whom I'd met on assignment as they guarded the entrance to Camp Victory (the big military base at Baghdad Airport). They invited me to come live with them, and so began my four-month embed—an unusually long stint. That summer the troop was sent to the Sunni triangle. The soldiers, who had led the ground war in Iraq, had expected to be sent home, but instead found themselves fighting a new kind of guerilla war—something cavalry was not specifically trained to do. House raids meant leaving the armored security of tanks and Bradleys. Their task was complicated by the fact that they didn't know anything about the insurgents they were meant to find and capture. When the troop was sent home in August 2003, I returned to New York with some of the first photographs of detained Iraqis. The insurgency, which had seemed at first to be a sideshow of the war, would move to center stage by the spring of 2004, by which time I was back in Iraq, this time unembedded.

Without the protection of the military I knew I would be taking greater risks, but I wanted to get a more complete picture of the story in Iraq. As the momentum of the insurgency increased, I took frequent trips to the south in search of the Mahdi Army. At that time, the Madhi Army was still feeling out its relationship with the media and did not seem to pose a deadly threat. However, many different insurgent groups were in play by then and some were not friendly to journalists, so when I was on my way back to Baghdad one day with my good friend Adnan Khan, a writer for Canada's *McLean's* magazine, we proceeded cautiously. But not cautiously enough.

On April 11, 2004, we drove into the tail end of an ambush in the Sunni stronghold of Latifiya. I snapped some quick pictures out the window—two tankers on fire, bodies lying in the road. Then we made an error: we got out of the car to get more photographs. Moments later I found myself in the middle of a firefight. Some neighborhood men and I huddled against a street corner, and it looked like there was no way out of open sight until a woman ushered us through a gate into a nearby house. I hid in the house and soon after, someone else led Adnan to me. We thought we (and my photographs) were safe, until five men crazed with anger and adrenaline burst through the gate, intent on killing "the Americans." We showed them our Canadian passports. A series of debates and screaming matches ensued between the men holding guns at our heads and the women of the house, who pleaded over and over again that they could not kill a Muslim (Adnan, who also had a Pakistani passport). Our driver, Ali, begged for our lives, swearing on the Koran that we were "good journalists." They spared us our lives and took all of our camera equipment and digital media.

Back at the hotel. I felt acute anxiety over losing my images and being without a camera. I already had several stories in the works. One on the Mahdi Army, but also a story on the women patients of the Rashad Psychiatric Hospital. I had come back to Iraq to get up close, to make portraits of individual people, as I had with the Cavalry soldiers. The abduction only drew me closer to what was going on in Iraq, involving me more intimately than ever in the lives of those affected by the ongoing conflict. So I went back to New York to replace my gear and returned as soon as possible. My unembedded tour had just begun.

—— *from* ——

The End of America
Letter of Warning to a Young Patriot
Naomi Wolf

2007

In this book bestselling author Naomi Wolf (The Beauty Myth) lays out her case for saving American democracy. Through authoritative research and documentation Wolf explains how events of recent years parallel steps taken in the early years of the twentieth century's worst dictatorships such as Germany, Russia, China, and Chile. The book cuts across political parties and ideologies and speaks directly to those among us who are concerned about the ever-tightening noose being placed around our liberties. A New York Times bestseller and Nautilus Book Award Silver Winner in Social Change/Activism.

IN COLLEGES WITH PROGRESSIVE CURRICULA, the Founders are often portrayed as "dead white men," whose vision was imperfect, who denied women and the poor civil rights, and who defined an African slave in America as being three-fifths of a person; old guys in wigs who wrote documents that are now dusty in language that seems to us to be either arcane or to offer sentiments that are so obvious now they have become clichés (". . . life, liberty, and the pursuit of happiness . . .").

Here's what we're not taught: Those words at the time they were written were blazingly, electrifyingly subversive. If you understand them truly now, they still are. These men and the women who supported their work were walking further out into the unknown—betting on ordinary people's capacities—than anyone had ever walked in the history of the human race. You are not taught—and it is a disgrace that you aren't—that these men and women were radicals for liberty; that they had a vision of equality that was a slap in the face of what the rest of their world understood to be the unchanging, God-given order of nations; and that they were willing to die to make that desperate vision into a reality for people like us, whom they would never live to see.

You weren't taught that the way they brought the freest nation in the world into being was by reading passionately about fledgling democracies of the past; by positioning their imaginations directly against the violent repressions they had fled; and by carefully, delicately crafting a mechanism of checks and balances, and a bill of rights, that would protect these extreme manifestations of freedom. The Founders set out to prove that ordinary people could be entrusted with governing themselves in a state where no one could arbitrarily arrest them, lock them up, or torture them.

Living against the backdrop of violent repression, these men and women saw the democracy they were seeking to establish, and the checks and balances that protected it, as being in need of continual rededication against potential tyrants in America who would want to subjugate Americans.

Thomas Jefferson's initial reaction to the proposed Constitution was negative, for, as he wrote to James Madison, he feared the possibility of the rise of an American tyrant: ". . . Roman emperors, popes, German emperors, deys of the Ottoman dependencies, and Polish kings—all were elective in some sense." Indeed, historian Bernard Bailyn sees that "[T]he fear of power—the very heart of the original Revolutionary ideology—was an animating spirit behind all of [Jefferson's] thinking."

Jefferson wasn't alone in the Revolutionary generation in fearing an American despot. After the publication of the proposed Constitution in 1787, critics shared his apprehension. They feared a president's treaty-making power, because they were worried he might make deals in secret. They worried about his power to make certain decisions without a two-thirds majority, because they feared he might do anything he wanted with that power. They argued that an American executive would not be immune to despotic temptations, just as an unchecked Congress would not be immune.

The authors of *The Federalist Papers*—Alexander Hamilton, James Madison, and John Jay—wrote that series of essays to help reassure their fellow Americans. They did so by explaining that the complex web of tensions they were proposing—these "checks and balances"—would prevent a person or a group united in "a common interest or passion" from depriving others of their rights. Hamilton, Madison, and Jay did not think that this web was self-sustaining. They thought that the delicate mechanism of the interdependent executive, legislative, and judiciary branches was only as reliable as the character of the people who were either protecting or abandoning it. They saw all people as corruptible and so set up the system to keep anyone from having unconfined power.

It was a truism to the Revolutionary generation that if the fragile mechanism became unbalanced, American leaders too—of course—would revert to brutality. We are so removed from the tyranny that the nation's first patriots experienced personally that we have not only forgotten this crucial insight, we have even forgotten to consider how obvious it was to the fathers and mothers of our country.

The Founders never expected us to fall asleep or get lazy. They counted on us to keep the web of the precious system intact so that an American despot could never arise. They trusted us to cherish liberty as they did.

The price of liberty, the generation that debated and created the Constitution understood, is eternal vigilance.

—— *from* ——

Inquiries into the Nature of Slow Money
Investing as if Food, Farms, and Fertility Mattered
Woody Tasch

2008

Could there ever be an alternative stock exchange dedicated to slow, small, and local? Could a million American families get their food from CSAs? What if you had to invest 50 percent of your assets within fifty miles of where you live? Such questions—which lie at the heart of Slow Money—represent the first steps on our path to a new economy. Woody Tasch, widely regarded as a pioneer of the concepts of patient capital, mission-related investing, and community-building venture capital, and founder and chairman of Slow Money, offers a call to action for designing capital markets around not extraction and consumption, but preservation and restoration.

THERE IS SUCH A THING AS MONEY that is too fast.

Money that is too fast is money that has become so detached from people, place, and the activities that it is financing that not even the experts understand it fully. Money that is too fast makes it impossible to say whether the world economy is going through a correction in the credit markets, triggered by the subprime mortgage crisis, or whether we are teetering on the edge of something much deeper and more challenging, tied to petrodollars, derivatives, hedge funds, futures, arbitrage, and a byzantine hypersecuritized system of intermediation that no quant, no program trader, no speculator, no investment bank CEO, can any longer fully understand or manage. Just as no one can say precisely where the meat in a hamburger comes from (it may contain meat from as many as hundreds of animals), no one can say where the money in this or that security has come from, where it is going, what is behind it, whether—if it were to be "stopped" and, like a hot potato, held by someone for more than a few instants—it represents any intrinsic or real value. Money that is too fast creates an environment in which, when questioned by the press about the outcome of the credit crisis, former treasury secretary Robert Rubin can only respond, "No one knows."

This kind of befuddlement is what arises when the relationships among capital, community, and bioregion are broken:

> There is an appropriate velocity for water set by geology, soils, vegetation, and ecological relationships in a given landscape. There is an appropriate velocity for money that corresponds to long-term needs of communities rooted in particular places and to the necessity of preserving ecological capital. There is an appropriate velocity for information, set by the assimilative capacity of the mind and by the collective learning rate of communities and entire societies. Having exceeded the speed limits, we are vulnerable to ecological degradation, economic arrangements that are unjust and unsustainable, and, in the face of great and complex problems, to befuddlement that comes with information overload.

As long as money accelerates around the planet, divorced from where we live, our befuddlement will continue. As long as the way we invest is divorced from how we live and how we consume, our befuddlement will worsen. As long as the way we invest uproots companies, putting them in the hands of a broad, shallow pool of absentee shareholders whose primary goal is the endless growth of their financial capital, our befuddlement at the depletion of our social and natural capital will only deepen.

On a societal level, momentum toward an incipient epiphany about money, enterprise, and nature has been building for a few decades.

Perhaps the poster child for this process is Ray Anderson, whose self-described epiphany upon reading Paul Hawken's *The Ecology of Commerce* has reached the status of legend in the field of sustainable business. Anderson's "spear in the chest" impelled him, at the age of sixty and after decades at the helm of his mature manufacturing company, to move from "the way of the plunderer" to the way of the sustainability pioneer, systematically working to reduce the ecological footprint of his company. Ray has been out front, but he has certainly not been alone.

Al Gore and Muhammad Yunus have brought climate change and social enterprise to the fore. Paul Hawken has evoked the "blessed unrest" of one hundred million citizens around the world working to promote sustainability. The once-wild eco-efficiency ideas of Amory Lovins are increasingly recognized. Jenine Benyus, Bill McDonough, and others are popularizing biomimicry, design ideas from nature. Not as much in the limelight, but equally important, the birth and maturation of such organizations as Business for Social Responsibility, CERES, Social Venture Network, Investors' Circle, the Social Enterprise Alliance, the Business Alliance for Local Living Economies, Ethical Markets, and a host of for-profit and nonprofit community-development financial intermediaries have been broadening traditional notions about the responsibility of business and the nature of private enterprise. Assets under management by social investment funds have grown dramatically. Fifty thousand people attend the Natural Products Expos East and West each year to see the latest in organics and natural products. Entrepreneurial companies such as TerraCycle and Stonyfield Farm and Farmers Diner and Dancing Deer Baking Company and United Villages and Energia Global and Sun Edison and IceStone and thousands more are pioneering businesses that create not only shareholder value, but also public benefit.

With all these developments and the growing momentum of such "blessed unrest," and with the crucible of environmental and economic crises ratcheting up the immediacy of these concerns every day, why hasn't the epiphany fully epiphanized?

My answer is: The Other Hundred Million.

That is, while one hundred million citizen activists are promoting sustainability, another one hundred million individuals—investors and the intermediaries who represent them—are stubbornly and intently affixed to their computer screens, maximizing the growth of financial portfolios and the speed of capital, promoting a culture of moneytheism and short-term thinking, maximizing circulation, minimizing percolation, diverting irrigation from the seeds of sustainability.

—— *from* ——

The Looting of America

How Wall Street's Game of Fantasy Finance Destroyed Our Jobs, Pensions, and Prosperity, and What We Can Do About It

Les Leopold

2009

How could the best and brightest in finance crash the global economy and then get us to bail them out as well? What caused this mess in the first place and what can Main Street do about it? Co-founder and director of the Labor Institute Les Leopold writes a page-turning narrative of how we all fell victim to Wall Street's exotic financial products, how even school districts were taken in by "innovative" products like collateralized debt obligations, and how they sucked trillions of dollars from the global economy when they failed. The Looting of America also tells us what average Americans can do to ensure that fantasy finance never rules our economy again.

WHO ARE THE BIG WINNERS at the fantasy-finance casino? Many of the very richest people in America. In 1982, the top 400 individuals held an average net worth of $604 million each (in 2008 dollars). By 1995, their average wealth jumped to $1.7 billion. And in 2008, the 400 top winners averaged $3.9 billion each. Just imagine. Your Lear Jet lands on the private runway out back and you are whisked to a gold-plated game room. You and 399 other multibillionaires take your drinks and settle into the plush leather chairs at the gaming tables. In front of each of you are your chips—3,900 of them, with each chip worth $1 million! The total for the 400 high rollers adds up to a cool $1.56 trillion. That's equal to about 10 percent of the entire gross domestic product of the United States.

Has fantasy finance been good to you or what?

This year you sense the crackling excitement as the top 25 hedge fund managers arrive at the casino. In 2008, a year that saw the collapse of the stock market, the implosion of pension funds, 401(k)s, and college endowments, the destruction of millions of jobs, and the worst recession since the 1930s, the top 25 hedge fund managers received $11.6 billion in compensation. You join in the thunderous applause as these guests of honor waltz in.

But just outside the window, if you dare to look, are 94.6 million non-supervisory workers who earn less than the average worker did in 1973. Also out there are about 44 million Americans with no health care. They could use some of those chips. If each billionaire inside the casino walked out with "only" $100 million per person, they would leave $1.52 trillion sitting on the table. If these chips landed in the public coffers, let's say via steeply progressive income and wealth taxes, we could invest $150 billion a year in developing and deploying renewable energy alternatives—ten times what President Obama called for during his campaign. Or we could provide free tuition for every student at every public college and university—in perpetuity.

Yet, we Americans are skittish about redistribution. As President Obama said, "This is America. We don't disparage wealth. We don't begrudge anyone for achieving success." In fact, we believe both in the equality of opportunity and in the inequality of income. Nearly all of us would agree that those who have talent, study hard, and work hard should earn more than those who don't. We admire the most successful in every field. We more or less agree that it's fine to be rich. Most of us would like to be rich as well. But we also have a sense of fairness. We worry when the gap between the superrich and the rest of us grows and grows, especially while most of us run in place. And there's that nagging feeling that the billionaire CEO who makes 1,000 times more money than his average employee isn't actually 1,000 times smarter, 1,000 times more studious, or 1,000 times harder-working. In other words, the extent of inequality we see today in America cannot possibly be due to merit. It comes, largely, from those who are in the right positions at the right times to game the casino.

The more their wealth accumulates, the more the superrich are able to lobby for reducing taxes on capital gains, on inheritance, and on the highest incomes. In 2008, corporate recipients of our tax dollars, in the form of Troubled Asset Relief Program (TARP) bailouts, spent $77 million on lobbying and $37 million in campaign contributions. According to the Center for Responsive Politics, their return on that investment was 258,449 percent. It's hard to get elected to anything without the financial backing of these elites. In fact, the best way to get elected is to be one of them.

We also worry that the superrich are severing their social connections with the rest of us. They no longer live anywhere near us (or if they do, it is behind well-protected walls, fences, and gates). Their kids don't go to our schools. They don't ride on our buses and trains, and they're not in line with us at the airport either. They don't see our doctors or go to our hospitals. So they don't suffer the indignities of our crowded services and collapsing infrastructure. Do they have any idea what our lives are like?

After the December 2008 auto-industry bailout, Bob Lutz, the vice-chairman of GM, was suffering from culture shock. He found himself in a strange land—America. He had been forced to go native. "I've never quite been in this situation before of getting a massive pay cut, no bonus, no longer allowed to stay in decent hotels, no corporate airplane. I have to stand in line at the Northwest counter. I've never quite experienced this before. I'll let you know a year from now what it's like."

—— *from* ——

The End of Money and the Future of Civilization

Thomas H. Greco, Jr.

2009

In this timely work Thomas H. Greco Jr., consultant and director of the Community Information Resource Center, demystifies the subjects of money, banking, and finance by tracing historical landmarks and important evolutionary shifts that have changed the essential nature of money. Greco provides the necessary understanding to implement approaches toward monetary liberation that would empower communities, preserve democratic institutions, and begin to build economies that are sustainable, democratic, and insulated from the financial crises that plague the dominant monetary system.

JUST AS IT IS VAIN TO JUDGE HISTORY, it is equally vain to try to predict its future course. While one can try to discern patterns and causal relationship from the past and extrapolate trends out into the future, it is very likely that even relatively short-term predictions will prove to be erroneous. We simply cannot account for what Nassim Taleb calls the "black swans"— those highly improbable events that virtually no one sees coming, that take us by surprise, and often change the course of history. Yet we can see that particular conditions bring about particular kinds of outcomes, and we are not entirely powerless to change those conditions.

I have described in this book a particular worldview and traced the development of significant human institutions that have enabled the ever-increasing concentration of power and wealth. By projecting this long-standing trend we can arrive at some very disturbing possibilities. It appears that the fate of the world, and everyone in it, is now to be determined by a very small group of individuals who have the power to decide for all of us without consulting any of us. They have their own worldview, their own values, and their own agenda that is mostly hidden. We have seen the development of a mode of governance in which, as C. Wright Mills described it, "Public relations displace reasoned argument; manipulations and undebated decisions of power replace democratic authority." At the same time, the world is being confronted with geophysical changes, human-made or otherwise, that are bound to have major impacts on how we live.

Fortunately, we still have a little bit of wiggle room in which we are free to act, but time is running out. Most of our political, economic, and religious leaders seem to be taking us in the wrong direction. That makes expressions of dissent more important than ever. There is always some risk in expressing contrary views, but it is the dissidents who are the most valuable in society and politics—for it is their dissent that focuses attention on the matters that, if left unattended, will rend the social fabric and cause greater pain to the body politic later on. It is the dissidents who force those in positions of power to justify themselves and their actions to their constituencies. The British notion of the "loyal opposition" probably had much to do with the success of British civilization, but such opposition is barely noticeable these days, either in Britain or America or elsewhere. The increasing suppression of dissent is making it necessary to devise ever more creative forms for peacefully expressing it. There is a facetious aphorism that says that, "No good deed goes unpunished." While as a general statement that may be overly cynical, it seems to bear a lot of truth when the good deed threatens the agendas and narrow self-interests of the power elite.

In assessing the current prospects for civilization, I think we need to take very seriously Carroll Quigley's observations and conclusion that, "sooner or later, an authoritarian political system that reflects the inequality in control of weapons will be established," just as Supreme Court Justice Louis Brandeis warned that, "We can have a democracy in this country or we can have great wealth concentrated in the hands of the few. We cannot have both." It appears that western civilization has already arrived at that point. Neither man lived to see the virtual shredding of the Bill of Rights and negation of the Constitution that has transpired over the past few decades, largely under the guise of the War on Drugs and then drastically worsening in the "war on terror" following September 11, but even from his vantage point of the mid-1960s Quigley had concluded that "there is little reason to doubt that authoritarian rather than democratic political regimes will dominate the world into the . . . foreseeable future."

Civilization is at a critical juncture where circumstances require that each of us take greater responsibility—not only for ourselves and our close communities, but also for the common good. We are, after all, one human family sharing one planetary home. Giving our leaders the benefit of the doubt and assuming the best of intentions on their part, I share the opinion of Mahatma Gandhi that, "Good government is no substitute for self-government." My own preference follows that of President Woodrow Wilson who said, "I do not want to see the special interests of the United States take care of the working-men, women, and children. I want to see justice, righteousness, fairness and humanity displayed in all the laws of the United States, and I do not want any power to intervene between the people and their government. Justice is what we want, not patronage and condescension and pitiful helpfulness. The trusts are our masters now, but I for one do not care to live in a country called free even under kind masters. I prefer to live under no masters at all."

What needs to happen to reverse the destructive and despotic trends, and prevent our sliding into a modern form of materialistic feudalism? In my opinion, we need (at a minimum) to find ways of achieving a number of goals.

- Power and control need to be decentralized
- Wealth must be more fairly distributed
- Local economies must be nurtured
- The commons, especially the credit commons, must be restored
- Monopolies must be eliminated or circumvented

- The basic necessities of life—especially water, air, food, and energy—must be brought under popular control
- Ecological restoration must be a high priority

As I have argued throughout, none of this can be achieved to any significant degree under the present politicized global debt-money regime. It is therefore essential that the processes of exchange and finance be recreated. None of this needs to involve coercive measures or violent confrontation, but simply the assumption of personal responsibility, voluntary cooperation, and organization. The greatest results will derive from a willingness to share and to work together. Still, these are a few things that we can do as individuals to reduce our dependence upon the dominant institutions and to prepare the way.

- You've certainly heard this numerous times before, but it bears repeating: every dollar spent is a vote. Think before you spend your money—consider more than price.
- Promote the establishment of private complementary exchange systems—and *use them*.
- Buy from your friends and neighbors whenever possible.
- Contribute your time, energy, and money to whatever moves things in the right direction.

We will either learn to put aside sectarian differences, to recognize all life as one life, to cooperate in sharing earth's bounty, and yield control to a higher power—or we will find ourselves embroiled in ever-more-destructive conflicts that will leave the planet in ruins and avail only the meanest form of existence for the few, if any, who survive. The only rational course now is for the people of the earth to embrace one another in familial love and without judgment, sharing what we have and supporting one another to each realize our fullest potential while at the same time dedicating ourselves to nurture our Mother Earth so that she may continue to nurture us. For it is, as always, the same fundamental choice that creation puts before us, so plainly expressed in the Mosaic scriptures: "I call heaven and earth to record this day against you, that I have set before you life and death, blessing and cursing: therefore choose life, that both you and thy seed may live" (Deuteronomy 30:19).

As for the elite rulers, grudges will do us no good and only create new hurdles. Let us thank them for their service and bid them welcome as members of our human family.

—— from ——

Howard Dean's Prescription for Real Healthcare Reform

How We Can Achieve Affordable Medical Care for Every American and Make Our Jobs Safer

Howard Dean with Igor Volsky and Faiz Shakir

2009

Over the years Chelsea Green has worked swiftly to get books on crucial political issues out during the heat of a debate. And so it was that, in 2009, as the nation was deciding the future of healthcare legislation, we published Howard Dean's Prescription for Real Healthcare Reform, *in which the physician and former governor widely credited for reviving the Democratic Party after the 2004 elections told Americans what real healthcare reform would look like and how they could trump big money and put health care back on track. The public option that Dean initially recommended did not come to pass, but healthcare reform did, and the book was a widely used tool in the halls of Congress and in the hands of healthcare reform advocates and everyday Americans as the debate raged on.*

AMERICANS NEED REAL HEALTHCARE REFORM, not just insurance reform, and nobody should mistake the two. If we get reform that requires insurance companies to provide coverage to everyone who applies, charge everyone the same premiums, and end their predatory practices, that would be great insurance reform. But that is not healthcare reform.

Real healthcare reform should offer coverage to the employed, the unemployed, the sick, the healthy, the young, the old. Everyone. Health reform should give all Americans the choice between private and public health coverage and break the monopoly that private insurers have on our healthcare system.

Real healthcare reform prohibits insurance companies from rescinding the coverage of cancer patients undergoing chemotherapy. Real healthcare reform protects American families from crushing medical debt, requires insurance companies to spend almost all of our premium dollars on healthcare benefits rather than costly administrative overhead or slick marketing campaigns, and provides us with adequate coverage when we need it most. And it does this always.

Real healthcare reform would give us portable, affordable, and adequate insurance. It would patch our checkered healthcare system by establishing a public plan to complement the private insurance market. It would lower costs by restoring real competition and price transparency to healthcare markets and establish new principles of innovation and health quality.

In short, real healthcare reform, unlike health insurance reform, frees our national health care and well-being from the stranglehold of private insurers and gives it back to the American people.

Recall that the purpose of health insurance is to provide coverage when it is needed most. Yet for many Americans, health insurance is either too expensive or simply inadequate. As more and more workers lose their employer-sponsored health insurance coverage, they turn to existing public programs and try—often unsuccessfully—to find coverage in the individual market. Nearly nine out of every ten people seeking such individual coverage can't find an affordable option, and most Americans are too young for Medicare, too old for the State Children's Health Insurance Program (SCHIP), and too rich for Medicaid. In fact, if you're an adult with no dependent children, in forty-three states you can be penniless but still ineligible for Medicaid coverage.

Therefore, any real healthcare reform must include the following principles:

Principle 1: Everybody In, Nobody Out

Everyone should have health insurance. As President Obama has explained, "The only way to eliminate cost-shifting, gross disparities between insurance practices, inefficient medical care, and unnecessary procedures is to have a system that includes everyone."

Principle 2: No More Healthcare Bankruptcies

Americans' financial health must be protected. This means that healthcare coverage ought to be affordable. More than 50 percent of all bankruptcy filings result at least in part from medical expenses; every thirty seconds, someone files for bankruptcy in the aftermath of a serious health problem.

In surveys in Canada, where there has been universal health insurance since 1966, the sense of security is often listed as the highest value of the system. All Canadians know that if something happens to them, they will have health insurance that they can't lose and that will take care of their basic needs. Health insurance reform must make that true in the United States.

Principle 3: Take It to Go

An employer-based healthcare system means that healthcare does not travel with employees if they change jobs. This creates one of the most urgent problems facing ordinary Americans who have insurance: They are locked into their current jobs, particularly if they have a medical condition or if they are older. Essentially they are denied promotion or advancement because they can't afford, for health insurance reasons, to take a better job.

There are two ways to solve this problem, and both should be instituted. The first is to guarantee issue. If you leave your job for a better one or one in a different state, an insurer shouldn't be able to deny you coverage because you are too old or suffer from a preexisting medical condition. The second is to give Americans the choice of either subscribing to a private insurance plan with guaranteed issue or using a public healthcare plan (similar to Medicare) that will cover them no matter where they are in the fifty states and territories. Portability is essential for fairness in our system.

Principle 4: Choose or Lose

Americans should be able to keep what they have if they like it or choose something different.

Principle 5: Improved Care, Quality, and Efficiency

Quality of patient care must be improved. I believe this will be an actual consequence of a more rational system—one in which fewer Americans with insurance can fall through the cracks. It will also be a consequence of a system that reorients its payment priorities so that unnecessary care is no longer profitable. And finally, improved care will be a consequence of a system that has reduced duplication by means of a reasonable and universal technology for electronic medical records, hopefully put together by people who know as much about doctors and healthcare providers as they do about technology and software.

—— *from* ——

Marijuana Is Safer

So Why Are We Driving People to Drink?

Steve Fox, Paul Armentano, and Mason Tvert

2009; second edition, 2013

On July 26, 2014, The New York Times became the first major news media outlet to endorse the legalization of marijuana. In the opening paragraph of their landmark column, the paper's editorial board indicted marijuana prohibition for "inflicting great harm on society just to prohibit a substance far less dangerous than alcohol." The "marijuana is safer" message originated in this 2009 book by Steve Fox, Paul Armentano, and Mason Tvert, which was updated and expanded in 2013 following the legalization of marijuana in Colorado. Not only was the book the source material for the Times's historic call to arms, but the editorial board consulted with the authors in the months leading up to the publication of their article. By providing an objective examination of marijuana and alcohol and persuasive arguments for the millions of Americans who want to advance the cause of marijuana reform, Marijuana Is Safer exemplifies the cutting-edge political thinking that has come to characterize Chelsea Green books.

Marijuana Jujitsu:
Using the Adverse Effects of Alcohol to Our Advantage

One would think that marijuana legalization advocates would enthusiastically embrace the pot-versus-alcohol comparison. After all, when one steps back and objectively evaluates the potential risks of pot and booze, marijuana's side effects are relatively insignificant. Nevertheless, some advocates have been hesitant to make direct comparisons between the two substances, fearing that discussions about the harms of alcohol will only serve to remind the public that marijuana might pose similar detrimental effects. Others have been reluctant to position cannabis as a less harmful alternative to alcohol, assuming that making such a comparison might appear as if they are promoting marijuana use.

Interestingly, the same advocates who shy away from comparing the effects of pot to the effects of alcohol typically do not hesitate to compare marijuana prohibition to alcohol prohibition. Listen to almost any speech by a prominent drug-policy reformer and you are likely to hear a reference to the failure of America's so-called Noble Experiment. The purpose is to remind the audience that the federal prohibition of alcohol did not stamp out alcohol use; rather, it significantly increased the crime associated with alcohol and drove its use underground where the lack of regulations made its consumption more dangerous. Yet when reformers make this comparison, they downplay that the use of alcohol increased once Prohibition ended. Their goal is simply to convince the audience that prohibition is counterproductive, and since it was deemed a failure for alcohol, it should also be deemed a failure for marijuana.

Of course, whether it is emphasized or not, most everyone in the audience will assume that ending marijuana prohibition would increase the availability and use of cannabis, perhaps significantly. If this audience is made up of individuals already familiar with the relative harms of marijuana and alcohol, then the likely prospect of an increase in the public's use of pot will not necessarily be much of a concern to them. But if those listening believe that cannabis is potentially as harmful as alcohol—which is what most swing voters who will ultimately decide whether marijuana should be legal in the future are likely to believe—they will not be thrilled by the prospect of marijuana storefronts opening up in their neighborhoods. When you consider this fact, it becomes almost shocking that any advocate would intentionally avoid educating the public that marijuana has been proven to be less harmful than alcohol.

Instead of avoiding comparisons between pot and booze, we propose that proponents of marijuana legalization engage in some verbal jujitsu. Jujitsu is a fighting technique involving the use of balance and leverage to turn your opponent's strength and momentum to your own advantage. As things stand today, Americans' concern over the ill effects of alcohol—as exhibited by the question, "Why add another vice?"—is a force against marijuana-policy reform. Advocates for cannabis regulation want the public to accept legalization despite the fact that a substantial portion of the public considers marijuana to be at least as dangerous as alcohol. In short, reformers are calling for a society where adults will have legal access to alcohol and marijuana at a time when the public is becoming increasingly aware of the health and societal problems associated with booze. This is an uphill task to say the least.

Sure, it may be possible to legalize marijuana despite this sentiment, but it will not be easy. In order to turn the tide after more than seventy years of marijuana propaganda and prohibition, the American people must be inspired to change the status quo. But if they believe—or are allowed to continue to believe—that the legal access to cannabis for adults will only compound many of the alcohol-fueled problems our society already faces, they will support keeping the system the way it is. This is where we need to apply our jujitsu. We will take our opponents' strongest argument—that alcohol is associated with a wide variety of social ills—and twist it to our advantage. How will we do this? By responding to our critics, over and over again, that we are not seeking to add a vice. Instead we are providing adults with a safer and less harmful recreational alternative to alcohol.

In sum, the fact that alcohol causes so many problems in our society is not a reason to keep pot illegal; rather, it is the reason we must make it legal. Unless our opponents are going to argue for a return to alcohol prohibition, they will be forced to explain why they wish to compel adults to use the more harmful recreational intoxicant.

—— *from* ——

Bye Bye, Miss American Empire

Neighborhood Patriots, Backcountry Rebels, and Their Underdog Crusades to Redraw America's Political Map

Bill Kauffman

2010

Secession movements and political reorganization have been perennial themes in American politics, and remain so to this day, from people who want to form the Second Vermont Republic to ballot initiatives aimed at splitting big states like California into supposedly more manageable, representative regions. Bill Kauffman's "exploration in political heresy," as one reviewer wrote, is a "vocabulary-bending jeremiad that exalts the local over the global." It challenges the reader to think outside the box and serves as an intellectual bookend to Chelsea Green's first political book, The Vermont Papers.

FIVE DECADES OF STATEHOOD FOR ALASKA AND HAWAII, and what do we have to show for it? The Iditarod, countless bad puns about getting lei'd, and a sweatshop Betsy Ross stitching a fifty-first star for Puerto Rico.

We can't say we weren't warned.

A chorus of reactionaries and wise liberals, from Senator William Ful-
bright (D-AR) to Columbia University president Nicholas Murray Butler,
cautioned that admitting noncontiguous states—abandoning the "united"
part of the United States—would be venturing down "the road of empire"
and "the road to colonialism," as Senator James Eastland (D-MS) said. "We
must not take it. If we go down this road . . . there will be no turning back."
To President Butler, writing in 1947, bringing in Alaska or Hawaii "would
be the beginning of the end of our historic United States of America . . .
We now have a solid and compact territorial Nation bounded by two great
oceans, by Canada, and by Mexico. This should remain so for all time."

It was "folly," said North Carolina representative Woodrow Jones of the
Hawaiians, "to believe that these people some 5,000 miles from Washington
and 2,100 miles from the mainland of America" can possibly "be imbued
with the national spirit." Congressman William Wheeler (D-GA) predicted
that "in a few years, if we follow the precedent we seem to establish here,"
the House would teem with "the gentleman from Guam, the gentleman
from the Virgin Islands, the gentleman from Liberia, the gentleman from
Israel . . . I have grown up thinking that this is the United States of America,
not the United States of the entire globe."

Mississippi Democratic senator John Stennis, the principal foe of statehood for Alaska, wondered "whether we shall take a disconnected area,
whether it be in the Pacific, in South America, in Africa, or anywhere else . . .
in the bosom of our nation? We are changing the pattern of our Union once
we launch out on this program."

Now, you may write off Stennis as a segregationist apparition, but if you
are going to discount the considered opinions of every man and woman of
the past who fails to meet your elevated moral standards, then you have cut
yourself off from all that has come before. You're navigating blind, man—
blindly and arrogantly. I hope you've brought a life jacket. The River Styx
is mighty deep.

The rest of us, sinners to be sure, might listen to Senator Stennis. (Who
was a courtly gentleman, by the way—yes, he was a servant of the mili-
tary-industrial complex, but he escorted my grandmother and great-aunt
onto the Senators Only elevator and sent them on their way to visit me in
Senator Moynihan's office with kindness and good directions. That counts
for something.)

A handful of Southern Democrats, Taft Republicans, and independent
liberals could not save the flag from its forty-ninth and fiftieth stars. They
foresaw another constellation's worth down the road. That old South Car-

olina horndog Strom Thurmond, then a segregationist Democrat, declared: "Once these two Territories are admitted to the Union, the precedent will have been set for the admission of offshore Territories which are totally different in their social, cultural, political, and ethnic makeup from any part of the present area of the United States. Would we then be in a position to deny admission to Puerto Rico, Guam, American Samoa, the Marshall Islands, or Okinawa?"

Probably not. Though whether or not Puerto Rico—or the native populations of Hawaii and Alaska—wanted in was an open question.

Statehood for Alaska and Hawaii, grafted onto the union largely for dubious "national security" reasons and in egregious violation of the contiguous integrity of the forty-eight United States, is being reexamined by a surging native Hawaiian movement and by a feisty if still fringe band of Alaska secessionists. Why not do jigsaw-puzzle makers a favor and grant these two remote colonies their independence? Let us give their stars to worthier places—say, West New York and Superior California.

--------- *from* ---------

Killing the Cranes

A Reporter's Journey Through Three Decades of War in Afghanistan

Edward Girardet

2011

Few reporters have covered Afghanistan as intrepidly and humanely as Edward Girardet. He arrived there as a young foreign correspondent just three months before the Soviet invasion in 1979. Over the next decades he trekked hundreds of miles across rugged mountains and deserts on clandestine journeys, following Afghan guerrillas as they smuggled French doctors into the country and battled with one another as well as invaders. He witnessed the world's greatest refugee exodus, the bitter Battle for Kabul in the early 1990s, the rise of the Taliban, and, finally, the US-led Western military and recovery effort that began in 2001. Killing the Cranes—winner of the prestigious Helen Bernstein Award for Excellence in Journalism—sheds extraordinary light on the personalities who have shaped Afghanistan and provides crucial insights into why the West's current involvement turned into such a disaster, not only rekindling a new insurgency but also squandering billions of dollars on a recovery process that has shown scant success.

IT IS EARLY 2011. THE AFGHAN CAPITAL is in partial shutdown until the security monitors can decide whether a reported threat is real or not. "Shutdown" is when the internationals—the UN, foreign missions, aid agencies, contractors—prevent their personnel from going out. Kabul goes into full shutdown whenever there is a confirmed incident. One was the suicide attack against ISAF headquarters in early August 2009, killing seven and injuring ninety-one. Another was the assault against a United Nations guesthouse in late February 2010. At least sixteen people, mainly foreigners, died. It was up to a lone UN staffer to ward off the attackers until the police arrived, an hour late. They then shot him dead in the confusion, believing him to be a Talib.

The Taliban and their allies are after symbolic targets. ISAF and the United Nations are certainly these. The rebels are also seeking anything US-related. *ISAF*, a running joke goes, stands for "I Saw Americans Fighting." There's not much enthusiasm for combat among most NATO partners. The Swedes, Norwegians, and other Western armies, under pressure from their own electorates, have all indicated their desire to pull out.

The US surge, which came in with President Obama, has made life more difficult for the insurgents. So they are now after easy objectives that will have a strident impact on the international community. The rebels want to show that they can still operate when and where they like, regardless of American military might.

The Taliban and other anti-Western insurgents have made IEDs [Improvised Explosive Devices] their most lethal—and effective—weapon: some 7,228 attacks in 2009, a 120 percent rise over the previous year. By the end of 2011, it was 16,000. The most striking change, however, was the rise in suicide assaults. These alone had tripled. A June 2010 United Nations report cited an average of one assassination a day, with a suicide attack every two or three days. These represent the most murderous form of violence in Afghanistan today. They also account for an estimated 70 percent of civilian deaths. Furthermore, mines or bombs are hazardous for reporters and aid workers. The expats in Afghanistan today are nervous. The guerrillas are hitting innocent civilians with IEDs or suicide attacks in Kabul, Kandahar, and other cities. One of the worst was in Jalalabad in mid-February 2011, with over thirty Afghans killed and seventy wounded outside a bank. Some of them were police waiting to pick up their paychecks. So devastating have been these assaults that some Taliban are worried that the indiscriminate killings are giving them a bad reputation among the local population; they are now trying to disclaim responsibility. Other insurgent groups—particularly those with foreign affiliations, such as the Haqqani Network—don't believe this matters. Anything to undermine the government and its outside backers. Ordinary Afghans simply have to bear it. The traffic in the city and the jostling in the bazaars go on as usual. War becomes relative. One lives with it. And Afghans have lived with it for nearly three and a half decades.

Most expats have little idea about the real Afghanistan. Holed up in their heavily fortified compounds for weeks—even months—on end, only the chosen few are allowed out. Life in the Kabul dust bowl is too dangerous, or at least that's the impression conveyed. People are shocked when they hear that I walk through the city, but I am the first to admit I don't walk complacently. I am perpetually scanning the road for danger signals, such as idling cars. If I see a NATO convoy, I turn the other way. Foreign soldiers are the preferred targets for IEDs. Something could always happen.

Much has indeed changed in Kabul, but not the way many had hoped. The airport is the most noticeable. New beige or gray-tinged hangars and office blocks for NATO forces have been constructed, while dozens of military, civilian, and aid planes and helicopters line the runway aprons. Many helicopters are ex-Soviet Mi-8s, often with Russian or Ukrainian crews. I have to look hard to find the traces of all those aircraft wrecks from shelling of the 1980s and '90s that used to litter the ground like meteor-punctured dinosaurs. They have all been cleared away. Today there is a new marble-fronted terminal heralding the new age of "post-conflict recovery." The only problem is that Afghanistan's wars have yet to end.

On a recent trip to Afghanistan I find that my airport pickup has not arrived. I cadge a lift from Tom, a bearded American logistical coordinator wearing a *shalwar-kamiz* and a woolen *kola*. He has been here since 2005 and worked previously in Uzbekistan. He is waiting to pick up two young consultants coming in from Dubai. Tom is not optimistic and believes NATO is losing the war. There are too many contradictory interests, he maintains. The security companies simply make the expats more paranoid. Everyone is out to make money. "They need to be talking to the Taliban," Tom adds with the weary authority of an old hand.

On leaving the airport with its armored vehicles, Afghan soldiers in American-style uniforms, and police with blue bulletproof vests, one crosses into the sprawling beyond, a totally different scenario. The international obsession for security has turned Kabul into a city of siege. Whole streets have been cut off by crash barriers, concrete walls, and police checkpoints, angering numerous residents forced to make wide detours to take their children to school or get to work.

Tom drops me off at Gandamack lodge, Peter Jouvenal's guesthouse— though it's not the same building as before. The previous landlord wanted to sell it for nine million dollars, so Peter moved. Still a cameraman-producer, Peter is also a full-fledged entrepreneur. He remains one of the best-informed foreigners on Afghanistan, always blunt with his opinions. Lack of commitment is the principal reason why the international recovery effort is failing, he explains. "They all have their own agendas. They're not here for the Afghans." The British army has embraced a far more realistic but pessimistic approach, in his opinion. They know they are fighting an impossible war. As for the UK's international aid agency, and other diplomats isolated at the British embassy, Jouvenal says, "They're living on another planet. They've no idea what's going on."

Peter and I have worked in Somalia, Liberia, and Sri Lanka, but now we're back in Afghanistan. Again. He offers to take me over in his Land Rover to Bada Bir, an agricultural research center on the outskirts of the capital, where his wife, Hassina, is training women to pick quality crops at the farm for hotels and restaurants so that they have a bit of income.

As we drive through the city, I notice that there has been even more construction since my last visit to this part of town several years earlier.

Whole sectors are now studded with garish Dubai-style villas with high walls and razor wire, armed guards sitting outside. There is a lot of money in Kabul these days, much of it in the wrong hands. The farm is a government initiative started in the Soviet era. Several fields are being cultivated as part of a USAID-funded project for sweet corn, cherry tomatoes, and peppers. They are using different types of irrigation, such as drip, flooding, and furrow, to see what can be replicated easily by the Afghan farmer.

Hassina, an energetic Afghan entrepreneur, has also set up a nonprofit NGO—the National Organization for Women (NOW)—to help women establish their own businesses. It is hard for Afghan women to earn a living. At the farm, there is resistance from the male employees, who steal the crops to make money and deeply resent the women—who remind me of Latin American migrant workers with their straw hats bending over the pepper plants in the hot late-morning sun.

We head back for lunch. Gandamack is located off a busy road near the UNHCR and Iranian embassy. There is no sign indicating a hotel and restaurant behind its walls. It's best to be discreet. But the guesthouse is a well-known watering hole and eating place for expats. It's a small world, and immediately upon entering it I am bumping into people I know from before or from other wars. One of them is a British neighbor from a nearby village in France working for the UN. We never seem to find the time to get together back home, so we arrange to have dinner in Kabul. Gandamack is not like many of the embassies and international missions, whose barriers have become so high you can no longer see the buildings. Security has defeated the whole purpose of being here. Most experienced NGOs refuse to have armed protection. Their best security, they maintain, is good relations with the communities they work in. If you lose touch, there's no point.

It is evening as I walk back to my room at the American Institute for Afghanistan Studies, a quiet place to write. Kabul may have changed with the constant traffic and well-lit shops, but I still find the same hospitality. Always a greeting coupled with a gesture beckoning me over for tea.

Nearby, just a few hundred yards from the British and German embassies, I nip into the Finest Supermarket, which caters to foreigners and wealthy or diaspora Afghans. I purchase some batteries, the equivalent to three days' wages of an Afghan laborer, and hurry out. I am wary about lingering. Months later, in January 2011, a suicide bomber blew himself up at Finest Supermarket, killing five Afghans—including a young child—and three foreign women.

Overhead, an enormous billboard flashes. A wide-screen TV the size of two trucks relentlessly advertises new Toyota cruisers, Visa cards, and Kam Air—now the preferred airline carrier for most expats. The weekend flights are also filled by well-heeled Afghans, including government officials, who have made fortunes from the international recovery process and make regular trips to Dubai and the other Gulf countries where they have homes.

How many Afghans can afford such luxuries, particularly destitute migrants from the countryside in search of jobs? The bulk of rural Afghans have benefited little from the billions of dollars poured in over the past years. Ordinary Afghans may also wonder what on earth all these foreigners are doing here. Despite the propaganda about how the internationals have come to help promote democracy and recovery, the Afghans are no longer buying it. Even most foreigners, if they are honest, know that their intervention has proved largely a failure. Afghanistan has become one great pretend game.

—— *from* ——

Get Up, Stand Up

Uniting Populists, Energizing the Defeated, and Battling the Corporate Elite

Bruce E. Levine

2011

Polls show that the majority of Americans oppose recent US wars and Wall Street bailouts, yet most remain passive and appear resigned to powerlessness. In Get Up, Stand Up, *clinical psychologist Bruce Levine offers an original and convincing explanation for this passivity and describes how we can recover dignity, confidence, and the energy to do battle. That achievement fills in the missing piece that, until now, has undermined so many efforts to energize genuine democracy.*

I WILL PROVIDE EVIDENCE . . . that the majority of Americans are actually populists, in the sense that they are anti-elitists who trust the American people's judgment more than the corporate-government alliance. I will also describe differences among populists. I believe it is possible that populists can overcome their divides and together battle against elite control, and I will offer suggestions as to how to create this unity.

The corporate media routinely divides Americans as "liberals," "conservatives," and "moderates," a useful division for the corporatocracy because no matter which of these groups is the current electoral winner, the corporatocracy retains power. In order to defeat the corporatocracy, it's more useful to divide people in terms of "elitism" and "anti-authoritarianism"; and in order to unite anti-authoritarians, it's important to understand the psychological differences among them.

One example of an anti-authoritarian movement that I am personally familiar with is the mental health treatment reform movement, which comprises people who identify themselves as "on the left," others who identify themselves as "libertarians," and still others who disdain any political labels. I can tell you from my nearly two decades of working with these reformers that they certainly have different political views, but they all share a distrust for Big Pharma, a contempt for pseudoscience, and a belief that people deserve truly informed choice with respect to treatment. Most of these reformers respect

Erich Fromm, the leftist psychoanalyst, along with Thomas Szasz, the libertarian psychiatrist, both passionate anti-authoritarians who have confronted mental health professionals for using dogma to coerce and control people.

Similarly, the education reform movement includes anti-authoritarians across the ideological spectrum, from libertarian educators such as John Taylor Gatto to left educators such as Alfie Kohn. While there are political differences among them, they agree that most standard schools are oppressive environments that more often encourage obeying orders, apathy, and dependence on authorities rather than nurturing curiosity and critical thinking.

Among anti-authoritarians, there are both the more "afflicted" and the more "comfortable," and it's important to understand their differing psychological realities in order to better unite them. This comfortable-afflicted continuum, at its most fundamental level, is based on the magnitude of frustration and other pains that one has in getting through the day. In our money-centric society, the capacity to pay bills significantly affects people's level of comfort, but there are other important nonfinancial variables that can either mitigate or exacerbate pain. Pain is reduced by having a platform in which one's voice can be heard by others; pain is increased when one feels completely voiceless, impotent, and powerless. Pain is reduced by having a meaningful job, even if it's not lucrative; pain is increased when one is working *only* for a paycheck. Pain is reduced by having other people in one's life who are joyful about one's joy and sad about one's sadness; pain is increased by isolation and an absence of caring. Pain is reduced by a feeling of connectedness with one's locale and natural world; pain is increased when one feels completely alienated from one's surroundings.

The afflicted are pained by some combination of their money worries, their employment, their unemployment, their isolation, and their alienation. In contrast, one is in the comfortable group if, all in all, the satisfactions of life outweigh the frustrations. One need not be financially well off to be in the comfortable group. It may be enough to have a platform, a meaningful job, and/or a non-alienating locale.

At different times in my life, I have been at different points on the afflicted-comfortable continuum. I have been overwhelmed by the pains of money worries, a stupid job, an alienating environment, and isolation. But I also know what it feels like to not have these pains. And I have come to understand how my level of pain about everyday life affects my receptivity to ideas, my energy level, and my capacity to take action.

Among "comfortable anti-authoritarians," many may know that there are millions of Americans working mindless jobs in order to hold on to their health insurance, or hustling two low-wage jobs to pay college loans, rent, and a car payment, or who may be unable to find even a poorly paying, mindless job and are instead helplessly watching eviction or foreclosure and bankruptcy close in on them. Many comfortable anti-authoritarians may intellectually understand the plight of the afflicted, but unless they have been part of that afflicted class—and remember what it feels like—they may not be able to fully empathize and respect the afflicter's emotional state. One major symptom of this lack of empathy and respect is the assumption that passive people are politically inert because they are ignorant; for example, that they lack knowledge of how they are being victimized. This assumption of ignorance as the cause of passivity is a great source of resentment for the afflicted, and this resentment is a great source of disunity.

I don't presume to know what everybody in the afflicted class needs, but I can tell you what would have engaged me when I was a member. I certainly didn't need lectures or other easy ego-tripping advice on what I should do. From the comfortable, I would have liked to hear some recognition that human beings often become passive not because they are ignorant, stupid, lazy, or immature but because they are overwhelmed by their pain, and their primary goal is to shut down or divert themselves in order to function at all. So when I found myself watching too much stupid television to divert myself from the pain of my life, I *knew* that watching stupid television was destructive for me. People *know* that alcohol, drugs, gambling, and other shutdowns, escapes, and diversion are not healthy; but they also know that without these shutdowns and diversions, their pain can be so overwhelming that they feel suicidal, homicidal, or psychotic. Comfortable anti-authoritarians need to respect the reality of the effects of overwhelming pain. The assumption that people's inactions are caused by ignorance sounds and smells elitist to many in the afflicted class who lack the energy to be engaged in any activism. Instead of lecturing to the afflicted, the comfortable might try respecting them and, if possible, sharing resources with them. Respect, resources, and anything that concretely reduces their level of pain is likely to be far more energizing than a scolding lecture.

Other divides among anti-authoritarians have caused disunity. It's natural for us to come to different conclusions as to the causes of passivity as well as to have different strategies for transforming it. Spirited debate is what democracy is all about. But when debate turns to mutual antipathy and divides anti-authoritarians, it plays into the hands of the elite. When advocates become so ego-attached to their analyses that they're unwilling to hear other explanations and other solutions, then they have forgotten the spirit of democracy. All of our experiences are limited, and so none of us has all the answers. The spirit of democracy is one of mutual respect and confidence that others can have truths and solutions that any one of us may not have yet considered.

Most of us understand the reality that we are governed by a corpora- tocracy, and for many of us it's a truth that triggers frustration and anger. Some of us are able to use that frustration and anger to energize construc- tive actions. However, there is a large group of anti-elitists who have been so worn down by decades of personal and political defeats, by financial struggles, by social isolation, and by daily interaction with impersonal and inhuman institutions that they no longer even feel the urge to act; for them, the truth of elitist control does not trigger resistance. Instead, their pain results in an ever-increasing withdrawal from the political sphere.

This is a different explanation for widespread political inaction by Amer- icans than is routinely offered, and some activists struggling for democracy disagree. They insist that people are inactive because they are ignorant of what's going on, or that flawed organizations that should be channeling the desire for change are failing us. I am certainly in favor of getting truths out there and improved organizing efforts. However, I believe that missing from these oft-preached solutions is a vitally important piece of the puzzle—the problem of demoralization. The aim of this book is to deal with that piece so all who believe in democracy can have a better chance of achieving it.

—— *from* ——

Local Dollars, Local Sense
How to Shift Your Money from Wall Street to Main Street and Achieve Real Prosperity
Michael H. Shuman

2012

In 2010 Chelsea Green and the Post Carbon Institute teamed up to concep- tualize the Community Resilience Guides, which would provide cutting-edge guidance on local and regional economic, food, and energy solutions. Local economy pioneer Michael Shuman's Local Dollars, Local Sense *was the first release in the series, and James Howard Kunstler summed up its worth when he said, "This book should be required reading for Americans." That's because, still reeling from an economic crash caused by reckless behavior on Wall Street, Americans needed to understand why they should move their money to Main Street, and how they and their communities could profit in the process. A revolutionary toolbox for social change, the book delivers the most thorough overview available of local investment options, explains the obstacles, profiles investors who have paved the way, and demystifies the growing realm of local investment choices.*

AMERICA'S INVESTMENT SYSTEM IS BROKEN. Even though roughly half the jobs and the output in the economy come from local small business, almost all our investment dollars go into big corporations on Wall Street. The overall wealth of the country is more than $150 trillion. Some of this wealth is held in the form of land, buildings, and machinery and is considered "illiquid"—not very easy to convert into dollars. The most liquid assets held by households and nonprofits are stocks, bonds, mutual funds, pension funds, and life insurance funds, and at the end of 2010 these totaled about $30 trillion. To put this number in perspective, all the production in the United States each year—the gross domestic product (GDP)—currently totals about $15 trillion. So Americans have double their GDP in long-term savings. *Not even 1 percent of these savings touches local small business.*

Were local businesses uncompetitive, unprofitable, and obsolete for the U.S. economy, this gap would be understandable. But as we will see, local businesses are actually more profitable than larger corporations—and their competitiveness is impressive despite decades of inattention from policymakers and economic developers. This investment gap represents a huge market failure. It means that Americans are systematically overinvesting in Wall Street and underinvesting in Main Street. Were this $30 trillion allocated efficiently, at least $15 trillion would move into locally owned small businesses.

Imagine the kinds of new businesses and economic revitalization that would be possible with a $15 trillion shift. To put this number in perspective, it represents twenty times more money than all the funding the federal government allocated in the first national stimulus program of 2009–2010. It represents about $50,000 for every American man, woman, and child. For even a small town of five thousand, this shift would make $250 million available for starting or expanding local business. For a suburban town of fifty thousand, it would mean $2.5 billion more of capital. For a metro area of half a million, $25 billion more would be available.

What stands in the way of this shift is obsolete institutions and laws that make local investment extremely difficult and expensive. Securities laws from the Great Depression effectively enacted a system of investment apartheid, with "accredited investors" being able to invest in any business they wish and unaccredited investors being essentially told to get lost. Accredited investors make up the richest 2 percent of Americans—those who earn more than $200,000 (or $300,000 with a spouse) or have more than $1 million in assets, excluding their primary residence. As long as entrepreneurs don't lie about their business plans, governance, and numbers, they can easily approach any "accredited" investor for money. The other 98 percent of us are "unaccredited" and presumed too gullible to invest in a company without massive legal paperwork. Before a business can make an investment "offering" to even a single unaccredited investor, it must pay an attorney to produce a private placement memorandum and various regulatory filings and documents; legal, accounting, and government fees could easily run $25,000 to $50,000. If a company wants many unaccredited investors, it must create a public offering that could cost another $50,000 or more, and it then must make ongoing, exhaustive filings to the SEC.

The thick offering documents are frankly worthless to the layperson for whom they were written to protect. They are filled with turgid, legalistic prose that lives on lawyers' hard drives. Often these documents are printed IN A TINY FONT IN ALL CAPITAL LETTERS THAT NO HUMAN BEING HAS EVER BEEN OBSERVED TO READ. Besides ensuring full employment for attorneys, securities law can claim one stunning achievement: It has managed to keep small investors away from small businesses. Again, 98 percent of the American public cannot invest in more than half of the economy.

This exclusion is especially galling given that there's overwhelming evidence that local businesses are the most important sources of new income, wealth, and jobs for communities. At a time when *official* U.S. unemployment is at its highest levels since the Great Depression, the sluggishness with which either political party has sought to fix this problem by reforming securities law and promoting local investment is stunning.

Most Americans, of course, don't really invest in individual companies. They take advantage of tax laws to place small percentages of their paychecks into their individual retirement accounts (IRAs) and 401(k) accounts sheltered from income taxes. But for any investor—accredited or unaccredited—who wishes to put this money into a portfolio of local businesses, the market failure is just as bad. There is not a single mutual fund or investment broker in the country that gives "retail" investors the opportunity to invest in a portfolio of local businesses. The curious investor who presses her broker or financial advisor for some local-investment options is told, condescendingly, that these small businesses are too risky and their profits too insignificant to bother with, even though there's compelling evidence, as we'll see, that they are less risky and more profitable than the Fortune 500.

—— *from* ——

The New Feminist Agenda

Defining the Next Revolution for Women, Work, and Family

Madeleine M. Kunin

2012

Winner of a ForeWord Book of the Year Award (Bronze) and the Ernesta D. Ballard Book Prize, former Vermont governor Madeleine Kunin's incisive treatise on the state of feminism shows that, despite opening up thousands of doors in the 1960s and 1970s, US women are not where they thought they'd be—and on several fronts are far behind women in other countries. It's time, says Kunin, to change all that. Looking back over five decades of advocacy, Kunin analyzes where progress stalled, looks at the successes of other countries, and charts the course for the next feminist revolution—one that mobilizes women, and men, to call for the kind of government and workplace policies that can improve the lives of women and strengthen their families. Kunin, the first woman in the United States to serve three terms as a governor, also served as deputy secretary of education and as an ambassador in the Clinton administration.

FIVE OF US WERE MEETING FOR LUNCH and reminiscing about the women's movement. "I was never one of those angry women," one said. "I'm still angry," I blurted. My reaction surprised both me and my friends. Where did that come from? A source I hadn't tapped before. Upon reflection, I realized that I'm not angry enough to carry a placard down hot macadam streets in front of the nation's Capitol, like I did in my thirties when I marched for women's rights. But now in my seventies I'm still dissatisfied with the status quo and harbor a passion for change. Old age allows me the luxury of being impatient—there is not so much time left—and it permits me to say what I think, to be demanding, and, best of all, to imagine a different world where there is true gender equality in the workplace, the home, and the political arena.

Why the anger? What did I expect?

I expected that the women's movement of the 1970s would give me a good answer to the question my students regularly asked: how do you manage to have a family *and* a career?

I expected that affordable, quality child care would be widely available, that paid family leave would be the law, and that equal pay for equal work would be a reality. I did not expect that women would still make 77 cents for every dollar that men earn.

I expected that one-third to one-half of our Congress, governors, state legislatures, and mayors would be female. I did not expect that in 2010 that number would be 17 percent in the Congress, and the United States would be tied at 69th place in the percentage of women in parliaments, out of 178 countries.

I expected that one-third to one-half of corporate board members would be women. I did not expect to see that proportion stuck at 17 percent.

I expected that a high percentage of the Fortune 500 companies would be led by women. I did not expect that figure to be 3 percent.

I expected that misogyny, rape, and other acts of violence against women would be widely condemned and sharply reduced. I did not expect that a female journalist could be sexually abused in the middle of Cairo's Tahrir Square and then blamed for bringing it on herself, as Lara Logan of CBS News experienced in February 2011.

I expected that *Roe v. Wade* would remain the law of the land. I did not expect that it would be eroded, state by state.

I expected that by the year 2011 grandmothers like myself would be able to tell their grandchildren of how life used to be "long ago," when families had to figure out for themselves how to be both wage earners and caregivers.

Some changes occurred that I had not expected and could not have imagined: that women would comprise nearly 60 percent of college undergraduates, that women would comprise half of the medical and law students, that women would enter the workforce in record numbers, and that the traditional family supported by the father would be overtaken by the two-wage-earner family.

That's the good news. The bad news is that many women who have careers that we never could have imagined for ourselves are still flummoxed by the most age-old problem: how to have a job and take care of the children, the elderly, the sick, and the disabled. Until we find a way to sort out how to share these responsibilities—between spouses, partners, employers, and governments—gender equality will remain an elusive goal. Progress for women will remain stalled. But it's not only about gender anymore.

—— *from* ——

What Then Must We Do?

Straight Talk About the Next American Revolution

Gar Alperovitz

2013

Never have Americans been more frustrated with our economic system, more fearful that it is failing, or more open to fresh ideas about a new one. But what might that next system be? Not corporate capitalism, says author Gar Alperovitz, and not state socialism, but something else—something entirely American and something for which he boldly lays the groundwork in What Then Must We Do? *The author argues passionately that the time is right for a revolutionary new economy, and explains what it means to democratize the ownership of wealth, what it will take to build a new system to replace the decaying one, and how to strengthen our communities through cooperatives, worker-owned companies, and publicly owned enterprises. Alperovitz's long career in social change has spanned decades, in which he has worked in both academia and government and has co-founded The Democracy Collaborative.*

PEOPLE TOSS AROUND the phrase *It's the system* pretty loosely in everyday language. Usually they mean that things are sort of set up, by either design or accident, to run the way they run—and that the game is pretty well rigged so that those at the top (and their organizations) control the action. You can't really buck the system: Too much power, too much red tape, too much bureaucracy—they'll wear you down.

And so on.

That's not a bad way to start thinking about the *big* system that defines the overarching contours of our national life—namely, the large corporate-dominated economic system and the heavily constrained political system that set the terms of reference for almost everything else.

I want to push a bit deeper, however. Here's the essential point: A system problem—as opposed to your usual garden-variety political problem—is one that isn't going to go away through politics as usual. It will require somehow changing the way things are rigged deeper down in the machinery of institutions, corporations, bureaucracy, and all the other elements of the system that produce the outcomes we experience.

A system problem is difficult. It runs deep.

Everyone knows we have problems in the United States: unemployment, poverty, environmental decay, global warming—to say nothing of whole cities like Detroit, Cleveland, St. Louis, and many others that have essentially been thrown away. If you are black or brown, your prospects are far worse. And wars keep happening, with little positive outcome and lots of dead American kids (to say nothing of dead Iraqis, Afghanis, and others). Civil liberties decay, day by day, year by year.

So much is obvious. Moreover, this wealthiest of all wealthy nations has been steadily falling behind many other nations of the world. Consider just a few wake-up call facts from a long and dreary list: The United States now ranks lowest or close to lowest among advanced "affluent" nations in connection with inequality (21st out of 21), poverty (21st out of 21), life expectancy (21st out of 21), infant mortality (21st out of 21), mental health (18th out of 20), obesity (18th out of 18), public spending on social programs as a percentage of GDP (19th out of 21), maternity leave (21st out of 21), paid annual leave (20th out of 20), the "material well-being of children" (19th out of 21), and overall environmental performance (21st out of 21).

Add in low scores for student performance in math (17th out of 21), one of the highest school dropout rates (14th out of 16), the second-highest per capita carbon dioxide emissions (2nd out of 21), and the third-highest ecological footprint (3rd out of 20).

Also for the record: We have the worst score on the UN's gender inequality index (21st out of 21), one of the highest rates of failing to ratify international agreements, the highest military spending as a portion of GDP (1st out of 21), and among the lowest spending on international development and humanitarian assistance as a percentage of GDP.

Such facts are pretty hefty elbow nudges in the direction I'd like you to think about, but they aren't (yet) much more than that. Everyone knows that if you don't like the way things are turning out, the thing to do is to "get involved"—elect a congressman, or senator, or president. We've all been told (and maybe even told others!) that things aren't going to change unless we all roll up our sleeves and get into the game.

I don't have any problem whatsoever with that kind of advice—nor . . . with advice suggesting that we need to build a political movement. The problem is not with what is being said, but with what is not being said.

What is usually being said is this (in only slightly oversimplified language): We know that the economic system is dominated by large and powerful corporate institutions—and we know that the political system is dominated by money and lobbying, and also, in practice, by large corporate institutions.

The fundamental judgment, however, is that it is possible (without altering "the above") to organize enough political power so that "the above" can be made responsive to the concerns of the vast majority of people in these United States.

Usually the way politics does this trick, it is hoped, is that enough power can be put together to tax "the above" and then spend for good things like schools, roads, bridges, and maybe even health care. Also, politics, it is hoped, can put together enough power to regulate "the above" to achieve health, a clean environment, safety, and other outcomes of importance to the people.

Now, it's surely possible that this can be done sometimes. Moreover, almost certainly something like this . . . has worked (sort of) in the past.

But there is a really interesting and challenging—and also profoundly important—matter I'd like you to ponder. Things seem to have changed. It no longer seems that "the system" can be managed in the old way. It is possible, of course, that this means that maybe it can't be managed at all. Alternatively, clearly some way other than the above formula must be found to get us out of the box we are in.

The best way to ponder this matter *at the outset* is to take a look at some of the long, long trends documenting the outcomes flowing from the traditional assumptions and traditional political theory of change. Then we can consider what they tell us about whether the underlying system is being managed or if it is managing us.

Note carefully . . . I am not saying that traditional politics never works, or has never worked in the past. That is a different question. Nor am I suggesting . . . what might be done about the way the world seems to be proceeding. . . .

What I'm asking you to ponder with me is the simple fact that the system (the way underlying institutional power is currently arranged) seems now to be producing outcomes, year in and year out, that do not much respond to the old theory of politics. Something deeper is going on.

EPILOGUE

——— *from* ———

Companies We Keep

Employee Ownership and the Business of Community and Place

John Abrams

Originally published as *The Company We Keep* in 2005; second edition, 2008

In 2012 Chelsea Green Publishing became an employee-owned company through the use of an ESOP (Employee Stock Ownership Plan). It seems especially fitting to end this collection with an excerpt from this important book. Written by John Abrams, co-founder and president of South Mountain Company, an employee-owned design, building, and renewable energy company on Martha's Vineyard, Companies We Keep *celebrates the idea that when employees share in the rewards as well as the responsibility for the decisions they make, better decisions result and the company is strengthened to remain independent and strong into the future. This excerpt is from the concluding chapter called "The Company We Keep."*

I'M COMMONLY ASKED WHY OUR NAME is South Mountain Company when there are no mountains on Martha's Vineyard. When we started out in New York State, we worked out of a shop we built on South Mountain Road. Chris carefully hand-painted the name on the door of our old flatbed truck. When we got to the Vineyard, we didn't want to bother to repaint, so we kept the name. Years later, I tried to change it, but people in the company reacted so negatively I never tried again. I suppose the name is endearing because it reminds us of our irregular beginnings. Perhaps it's also comforting that something—anything—stays the same, given the constantly changing nature of our business.

Tachi Kiuchi and Bill Sherman, in *What We Learned in the Rainforest*, say, "We don't believe change has to seem draconian to be fundamental: it's hard to build a tree but easy to plant a seed. Building a tree is draconian, desperate, and ineffective. Planting a seed is fundamental, serene, and easy." Having planted the seeds of shared ownership, democracy, and cathedral building, we can only guess at the shape of the trees that will result. What will the next generation of owners do?

The questions at hand are these: Can small business, supported by strong underlying principles and shared ownership, help make better lives and better communities? To go farther, and perhaps too far, can business conducted this way help us be kinder to ourselves and to one another, to the planet, and especially to our children? Is it a stretch to say that the more fully we are fulfilled in our work, the more fully we can love both our children and our community? And that the more fulfilled we are, the more we can help build a future that's sane and just? If I overreach, it is only my enthusiasm for the possibility that is to blame.

The arc of this book is an attempt to find answers to these questions by tracking back through the experiences I've had as part of South Mountain Company, and by considering this experience in the context of the work and thinking of others. This process has led to many hunches and conjectures and some new understandings, but no clear answers yet, as far as I can tell.

My good friend Lee Halprin says about writing:

> A lot of writing does not show that it knows the slightness of its knowledge. I think it is good to consider how one feels about the relation between what one can say and what one knows and between what one knows and what one doesn't, and between what is known and what isn't, and between what's knowable and what isn't. I think it's good to think hard enough about this for the thought to somehow color one's writing, somehow to seep into it.

That feels particularly right to me, but hard, too, to uphold. I've tried to remember the slightness of my own knowledge as I have written, and tried to separate what I think I know from what I'm certain I don't.

Here's what I'm thinking now.

What I think I know is that the process of telling this story has helped me to know more about where we have been and where we are headed, in the same way that my colleagues at South Mountain continue to help me know more, every day, about the community we build and the company we keep.

I thought, when I started writing, that I wanted to tell a complete story about something we had started, grown into, and become. I see now that the story is not about what South Mountain has become as much as it is about what we have begun. There are things that we have learned to do, that we can do, right now, reasonably well. We can make good houses. We can develop other enterprise that extends our primary endeavors. We can develop effective relationships with those who are connected to our business. We can support a community of employees and employee-owners, giving them the opportunity to make good livings. We can offer, to one another, ownership and a voice in the conduct of our work. We can contribute to the well-being of our community and create small successes that enhance it. We can carefully consider those decisions that affect the evolution of our enterprise. We can infuse our work with a cooperative spirit that feels better than competition. We are beginning to have the capacity to think long-term. We're off to a good start. But there is much more to do, and much more to know.

I think I know that the ongoing attempt to balance multiple bottom lines has been, and continues to be, a worthy, enriching endeavor.

I think I know, too, that our craftsmanship, in all things, is the central thread that makes visible and tangible the underlying principles that guide us. Surrounded by the things we make, we are constantly reminded of the expressions and collaborations from which they resulted. Our doors warp, windows stick, tiles crack, floors shrink, finishes blemish. We fix these so that what we produce is the best it can be. The aspiration is genuine. Craft is a guiding star.

I think I know that the idea of community entrepreneurialism has taken hold within this company. As we move from our decades-long concentration on affordable housing to a more active role in renewable energy and relocalizing the economy, there is new excitement.

I think I know, because the tenor is so pervasive, that there is a developing notion of legacy in the company that hints at a bright future. We will endure.

ACKNOWLEDGMENTS

*F*irst and foremost, all thanks and recognition go to our tremendous authors. Although this book celebrates our company and its history, it goes without saying that we would not exist without our authors' enormous and varied talents and provocative ideas.

Second, we thank all Chelsea Green employees, past and present, who have worked tirelessly to edit, design, produce, and sell our authors' work over the past three decades. Collectively, they are the co-creators and facilitators who make all things happen and keep the spark of independent publishing alive in an era of multinationals and consolidation.

Third, we thank Ian and Margo Baldwin, the co-founders of Chelsea Green, who had the foresight (or good fortune) to think that starting a small publishing house in Chelsea, Vermont, would be a great idea. In the 1980s, long before tablets and smartphones and telecommuting, the notion that a general trade publisher could survive (and thrive) outside New York City seemed more than a little naive. Witness the bleached bones of a lot of other "country publishers" who thought the same thing, and who either sold out or got out. Ian and Margo's tenacity and direction over the years have grown the company (but not too much), steering it into prominence and profitability.

Fourth, we thank all the talented freelancers—editors, copy editors, proofreaders, indexers, designers, illustrators, and others—who have worked with Chelsea Green over the years; without their efforts we would never have been able to produce such beautiful and important books.

Special thanks to all of the current Chelsea Green employee-owners who suggested specific excerpts, wrote many of the introductory comments, and helped make this labor of love possible in a remarkably short amount of time: Ian and Margo Baldwin, Joni Praded, Makenna Goodman, Brianne Goodspeed, Michael Metivier, Shay Totten, Darrell Koerner, and Michael Weaver. Our intrepid intern Lizzy Hardison also lent editorial support above and beyond the duty in helping to organize material coming at her from many directions and keep the book on schedule.

Finally, thanks to the many people who value the kinds of books we publish. It is always gratifying to run into our "fans" when we attend conferences or trade shows and meet readers who say they own not just one or two of our titles, but a whole shelf full of them. They, like us, value our "brand" and our commitment to sustainability, independent living, progressive politics, and a better world.

LIST OF ILLUSTRATIONS

Titles Published
── *by* ──
CHELSEA GREEN

1985

In a Pig's Eye by Karl Schwenke
The Man Who Planted Trees by Jean Giono
The Upper Valley by Jerold Wikoff

1986

First Light by Ethan Hubbard
Permanent Parisians by Judi Culbertson and Tom Randall
Words and Images of Edvard Munch by Bente Torjusen

1987

The Automotive History of Lucky Kellerman by Steve Heller
Backtracking by Ted Levin
Castaways by George Cadwalader
Permanent New Yorkers by Judi Culbertson and Tom Randall

1988

The Eight Corners of the World by Gordon Weaver
Free-Heel Skiing by Paul Parker
Goodbye Highland Yankee by Scott Hastings, Jr.
New York's Great Art Museums by Robert Garrett
On Watching Birds by Lawrence Kilham

1989

The New Organic Grower by Eliot Coleman
Permanent Californians by Judi Culbertson and Tom Randall
Schooner Master by Peter Carnahan
The Vermont Papers by Frank Bryan and John McClaughry

1990

Dangerous River by R. M. Patterson
Journey to Ollantaytambo by Ethan Hubbard
The Lure of the Labrador Wild by Dillon Wallace

Season of the Whale by Erich Hoyt
Voyage to the Whales by Hal Whitehead

1991

A Canoeist's Sketchbook by Robert Kimber
End of the Road by Wolfgang Zuckermann
Getting Back on Your Feet by Sally R. Pryor
Judevine by David Budbill
Permanent Londoners by Judi Culbertson and Tom Randall
Ski Vermont! by Jules Older
Strangers Devour the Land by Boyce Richardson

1992

Beyond the Limits by Donella H. Meadows, Dennis L. Meadows,
    and Jorgen Randers
Blood Brook by Ted Levin
Four-Season Harvest by Eliot Coleman
John Burroughs by Edward J. Renehan, Jr.
Loving and Leaving the Good Life by Helen Nearing
Set Free in China by Peter Heller
A Shadow and a Song by Mark Jerome Walters

1993

The Independent Home by Michael Potts
The Safari Companion by Richard D. Estes
Wind Power for Home and Business by Paul Gipe

1994

The Contrary Farmer by Gene Logsdon
Eco-Renovation by Edward Harland
Solar Gardening by Leandre Poisson and Gretchen Vogel Poisson
Solar Living Source Book by John Schaeffer and The Real Goods Staff
The Straw Bale House by Athena Swentzell Steen, Bill Steen, and
    David Bainbridge

1995

The New Organic Grower, Second Edition, by Eliot Coleman
The Northern Forest by David Dobbs and Richard Ober

Renewables Are Ready by Nancy Cole, P. J. Skerrett, and The Union of
   Concerned Scientists

1996
The Book of Masonry Stoves by David Lyle
Forest Gardening by Robert Hart
The Independent Builder by Sam Clark
A Patch of Eden by H. Patricia Hynes
The Rammed Earth House by David Easton
Who Owns the Sun? by Daniel M. Berman and John T. O'Connor
Whole Foods Companion by Dianne Onstad

1997
The Contrary Farmer's Invitation to Gardening by Gene Logsdon
The Flower Farmer by Lynn Byczynski
Global Spin by Sharon Beder
Hemp Horizons by John W. Roulac
The Passive Solar House by James Kachadorian
Passport to Gardening by Katherine Laliberté and Ben Watson
A Place in the Sun by John Schaeffer and the collaborative
   design/construction team
The Sauna by Rob Roy

1998
The Apple Grower by Michael Phillips
The Blooming Lawn by Yvette Verner
The Earth-Sheltered House by Malcolm Wells
Field Days edited by Angela King and Susan Clifford
From the Redwood Forest by Joan Dunning
Gaviotas by Alan Weisman
The Good Woodcutter's Guide by Dave Johnson
Hammer. Nail. Wood. by Thomas P. Glynn
The Hard Work of Simple Living by Edward Koren with contributions
   from The Invisible Universe
Mortgage-Free! by Rob Roy
Rainforest by Wade Davis
Scott Nearing by John A. Saltmarsh
Simple Food for the Good Life by Helen Nearing

1999

Believing Cassandra by Alan Atkisson
The Bread Builders by Daniel Wing and Alan Scott
Four-Season Harvest, Second Edition, by Eliot Coleman
Genetic Engineering, Food, and Our Environment by Luke Anderson
Good Spirits by Gene Logsdon
Judevine, Second Edition, by David Budbill
Keeping Food Fresh by The Gardeners and Farmers of Terre Vivante
The New Independent Home by Michael Potts
The Safari Companion, Second Edition, by Richard D. Estes
Seeing Nature by Paul Krafel
Sharing the Harvest by Elizabeth Henderson with Robyn Van En
The Soul of Soil by Grace Gershuny and Joe Smillie
Stone Circles by Rob Roy
Straight-Ahead Organic by Shepherd Ogden
The Toilet Papers by Sim Van der Ryn
Y2K and Y-O-U by Dermot McGuigan and Beverly Jacobson
Wind Energy Basics by Paul Gipe
Wise Words for the Good Life by Helen Nearing

2000

The Beauty of Straw Bale Homes by Athena and Bill Steen
Breed Your Own Vegetable Varieties by Carol Deppe
The Co-op Cookbook by Rosemary Fifield
Fast Lane on a Dirt Road by Joe Sherman
Gaia's Garden by Toby Hemenway
Grassroots Marketing by Shel Horowitz
Living at Nature's Pace by Gene Logsdon
The Making of a Radical by Scott Nearing
The Maple Sugar Book by Helen and Scott Nearing
The Natural House by Daniel D. Chiras
The Neighborhood Forager by Robert K. Henderson
The New Family Cookbook by Bill Eichner, MD
The New Settler Interviews edited by Beth Robinson Bosk
Only Connect selected by John Lane and Maya Kumar Mitchell
The Resourceful Renovator by Jennifer Corson
Restoring the Earth by Kenny Ausubel
The River's Voice edited by Angela King and Susan Clifford
    for Common Ground

Round-Trip to Deadsville by Tim Matson
Toil by Jody Procter

2001

The Bioneers by Kenny Ausubel
Building with Earth by Paulina Wojciechowska
A Cafecito Story by Julia Alvarez
Circle Houses by David Pearson
Gaia's Kitchen by Julia Ponsonby and friends at Schumacher College
Heirloom Flower Gardens by JoAnn Gardner
Living Well in the Age of Global Warming by Paul and Hazel Delcourt, PhDs
Money by Thomas Greco
The Serious Straw Bale by Paul Lacinski and Michel Bergeron
Slow Food edited by Carlo Petrini with Ben Watson and Slow Food Editore
This Organic Life by Joan Dye Gussow
Trees Be Company edited by Angela King and Susan Clifford
     for Common Ground
Treehouses edited by David Pearson
The Village Herbalist by Nancy and Michael Phillips

2002

Common Sense Forestry by Hans Morsbach
ElderHouse by Adelaide Altman
Extreme Simplicity by Christopher and Dolores Nyerges
Freewheeling Homes by David Pearson
The Grape Grower by Lon Rombough
The Hand-Sculpted House by Ianto Evans, Michael G. Smith, and Linda Smiley
A House of Straw by Carolyn Roberts
The Lost Language of Plants by Stephen Harrod Buhner
Organic Soil Fertility Management by Steve Gilman
Organic Weed Management by Steve Gilman
The Pesto Manifesto by Lorel Nazzaro
Secrets of Salsa by The Mexican Women of Anderson Valley
The Solar House by Dan Chiras
Trees, Rivers, and Fields edited by Angela King and Susan Clifford

2003

A Handmade Life by Wm. S. Coperthwaite
Images of Earth and Spirit edited by John Lane and Satish Kumar

Natural Home Heating by Greg Pahl
The Slow Food Guide to New York City by Patrick Martins and Ben Watson
Strangely Like War by Derrick Jensen and George Draffan
Wild Fermentation by Sandor Ellix Katz

2004

Biodiesel by Greg Pahl
The Culture of Make Believe by Derrick Jensen
Don't Think of an Elephant! by George Lakoff
Guantánamo by Michael Ratner and Ellen Ray
High Noon for Natural Gas by Julian Darley
A Language Older Than Words by Derrick Jensen
Limits to Growth, Second Edition, by Donella Meadows, Jorgen Randers,
    and Dennis Meadows
Listening to the Land by Derrick Jensen
The New Ecological Home by Daniel D. Chiras
Rehearsing with Gods by Ronald T. Simon and Marc Estrin
The Sauna by Rob Roy
The Slow Food Guide to Chicago by Kelly Gibson and Portia Belloc Lowndes
Voices of the Land edited by Jamie Crelly Purinton
Walking on Water by Derrick Jensen
Welcome to the Machine by Derrick Jensen and George Draffan
What Can I Do? by Lisa Harrow
Whole Foods Companion, Second Edition, by Dianne Onstad
Wind Power by Paul Gipe

2005

America, Fascism, and God by Davidson Loehr
American Farmstead Cheese by Paul Kindstedt with the Vermont
    Cheese Council
The Apple Grower, Second Edition, by Michael Phillips
The Basics of Permaculture Design by Ross Mars
The Beauty of Craft edited by Sandy Brown and Maya Kumar Mitchell
The Challenge to Power by John Harrington
The Company We Keep by John Abrams
Designing and Maintaining Your Edible Landscape Naturally by
    Robert Kourik
Edible Forest Gardens, Volumes One and Two, by Dave Jacke
    with Eric Toensmeier

The Herbalist's Way by Nancy and Michael Phillips
How Democrats and Progressives Can Win, DVD
Nobody Particular by Molly Bang
The Permaculture Garden by Graham Bell
Permaculture Plants by Jeff Nugent and Julia Boniface
The Permaculture Way by Graham Bell
Pinhook by Janisse Ray
Start Making Sense edited by Don Hazen and Lakshmi Chaudhry
Unembedded by Ghaith Abdul-Ahad, Kael Alford, Thorne Anderson, and
    Rita Leistner
An Unreasonable Woman by Diane Wilson
A Wood of Our Own by Julian Evans

2006

Animate Earth by Stephan Harding
Bayberry and Beau by Nita Choukas
Car Sick by Lynn Sloman
Cottage Economy by William Cobbett
Crashing the Gate by Jerome Armstrong and Markos Moulitsas Zúniga
Ecovillages by Jonathan Dawson
Edens Lost and Found by Harry Wiland and Dale Bell with Joseph D'Agnese
Ethical Markets by Hazel Henderson with Simran Sethi
Food Not Lawns by H. C. Flores
Full Moon Feast by Jessica Prentice
Gaia Girls: Enter the Earth by Lee Welles
Landscaping Earth Ponds by Tim Matson
Luminous Fish by Lynn Margulis
Mad Sheep by Linda Faillace
Mission Rejected by Peter Laufer
Not in His Image by John Lamb Lash
The Passive Solar House, Second Edition, by James Kachadorian
Ready, Set, Talk! by Ellen Ratner and Kathie Scarrah
The Revolution Will Not Be Microwaved by Sandor Ellix Katz
Serve God, Save the Planet by J. Matthew Sleeth, MD
Sippewissett by Tim Traver
The Slow Food Guide to San Francisco by Eleanor Bertino, Sylvan
    Brackett, Wendy Downing, and Sue Moore with Slow Food USA
The Spirit of Silence by John Lane
Through the Eye of the Storm by Cholene Espinoza

2007

The Atlas of American Artisan Cheese by Jeffrey P. Roberts
Chelsea Green Guides: *Composting* by Nicky Scott
Chelsea Green Guides: *Energy* by Jon Clift and Amanda Cuthbert
Chelsea Green Guides: *Reduce, Reuse, Recycle* by Nicky Scott
Chelsea Green Guides: *Water* by Jon Clift and Amanda Cuthbert
The Citizen-Powered Energy Handbook by Greg Pahl
Dazzle Gradually by Lynn Margulis and Dorion Sagan
The End of America by Naomi Wolf
Exposed by Mark Schapiro
Gaia Girls: Way of Water by Lee Welles
Getting Started in Permaculture by Ross and Jenny Mars
Growing Green by Jenny Hall and Iain Tolhurst
The Happiness Trip by Eduardo Punset
Javatrekker by Dean Cycon
The Man Who Hated Work and Loved Labor by Les Leopold
Mind, Life, and Universe edited by Lynn Margulis and Eduardo Punset
Natural Beekeeping by Ross Conrad
Notes From the Holocene by Dorion Sagan
Perennial Vegetables by Eric Toensmeier
Preserving Food without Freezing or Canning by The Gardeners and
    Farmers of Terre Vivante
The Rammed Earth House, Second Edition, by David Easton
Sharing the Harvest, Second Edition, by Elizabeth Henderson with
    Robyn Van En
Surviving America's Depression Epidemic by Bruce E. Levine, PhD
Visionaries edited by Satish Kumar and Freddie Whitefield
When Technology Fails by Matthew Stein

2008

Biodiesel by Greg Pahl
The Carbon-Free Home by Stephen and Rebekah Hren
Chelsea Green Guides: *Biking to Work* by Rory McMullan
Chelsea Green Guides: *Greening Your Office* by Jon Clift and
    Amanda Cuthbert
Climate Solutions by Peter Barnes
Companies We Keep, Second Edition, by John Abrams
Finding the Sweet Spot by Dave Pollard
The Flower Farmer, Second Edition, by Lynn Byczynski

Fresh Food from Small Spaces by R. J. Ruppenthal
Holy Roller by Diane Wilson
How the Rich Are Destroying the Earth by Hervé Kempf
Inquiries into the Nature of Slow Money by Woody Tasch
Mortgage-Free!, Second Edition, by Rob Roy
Not One Drop by Riki Ott
Obama's Challenge by Robert Kuttner
Pearls, Politics, and Power by Madeleine M. Kunin
Renewing America's Food Traditions edited by Gary Paul Nabhan
A Shelter Sketchbook by John S. Taylor
Thinking in Systems by Donella H. Meadows
The Transition Handbook by Rob Hopkins
The War on Bugs by Will Allen
When Technology Fails, Second Edition, by Matthew Stein

2009

Business Advice for Organic Farmers with Richard Wiswall, DVD
Chelsea Green Guides: *Climate Change* by Jon Clift and Amanda Cuthbert
Chelsea Green Guides: *Nontoxic Housecleaning*, Second Edition,
  by Amy Kolb Noyes
Chelsea Green Guides: *Sustainable Food*, Second Edition, by
  Elize McDonough
Confronting Collapse by Michael C. Ruppert
Death and Sex by Tyler Volk and Dorion Sagan
Devil in the Milk by Keith Woodford
The End of Money and the Future of Civilization by Thomas H. Greco, Jr.
Future Scenarios by David Holmgren
Gaia's Garden, Second Edition, by Toby Hemenway
The Gort Cloud by Richard Seireeni
Howard Dean's Prescription for Real Healthcare Reform by Howard Dean
In Late Winter We Ate Pears by Deirdre Heekin and Caleb Barber
Journey of the Pink Dolphins by Sy Montgomery
Libation, A Bitter Alchemy by Deirdre Heekin
Living above the Store by Martin Melaver
The Looting of America by Les Leopold
Marijuana Is Safer by Steve Fox, Paul Armentano, and Mason Tvert
The Organic Farmer's Business Handbook by Richard Wiswall
The Raw Milk Revolution by David E. Gumpert
Search for the Golden Moon Bear by Sy Montgomery

Small-Scale Grain Raising, Second Edition, by Gene Logsdon
Spell of the Tiger by Sy Montgomery
The Transition Timeline by Shaun Chamberlin
Waiting on a Train by James McCommons
Walking with the Great Apes by Sy Montgomery
Wind Energy Basics, Second Edition, by Paul Gipe
The Winter Harvest Handbook by Eliot Coleman

2010

Adobe Homes for All Climates by Lisa Schroder and Vince Ogletree
The Biochar Debate by James Bruges
Bye Bye, Miss American Empire by Bill Kauffman
The Case Against Fluoride by Paul Connett, PhD, James Beck, MD, PhD, and H. S. Micklem, Dphil
Chanterelle Dreams, Amanita Nightmares by Greg A. Marley
Cheesemonger by Gordon Edgar
Disaster on the Horizon by Bob Cavnar
DIY U by Anya Kamenetz
The Earth's Best Story by Ron and Arnie Koss
The Farmstead Creamery Advisor by Gianaclis Caldwell
Fermentation Workshop with Sandor Ellix Katz, DVD
Growing, Older by Joan Dye Gussow
Holy Shit by Gene Logsdon
Masonry Heaters by Ken Matesz
Meat by Simon Fairlie
The People v. Bush by Charlotte Dennett
Poisoned for Profit by Philip and Alice Shabecoff
A Presidency in Peril by Robert Kuttner
The Progressive's Guide to Raising Hell by Jamie Court
The Resilient Gardener by Carol Deppe
A Solar Buyer's Guide for the Home and Office by Stephen and Rebekah Hren
Terra Madre by Carlo Petrini
Up Tunket Road by Philip Ackerman-Leist
Year-Round Vegetable Production with Eliot Coleman, DVD

2011

Alone and Invisible No More by Allan S. Teel, MD
Chasing Chiles by Kurt Michael Friese, Kraig Kraft, and Gary Paul Nabhan

The Chinese Medicinal Herb Farm by Peg Schaffer
The Color of Atmosphere by Maggie Kozel, MD
Cooking Close to Home by Diane Imrie and Richard Jarmusz
Diary of an Eco-Outlaw by Diane Wilson
Get Up, Stand Up by Bruce E. Levine
The Holistic Orchard by Michael Phillips
It's Probably Nothing by Beach Conger, MD
Killing the Cranes by Edward Girardet
The Mystery of Metamorphosis by Frank Ryan
Old Southern Apples, Second Edition, by Creighton Lee Calhoun, Jr.
Organic Principles and Practices Handbook Series:
   Compost, Vermicompost, and Compost Tea by Grace Gershuny
   Crop Rotation and Cover Cropping by Seth Kroeck
   Growing Healthy Vegetable Crops by Brian Caldwell
   Humane and Healthy Poultry Production by Karma Glos
   Organic Dairy Production by Sarah Flack
   Organic Seed Production and Saving by Bryan Connolly; contributing
      editor: C. R. Lawn
   Organic Soil-Fertility and Weed Management by Steve Gilman
   Whole-Farm Planning by Elizabeth Henderson and Karl North
Passive Solar Architecture by David A. Bainbridge and Ken Haggard
Reinventing Fire by Amory B. Lovins and Rocky Mountain Institute
Sepp Holzer's Permaculture by Sepp Holzer
Sex and the River Styx by Edward Hoagland
Slow Gardening by Felder Rushing
The Small-Scale Poultry Flock by Harvey Ussery
The Transition Companion by Rob Hopkins
When Disaster Strikes by Matthew Stein
Wild Flavors by Didi Emmons
Wild Law, Second Edition, by Cormac Cullinan

2012

2052 by Jorgen Randers
The Art of Fermentation by Sandor Ellix Katz
Cheese and Culture by Paul S. Kindstedt
Community Resilience Guide: *Power from the People* by Greg Pahl
Community Resilience Guide: *Local Dollars, Local Sense* by
   Michael H. Shuman
Dreaming the Future by Kenny Ausubel

Farms with a Future by Rebecca Thistlethwaite
Home Baked by Hanne Risgaard
Lynn Margulis edited by Dorion Sagan
Mastering Artisan Cheesemaking by Gianaclis Caldwell
Natural Beekeeping with Ross Conrad, DVD
The Natural Building Companion by Jacob Deva Racusin and Ace McArleton
The New Feminist Agenda by Madeleine M. Kunin
Nuclear Roulette by Gar Smith
Occupy World Street by Ross Jackson
The Organic Seed Grower by John Navazio
Perennial Vegetable Gardening with Eric Toensmeier, DVD
A Sanctuary of Trees by Gene Logsdon
The Seed Underground by Janisse Ray
Slow Democracy by Susan Clark and Woden Teachout
Sowing Seeds in the Desert by Masanobu Fukuoka
Taste, Memory by David Buchanan
Top-Bar Beekeeping by Les Crowder and Heather Harrell
Top-Bar Beekeeping with Les Crowder and Heather Harrell, DVD

2013
Community Resilience Guide: *Rebuilding the Foodshed* by
    Philip Ackermann-Leist
Cows Save the Planet by Judith D. Schwartz
Desert or Paradise by Sepp Holzer
Flying Blind by Don Mitchell
From the Wood-Fired Oven by Richard Miscovich
Good Morning, Beautiful Business by Judy Wicks
The Grafter's Handbook, Second Edition, by R. J. Garner
The Greened House Effect by Jeff Wilson
Growing Food in a Hotter, Drier Land by Gary Paul Nabhan
Holistic Orcharding with Michael Phillips, DVD
Keeping a Family Cow, Second Edition, by Joann S. Grohman
Life, Liberty, and the Pursuit of Food Rights by David E. Gumpert
Marijuana Is Safer, Second Edition, by Steve Fox, Paul Armentano,
    and Mason Tvert
Market Farming Success by Lynn Byczynski
Natural Beekeeping, Second Edition, by Ross Conrad
The New Cider Maker's Handbook by Claude Jolicoeur
The New Horse-Powered Farm by Stephen Leslie

The Organic Grain Grower by Jack Lazor
Out on a Limb by Benjamin Kilham
Paradise Lot by Eric Toensmeier with contributions from Jonathan Bates
Raising Dough by Elizabeth Ü
The Resilient Farm and Homestead by Ben Falk
The Sugarmaker's Companion by Michael Farrell
What Then Must We Do? by Gar Alperovitz
The Zero Waste Solution by Paul Connett

2014

The ALL NEW Don't Think of an Elephant!, Second Edition,
   by George Lakoff
Angels by the River by James Gustave Speth
Carbon Shock by Mark Schapiro
The Chelsea Green Reader edited by Ben Watson
Defending Beef by Nicolette Hahn Niman
Extracted by Ugo Bardi
Farming the Woods by Ken Mudge and Steve Gabriel
Gene Everlasting by Gene Logsdon
The Gourmet Butcher's Guide to Meat by Cole Ward with Karen Coshof
Grass, Soil, Hope by Courtney White
The Heal Your Gut Cookbook by Hilary Boynton and Mary G. Brackett
Hemp Bound by Doug Fine
In the Company of Bears by Benjamin Kilham
Integrated Forest Gardening by Wayne Weiseman, Daniel Halsey, and
   Bryce Ruddock
Let the Water Do the Work by Bill Zeedyk and Van Clothier
The New Net Zero by William Maclay and Maclay Architects
Organic Mushroom Farming and Mycoremediation by Tradd Cotter
Slowspoke by Mark Schimmoeller
The Small-Scale Cheese Business by Gianaclis Caldwell
The Small-Scale Dairy by Gianaclis Caldwell
An Unlikely Vineyard by Deirdre Heekin
The Wild Wisdom of Weeds by Katrina Blair